THE AGE OF REASON

ROUSSEAU
"Contemplating the wild beauties of Switzerland."
Fr. *From an engraving published in 1797*

THE AGE OF REASON

THE CONTINENT OF EUROPE IN
THE EIGHTEENTH CENTURY

BY

R. B. MOWAT

PROFESSOR IN THE UNIVERSITY OF
BRISTOL
FORMERLY FELLOW AND TUTOR OF CORPUS
CHRISTI COLLEGE OXFORD

NEW YORK / RUSSELL & RUSSELL

TO

H. V. F. S.

&

W. R. S.

ARCADIANS

FIRST PUBLISHED IN 1934

REISSUED, 1971, BY RUSSELL & RUSSELL

A DIVISION OF ATHENEUM PUBLISHERS, INC.

BY ARRANGEMENT WITH

GEORGE G. HARRAP & CO. LTD., LONDON

L. C. CATALOG CARD NO: 74-102521

PRINTED IN THE UNITED STATES OF AMERICA

PREFACE

HISTORY, though it cannot give the student of it a means of foreseeing the future, is at any rate the experience of the past, the memory of mankind. This experience is at least as important for mankind as his own experience is for the individual; it is the material on which, after reflection, he can base judgments and make decisions, so that his present conduct will be right.

It is for this reason, because history is mankind's experience, that (as Benedetto Croce has pointed out in a remarkable essay [1]) there has grown up a kind of impatience with it, almost a hatred of it. Reformers who are determined to see nothing good in the existing organization of society, and who are in a hurry to remodel it at any cost, shut their eyes to history, and will rather go on blind to it than have their cherished theories confuted by its inexorable lessons. Yet surely no reasonable man will deny that to shut one's eyes to the past is simply to waste the wonderful experience, the infinite variety of life, which mankind in its recorded years has, with success or failure, passed through.

Democracy, government by the people, is justified because the people, in the long run, are sensible and make correct judgments—if they have the requisite data. History is the data. This experience of the past, however, is only available in the presentations of it which historians put before the public; and these presentations, if they are to be of use, must be continually tested and revised by the historians themselves. Among historical presentations which are ripe for revision is that of the period before the French Revolution, the *ancien*

[1] *Antistorismo*, delivered at the Congress of Philosophers at Oxford in 1930.

5

régime, which was boldly called the other day, in a leading article of *The Times*, the " admirable eighteenth century."

In a previous work, *England in the Eighteenth Century*, to which this is a companion volume, an endeavour was made to deal with certain misconceptions regarding that age. The " Historical Revisions " which have been published by various writers in the valuable periodical *History* have called attention to certain other misconceptions regarding events and movements of the past. The eighteenth century on the Continent, however, has received little attention from the historical revisers.

That the truth about the eighteenth century has not been fully realized can scarcely be denied. A teacher commonly finds, for instance, a view prevailing in schools and colleges to the effect that the Industrial Revolution occurred much later on the Continent than in England because frequent warfare retarded the development of the Continental peoples. Now, this obviously is an impossible explanation, because all through the eighteenth century, except on one occasion (the Polish Succession), whenever the Continental peoples went to war Great Britain went to war too. Nor can it be said that Great Britain differed in being immune from devastating invasions; for between 1713 and 1792—the essential eighteenth century— France likewise was never invaded. Further, it could not have been warfare that prevented a Continental Industrial Revolution, because the demands of war increase the *tempo* of industrial development, and may change and dislocate—that is, revolutionize—the whole course of industry, as, indeed, the world has learned to its cost since the coming of the World War in 1914. The absence, or at any rate the late arrival, of an Industrial Revolution on the Continent is to be explained only by the persistence of certain ideals and habits bound up with the historical development of the Continental peasantry and petty *bourgeoisie* and their ideals of craftsmanship, *petite culture*, and small family businesses.

Fundamentally the explanation of the eighteenth century, its peculiar aspect and charm, is to be found not so much in economics or politics as in culture. France, Germany, Austria,

Italy, were (like England, as described in George Saintsbury's *Peace of the Augustans*) a happy valley with a pleasant town-metropolis. ' Town,' in the eighteenth-century meaning, was the men of letters, and the philosophers, and their friends the statesmen and the intellectual ladies—the people of the *salon* and the coffee-house. It was an age with an artistic ideal, a standard, and a genuine intellectual cosmopolitan *élite*; the characteristic men of the eighteenth century—Lessing, Rousseau, Montesquieu, Voltaire, Franklin, Dr Johnson (in spite of his prejudices), Mozart, Goethe—were citizens of the world, and their ability and their intellectual culture were genuinely first-rate. It was an age tolerant of everything except of the second-rate.

Tolerance and moderation are very near to each other, if they are not quite the same thing. The men of the eighteenth century, at any rate, were moderate as well as tolerant; and moderation has been called, rightly, " the supreme virtue of civilized man." Without this all his culture and all his enthusiasms are " nothing worth." There are those who believe that the decline of Europe began, not with the World War of 1914, but farther back, with the French Revolution, which aroused the consciousness of national honour, unknown to the eighteenth century, and the fierce competition of national egotisms, destroyers of Europe's civilization.[1]

In the present work the essential Continent in the eighteenth century has been regarded as a social whole. The endeavour of the author has been to present it in its chief cultural aspect and its natural background of society and politics. It is not the special business of the historian to draw morals, but it is legitimate on occasion to indicate the conclusion to which his researches may seem to have led. If asked to name, among the myriad qualities of an age, what may be taken as the outstanding feature of the eighteenth century on the Continent

[1] See Adalbert Wahl, *Deutsche Geschichte von der Reichsgründung bis zum Ausbruch des Weltkriegs* (1926), vol. i, p. vii. The above reference to moderation as " the supreme virtue of civilized man " was made by M. Politis in his concluding address as President of the Assembly of the League of Nations in the Thirteenth Ordinary Session, 1932.

I would venture to call it ' moderation,' and to affirm that this moderation expressed itself, even if somewhat elusively, in a ' sane cosmopolitanism.'

The list of the age's deficiencies is no doubt long; yet, to quote Saintsbury again, judgment must rest not upon its deficiencies, but on what it has of positive to offer, what is its own contribution to that glory of the past which is imperishably ours.

It is true that the peoples of the twentieth century have enormously outdistanced those of the eighteenth in the control of nature, in the management of natural forces; but have they greatly improved upon it in regard to the management of themselves? " The intelligent world," wrote Montesquieu in *De l'Esprit des lois*, " is far from being so well governed as the physical." I am inclined to think that the eighteenth century, even in comparison with the present age, did pretty well.

Besides learning useful lessons from the past we can have wholesome recreation. The eighteenth century is one of the playgrounds of the mind. It is the age of perfect balance, between man and nature, between production and consumption, between earnestness and indifference. The men of the age—so far as there are typical men and a typical age—felt that they had discovered the secret of life; they were satisfied and serene.

Of these at any rate comparatively happy peoples the Italians were the blithest. Italy in the eighteenth century—its masks and carnivals, its shows and operas, its moderately opulent towns, with their streets a little grass-grown, their comfortable villas, secluded gardens, cultured democratic nobles and *bourgeoisie*—was like the Italy of the last century of the ancient world before the age of the barbarians. It enjoyed all the benefits of inherited civilization. All the cultured people of Europe came there to participate in a country where war scarcely ever occurred, and where the sound of politics was never heard. Every town had its literary, artistic, musical circle. Arcadia, the fashionable academy, was everywhere, a republic of letters.

Amid the academic groves of Oxford, in a college of which the Palladian architecture is in the finest style of the age, a small group used to meet—indeed, still meets—for a modest repast and conversation about men and letters. The members of this group are pleased to regard themselves as continuing the tradition of Dr Johnson. They love the eighteenth century; they are Arcadians. *Et ego in Arcadia* . . .

It is needless to say that this book could not have been written without their happy inspiration, their wit, their sympathy, their knowledge. The sunny quadrangle, the park-like garden of flowers and lawns and lake, the scholar's room, the books, pictures, musical scores, the cheerful, friendly group— there is the essential eighteenth century still untroubled, complete.

R. B. M.

CLIFTON
1934

CONTENTS

ILLUSTRATIONS

THE AGE OF REASON

CHAPTER I

THE ADMIRABLE EIGHTEENTH CENTURY

TO-DAY men of letters and society have an ideal of sincerity which sometimes has led them along strange paths. They face facts of life without a blush and probe down to the innermost springs of conduct. " The ideal of the twentieth century," Mr Chesterton has said, " is something which the eighteenth century would have called candour. The ideal of the eighteenth century was something which the twentieth century would have called art, in that full sense in which the completed work of the artist speaks for the common man better than his own mere candour could speak for him." [1] It is, naturally, impossible to epitomize a whole age of mankind in one word; and if Mr Chesterton is right in calling the eighteenth century an age of artistry, others might prefer, and equally justly, to call it an age of serenity. The characteristic of the old Hellenic culture is found in the scholar and historian of Greek art, Winckelmann; and Winckelmann was no mere exception. He was a man of the eighteenth century, the product of ' enlightenment,' of the classicism of the age; he was Goethe's master.[2] He may be, as Walter Pater wrote, " the last fruit " of the fifteenth-century Renaissance, which survived into the eighteenth century and reached its climax with Goethe.

It is only fair to point out that there have been other verdicts on the eighteenth century. In particular, in Carlyle's judgment

---

[1] G. K. Chesterton, in *Illustrated London News*, November 5, 1932.
[2] See Walter Pater, *The Renaissance* (1901), pp. 213 ff.

it was an age of shams—" A decadent age . . . in which no
ideal either grows or blossoms, when Belief and Loyalty have
passed away, and only the cant and false echo of them remains,
and all solemnity has become Pageantry." [1] Carlyle was a
great writer, but his judgment is not wholly to be trusted
concerning an age where he discovered, with so much assurance, supreme grandeur in Frederick the Second of Prussia,
commonly called Frederick the Great.

In a remarkable passage in *Émile* Rousseau declares, as a
fact obvious to all his contemporaries, that there was constant
movement within eighteenth-century society. He is speaking
of the training of children by parents, and points out that
Europe is not like ancient Egypt, where professions and crafts
were hereditary, and a father could be perfectly secure in
giving his son a special training. " In Europe," says Rousseau,
" the ranks alone remain ; the men in them continually change
[*les hommes en changent sans cesse*]." He seems to mean by this,
change within each class, rather than change between classes.
Commoners were not often raised to the noble class, though
this happened from time to time. Outside the *noblesse* the
vast ' middle class,' or *bourgeoisie*, included everybody except
the smaller peasants ; and within this *bourgeoisie* there was
continual movement. Rousseau himself, the son of a small
watchmaker, became a man of letters, diplomatic secretary,
tutor. Instances of men rising in life in the eighteenth century
are innumerable. Boys rose out of the peasant class too, like
Haydn, who was the son of a gamekeeper. Promotions took
place within the same class and country, and also between
countries. Europe has never been so ' cosmopolitan.' Nobody
was excluded from employment, even from the highest official
positions, on account of nationality. The Austrian army,
officers and men, described by the Prince de Ligne, fighting
the Turks in Wallachia in 1788, was an international force of
French, Germans of all sorts, Dutch, as well as the numerous
races in allegiance to the Habsburg monarch.[2] The Pasha

---

[1] Thomas Carlyle, *French Revolution*, Book II, Chapter II.
[2] Prince de Ligne, *Mémoires* (ed. 1827), vol. i, pp. 173–233

Bonneval was not by any means the only ' Gentleman Errant.'
Wandering craftsmen were naturally still more numerous.
William Cockerill, engineer in Russia and Sweden, founder of
the great ironworks at Liége, is a famous instance. It is
possible that the theory of the social leaders of the eighteenth
century may have been (as the historian Lecky says it was)
that there should be a disciplined and industrious lower class
and an intelligent and managing upper class; but practice did
not conform to the theory.

Another common idea of the eighteenth century is that it
was infidel—*Voltairean*; and Gibbon (after Voltaire) is taken
as the classic example of this. An unbiased examination of
the people who emerge into history in that age will prove that
it contained no greater infidel element than the present, nor
a smaller proportion of saintly characters. High Society was
shockingly immoral; but the Christian life flourished in many
quarters, if mainly among the smaller *bourgeoisie*.

A third charge against the eighteenth century is that it
was an age of wars. It must be admitted that war was its
great failure. The age was sufficiently reasonable and intelligent
to want to abolish war, and certainly should and would have
greatly reduced the scourge, but for the evil step of Frederick
the Great in 1740. Nevertheless, the wars in the eighteenth
century (down to the opening of the French Revolution) were
fewer and less destructive to human life than in any previous
age.

A fourth charge is that the eighteenth century was formal
and rigid—a ' classical age,' an age of peruke, powder, and the
dress-sword, an age of the ten-syllabled couplet and the
dramatic unities. All these things existed, yet they never
absorbed the mind and spirit of man; for there never was a
year in the eighteenth century, from the time of *Robinson
Crusoe* and *Gulliver's Travels* to that of *Werther*, the *Contrat
social*, *Paul et Virginie*, and *Lyrical Ballads*, when the call
of the ' romantic ' was dead. The eighteenth century was
a ' classical age,' sweetened by a persistent renaissance of
the romantic spirit. Goethe's hexameter idyll, *Hermann und*

Dorothea, at the end of the century, combines German sentiment, the German heart, with classical art—the *deutsches Herz*
with the *antike Kunst*.

What is the secret of its charm? The answer is that the
eighteenth century was the time when all the gains made by
civilization before the industrial age were at the disposal of
mankind. The perfect balance between man and nature,
between town and country, had been attained. Industrialism
had to come, but it would have come gradually, adapted to a
growing society, conformed to the needs of each succeeding
generation. What prevented a gradual rhythm in the process
of establishing the Age of Steam, what produced the over-rapid
development, the congestion of urban populations, the over-
production, the under-consumption, the ' disequilibrium,' to
use a modern expression? These things were all produced by
the world war which came in 1792, just as the *disequilibria*
of the twentieth century have come from the World War of
1914. *La guerre, voilà l'ennemi.*

That war was the enemy was the opinion of Swift and
Voltaire, the age's greatest satirists—men who by their wit
incline mankind towards their wisdom. Swift and Voltaire
both agreed in holding that more estimable than all the great
captains were the men who helped people to grow " two
blades of grass upon a spot of ground where only one grew
before," who assisted mankind to " cultivate its garden."
Nobody can pretend that Swift and Voltaire meant only the
material garden.[1]

Ever since peoples became reflective about themselves and
their position in the world or in the universe they have tended
to believe themselves to be at the apex of civilization. The
peoples of Europe in the Middle Ages had not this kind of self-
consciousness. It was probably the fifteenth-century Renaissance that made them conscious of their capacity for progress,
intellectual, moral, material. Thereafter from generation to
generation wealth increased, and magnificent things were

---

[1] See Swift, *Travels to Brobdingnag*, Chapter VII; Voltaire, *Candide,*
ad fin.

achieved in letters, art, science. No wonder that in each succeeding century the peoples of Europe felt themselves to be the heirs of all the ages, the race of mankind in whom all the ends of the earth were met. They believed that there was such a thing as progress; they believed that they were progressing. For four hundred years Europe was, on the whole, blithe and optimistic; there was no pessimism, no general feeling of discouragement, until perhaps the last years of the nineteenth century, when the terms *blasé, fin de siècle,* came for a time into common use.

Of these four centuries, from 1500 to 1900, the eighteenth century was the most 'complete,' the least troubled by searchings of heart, doubts, longings, queries. Looking back upon history, we can see the eighteenth century placed between two 'great,' tremendous, but troubled ages—between the seventeenth century, on the one hand, an age of epic poems and epic struggles, the age of Milton, Cromwell, and Louis XIV, and, on the other hand, the nineteenth century, the age of scientific inventions, of Darwinism, Bismarckism, nationalist struggles, astounding material progress, vast cities, swift transport.

Between these two ages comes the tranquil, self-satisfied, complete eighteenth century. None of these terms can be used without qualification. There were doubters and rebels and disappointed men and women in the eighteenth century; and there were wars and riots occasionally; and bishops warned their flocks against the besetting habit of haste, against the growing intensity of life; and Jane Austen's ladies in *Mansfield Park* complain to each other of the difficulty of obtaining or keeping domestic servants. Nevertheless, we can see now, looking backward, that the problems of people of the eighteenth century were simpler than those of the present day, and that their lives were really less troubled, more nearly approached tranquillity. Taken as a whole, the men of the eighteenth century had a contented outlook upon life. They had a philosophy which satisfied them. Life offered certain definite good things—letters, art, good cheer, friends, congenial work. They asked for no more in this world; and for the next world—they were willing to take it as it came. They believed, as Spinoza said, that a free man should not think about death. Goethe is the supreme type of this ' complete ' man. Dr Johnson, though handicapped by a weak nervous system, came very near to it. Voltaire was only prevented by the possession of a persistently rebellious nature from attaining to it.

Tolerance is the mark, or at any rate one of the marks, of a civilized man. Gallio was civilized. " Tolerance is the test of true Europeanism." [1] It is a very difficult quality to acquire, for it demands knowledge, self-control, and the capacity for putting oneself mentally in the place of another. These things are only acquired by education, and in an enlightened society. The eighteenth century was the first tolerant age since the fall of the Roman Empire, and it was probably more tolerant than is the present age, the post-War twentieth century. It is true that the legal system in most states was not tolerant; the French law did not recognize Huguenotism, nor did English law give dissenters the full privileges of citizens. Nevertheless, there was religious tolerance in fact in most countries; and political tolerance was practically universal. There was no racial ' minority question ' in the eighteenth century, because nobody was nationally minded, and no people had the slightest desire to ' assimilate ' any other people to itself. Nobody claimed that his nation's culture was superior to that of another nation; nobody knew that his nation had a particular culture of its own, because culture was European, though expressed through different tongues. " To figure in polite learning," wrote Goldsmith in 1759, " every country should make their own language, form their own manners; nor will they ever succeed by introducing that of another which has been formed from manners which are different." [2] Goldsmith, surveying polite learning throughout Europe, never once uses the word ' nation '; but he describes learning, the joint

[1] Paul Cohen-Portheim, *The Discovery of Europe* (1932), p. 77.
[2] *An Enquiry into the State of Polite Learning in Europe*, Chapter V.

possession and contribution of the ' republic of letters,' as it
is shared by every ' country.' The type of eighteenth-century
tolerance was Frederick II of Prussia, against whom some
anonymous critic had posted a placard, high up, on a wall.
It was too high up for the King to read, so he told his
attendant to put it down lower.[1]

What was this ' Europe,' so complete, so sure of itself,
untroubled by doubts and yearnings? It was then, as it is now
(though no longer ' sure of itself '), a small area of the world's
surface, and even of the territory geographically called Europe.
For ' cultural Europe,' where Western civilization existed and
exists, has always been small. In the eighteenth century it
went no farther east than the Vistula, than Warsaw, where,
the Prince de Ligne wrote, " the best tone of France "
reigned, but " with an Oriental cast, the taste of Europe
and Asia." [2] Evidently Poland was the frontier-country.
Russia, though brought by Peter the Great and Catherine II
into close touch with ' Europe,' was outside; and still is. All
the Balkan lands were still subject to the Ottoman Turk, and
completely closed to Western influences. The Prince de Ligne
described from personal experience the amazingly Oriental
domestic life of the Moldo-Wallachian boyars and their ladies.
The British Isles, Scandinavia, Germany, Holland, and the
Habsburg lands, Italy, France, and the Iberian peninsula, were
all Europe, and, except for a small though vigorous people in the
English colonies of North America, were the sole repositories
of Western civilization. The Reformation had destroyed the
religious but not the intellectual unity of this Europe. The
real division had occurred in 1054, when Pope Leo IX ex-
communicated the Patriarch Michael Ceralarius. The division
between the Eastern and Western Churches became fixed and
permanent. This is one of the reasons why Western civilization stopped at the Vistula; Tatar invasions and the character
of Russian country had something to do with this too. For

[1] See below, p. 103.
[2] Prince de Ligne, *Mémoires*, vol. ii, pp. 50–51; the next Ligne reference is
from vol. i, pp. 210–213.

one reason or another Russia remained outside the European political ' system ' and outside European intellectual society down to the end of the eighteenth century, although the Imperial Court had cultural connexions with the West. Poland was the cultural frontier of Europe; and even here European culture was none too secure. It was established at Warsaw, where cultured Saxon kings reigned in the first half of the eighteenth century, but very little of the European spirit passed across the broad and deep Vistula.

This little Europe, this islet in a vast sea of strange races and cultures, had maintained the tradition of classical learning and taste since the fall of the Roman Empire; had brought this tradition to grand achievement in the Renaissance ; and had produced the epics of the seventeenth century. And now the eighteenth century was doing faultless work, highly finished in form, exquisite in thought. Tolerant, rational, a little sceptical; without prejudice; without political passion; a little worldly, perhaps, but serene; graceful in manner, neat in thought and expression, wholesome in body and sane in mind, the men of the eighteenth century felt that they had the secret of life, as far as they cared to inquire into it. " He who has not lived in the years near to 1789," said Talleyrand to Guizot in the later stormy age,[1] " does not know how sweet life can be." In spite of grave shortcomings in its moral and social economy the eighteenth century stands out in history as an admirable age.

[1] Guizot, *Mémoires* (1858), vol. i, p. 6.

CHAPTER II

COSMOPOLITANISM

WITHIN 'Europe'—that is, in the country between Lisbon and Warsaw—there was a vast amount of coming and going; a cosmopolitan spirit reigned. There was little or no race-consciousness. Peoples accepted rulers from other countries with equanimity. An Elector of Hanover became King of England. A Landgrave of Hesse became King of Sweden. An ex-King of Poland became Duke of Lorraine. A Duke of Lorraine became Grand Duke of Tuscany; and this Grand Duke of Tuscany became subsequently Emperor of Germany. A Spanish Infant became King of Naples; another Spanish Infant became Duke of Parma. Spain was ruled by a Bourbon, grandson of Louis XIV. The greatest of the Russian sovereigns after Peter I was a Princess of Anhalt. A prince of Brunswick-Wolfenbüttel was Guardian of the United Netherlands. Two Electors of Saxony, pure Germans, were successively Kings of Poland. The Pope was always an Italian; but this was the readiest way to ensure that the head of the Roman Catholic Church should be international. There being no Italian nation, and no great Italian state, a Pope of the Italian race was unlikely to have any pronounced or partisan political tendencies. Shortly after the close of the eighteenth century a French marshal was elected Crown Prince, to become the future King of Sweden. In fact, outside the 350 German states, mainly petty principalities, and all extremely patriarchal, it was the exception rather than the rule to find a native dynasty. States, like Venice or Holland, which elected their chief magistrate, being always controlled by a ring of aristocratic families, naturally chose a native, a member of one of these families; the 'Guardianship' of Duke

23

Ludwig Ernst of Brunswick-Wolfenbüttel in the Netherlands from 1751 to 1766 was exceptional. The military officers of the Dutch Army, however, including the commander-in-chief, were generally foreigners. The British Government had a notion of proposing Frederick II of Prussia for Stadtholder, but this design came to nothing. The French soldier (Marshal Bernadotte) who became Crown Prince of Sweden in 1810 and who founded the present reigning dynasty had not even a Swedish wife. His queen was Désirée Cléry of Marseilles. The number of generals and diplomatists who were not native to the states which they served is simply legion. Certainly ' high life ' was then (as, indeed, it always tends to be and still is) cosmopolitan.[1]

Everybody travelled, except those who, like the small tradesmen and the peasants, combined a well-assured position with lack of enterprise. In the eighteenth century, as in all ages, it was never lack of money which prevented people from travelling, but strong domestic ties and deficiency of enterprise and ambition. This explains why the small *bourgeois* and the peasant never travel. In the eighteenth century, however, all and sundry (apart from these two classes) moved incessantly, covering the broad, uneven highroads with a ceaseless stream.

[1] Among the persons referred to in the above paragraph were: (1) George Augustus, Elector of Hanover, George I of Great Britain from 1714 to 1727. (2) Frederick I, Landgrave of Hesse-Cassel, King of Sweden from 1720 to 1751. (3) Stanislaus Leczynski, King of Poland from 1704 to 1709, and from 1733 to 1734, Duke of Lorraine from 1736 to 1766. (4) Francis Stephen, Duke of Lorraine from 1729 to 1736, Grand Duke of Tuscany from 1737 to 1745, Emperor Francis I from 1745 to 1765. (5) Don Carlos, Charles IV of Naples 1735–59, Charles III of Spain from 1759 to 1788. (6) Don Philip, Duke of Parma from 1748 to 1765. (7) Philip, Duke of Anjou, King of Spain from 1700 to 1724 and from 1725 to 1746. (8) Sophia Catherina, Princess of Anhalt-Zerbst, Empress Catherine II of Russia from 1762 to 1796. (9) Ludwig Ernst of Brunswick-Wolfenbüttel, Guardian of William IV of Orange from 1751 to 1766, and Captain-General of the Netherlands from 1751 to 1786. (10) (a) Frederick Augustus I, Elector of Saxony from 1694 to 1733, Augustus II of Poland from 1697 to 1704 and from 1709 to 1733; (b) Frederick Augustus II, Elector of Saxony from 1733 to 1763, Augustus III of Poland from 1734 to 1763. (11) The last non-Italian Pope was Adrian Boyers of Utrecht, Pope Adrian VI, from 1522 to 1523. (12) Jean-Baptiste Bernadotte, Crown Prince of Sweden from 1810 to 1818, Charles XIV from 1818 to 1844.

The opening pages of *Jew Süss*, though it is not a contemporary authority, describe the eighteenth-century highway with accuracy and understanding:

A network of roads, like veins, was strung over the land, interlacing, branching, dwindling to nothing. They were neglected, full of stones and holes, torn up, overgrown, bottomless swamp in wet weather, and, besides, everywhere impeded by toll-gates. In the south, among the mountains, they narrowed into bridle-paths and disappeared. All the blood of the land flowed through these veins. The bumpy roads, gaping with dusty cracks in the sun, heavy with mud in the rain, were the moving life of the land, its breath and pulse.

Upon them travelled the regular stage-coaches, open carts without cushions or backs to the seats, jolting clumsily, patched and patched again, and the quicker post-chaises with four seats and five horses, which could do as much as eighty miles a day. There travelled the express couriers of Courts and Embassies, on good horses with frequent relays, carrying sealed despatches, and the more leisurely messengers of the Thurn and Taxis Post. There travelled journeymen with their knapsacks, honest and dangerous, and students as lean and meek as the others were stout and saucy, and monks with discreet eyes, sweating in their cowls. There travelled the tilt-carts of the great merchants, and the hand-barrows of peddling Jews. There travelled in six solid and somewhat shabby coaches the King of Prussia, who had been visiting the South German Courts, and his retinue. There travelled in an endless tail of men and cattle and coaches the Protestants whom the Prince-Archbishop of Salzburg had driven with insults from his country. There travelled gaily decked actors and soberly clad devotees, sunk in themselves; and in a magnificent *calèche* with outriders and a large escort the lean and arrogant Venetian Ambassador to the Court of Saxony. There travelled in disorder, on laboriously constructed vehicles, Jews deported from a Middle-German city of the Empire, making for Frankfort. There travelled schoolmasters and noblemen, silken harlots and woollen clerks of the Supreme Court. There travelled comfortably with several coaches the plump, sly, and jolly-looking Prince-Bishop of Würzburg, and on foot and out-at-elbows a Professor Landshut from the University of Bavaria, who had been dismissed for seditious and heretical opinions.

There travelled with the agent of an English shipping company a party of Swabian emigrants, wives, dogs, children and all, who wanted to go to Pennsylvania; and pious, violent, and bawling pilgrims from Lower Bavaria on the way to Rome; there travelled, with a rapacious, sharp, observant eye on everything, the requisitioners of silver, cattle, and grain for the Viennese War Treasury, and discharged Imperial soldiers from the Turkish wars, and charlatans and alchemists and beggars and young gentlemen with their tutors journeying from Flanders to Venice.

They all swept forward, backward, and across, came to a standstill, spurred on, stumbled, trotted easily, cursed the bad roads, laughed bitterly or with good-natured mockery at the slowness of the stage, growled at the worn-out hacks, the ramshackle vehicles. They all poured on, ebbed back, gossiped, prayed, whored, blasphemed, shrank in fear, exulted, and lived.[1]

One such poor man who travelled and earned a living in many countries of Europe was Ludwig Holberg (1684–1754). Goldsmith, who seems to have been inspired by Holberg's story himself to set forth penniless over Europe, narrates it in *An Enquiry into the Present State of Polite Learning*:

The history of polite learning in Denmark may be comprised in the life of one single man: it rose and fell with the late famous Baron Holberg. This was, perhaps, one of the most extraordinary personages that has done honour to the present century. His being the son of a private sentinel did not abate the ardour of his ambition, for he learned to read, though without a master. Upon the death of his father, being left entirely destitute, he was involved in all that distress which is common among the poor, and of which the great have scarcely any idea. However, though only a boy of nine years old, he still persisted in pursuing his studies, travelled about from school to school and begged his learning and his bread. When at the age of seventeen, instead of applying himself to any of the lower occupations, which seem best adapted to such circumstances, he was resolved to travel for improvement from Norway, the place of his birth, to Copen-

---

[1] L. Feuchtwanger, *Jew Süss, ad init.* (trans. Muir, 1926). Quoted by kind permission of Mr Martin Secker.

hagen, the capital city of Denmark. He lived there by teaching French, and at the same time avoiding no opportunity of improvement that his scanty funds could permit. But his ambition was not to be restrained, or his thirst of knowledge to be satisfied, until he had seen the world. Without money, recommendations or friends, he undertook to set out upon his travels, and make the tour of Europe on foot. A good voice and a trifling skill in music were the only finances he had to support an undertaking so extensive; so he travelled by day, and at night sung at the door of peasants' houses to get himself a lodging. In this manner while yet very young, Holberg passed through France, Germany and Holland; and coming over to England, took up his residence for two years in the University of Oxford. Here he existed by teaching French and music, and wrote his universal history, his earliest but worst performance. Furnished with all the learning of Europe, he at last thought proper to return to Copenhagen, where his ingenious productions quickly gained him that favour he deserved. He composed not less than eighteen comedies. Those in his own language are said to excel, and those which are translated into French have peculiar merit. He was honoured with nobility and enriched by the bounty of the King; so that a life begun in contempt and penury ended in opulence and esteem.[1]

William Cockerill, the founder of the great ironworks of Liége, was a Lancashire man, born of poor parents at Haslington in 1759. He was set to work in a cotton-mill, but soon found that he had more inventive capacity and more energy than were needed just to attend to a ' flying shuttle.' He found means to go off in 1794 to Russia, where the enlightened Empress Catherine II was always ready to employ men of talent, whether they were natives or foreigners. Unfortunately for Cockerill the Empress died in 1796, and the ups and downs of Court life under a despotism resulted in violent changes of administration under the rule of the ' mad ' Tsar Paul. Cockerill was put in prison, but managed to escape to Sweden. There he found employment under the Government on the work of constructing canal-locks. He wanted to introduce the

[1] *An Enquiry into the Present State of Polite Learning*, Chapter VI.

Industrial Revolution [1] into Sweden by setting up cotton-mills with machinery of his own inventing; but as this effort was not encouraged by the authorities he removed himself in 1799 to Belgium, where there was a fairly liberal *régime* under the French Revolutionary Directory. Establishing himself at Verviers, he entered into business with a native firm, and made spinning and weaving machines which created the modern prosperity of that town. In 1807 he moved his business to Liége, which is magnificently situated for exploiting the neighbouring iron- and coal-fields and for making use of the water-power and communications of the Meuse. At this time Liége and the rest of Belgium were in the Napoleonic Empire. Cockerill found ample scope for his powers of invention and organization and large markets for his woollen products. In 1809 he retired from business. The great ironworks at Seraing which bear his name were founded by his sons, who became what would now be called great ' industrialists,' or captains of industry. William Cockerill died in 1832, aged seventy-three, at the Château of Behrensberg, the seat of one of his sons, near Aix-la-Chapelle. The important Cockerill works at Liége (Seraing-on-the-Meuse) still continue in existence, and are among the chief Belgian industries.

If poor boys and workmen could see the world and make themselves at home in various countries, men of quite moderate means could, naturally, do so much more easily. Smollett, a ship's surgeon and successful novelist, had, of course, some money when he travelled in France and Italy in 1763-65. Laurence Sterne, though mostly in debt, had a clerical benefice, and made some guineas by writing. Although the French and English are supposed to have been enemies all through the eighteenth century (and, indeed, England fought France in five wars during that time), Sterne, who went to France in January 1762 (Great Britain being still engaged in the Seven Years War with France), found no sort of national antipathy or even coldness. He consorted with Diderot and Holbach,

---

[1] See pp. 6, 18 for further remarks upon the so-called ' Industrial Revolution.'

talked with Marshal Biron and with Madame d'Épinay; was invited to the celebrated suppers of Mademoiselle Clairon of the Comédie Française; and settled down for ten months at Toulouse, where he drank asses' milk and Frontignac among a resident English colony and attended the performance of a British troupe of actors. He had no illusions that his own people managed everything better than foreigners. " They order this matter better in France," he had said before leaving England, apparently after a dinner in London; and at his first dinner of *fricassée* of chicken at Calais he drank the King of France's health, " to satisfy my mind that I bear him no spleen." [1]

Moritz was a more respectable clergyman than Sterne, and, though not so sprightly, was by no means dull. If he had been just a dull, worthy man he would not have adventured to and through England, nor would he have written a sentimental novel, *Anton Reiser*, in his later years. Carl Philip Moritz was born at Hameln in 1757, the son of a regimental oboist. He was apprenticed to a hatter at Brunswick. After this his friends, who were almost as poor as himself, provided him with some schooling at Hanover. He lived meagrely, and read widely in German and English poetry. He tried to be an actor at Erfurt, Gotha, and Weimar; was a student at Erfurt University; and went with an acting company to Leipzig. For two years he was a student of theology at Wittenberg, and, failing to become a military chaplain, obtained a position as teacher at the Gymnasium Zum Grauen Kloster in Berlin. From there, in 1782, he made his great journey to England. After this he taught at the *Gymnasium* in Cologne, and from there in 1786 visited Italy, where he and Goethe were together for a considerable time. Later, through the friendship of Goethe and Duke Carl August of Saxe-Weimar for him, he obtained the position of Professor of Fine Art and Classical Learning under the Royal Academy of Berlin. He died in 1793.[2] On his

---

[1] Laurence Sterne, *Sentimental Journey, ad init.*
[2] See Carl Philip Moritz, *Travels in England* (1924), Introduction by P. E. Matheson, pp. xvii–xviii.

travels in England he went mostly afoot. The passage from Hamburg to London, including his food in the cabin, cost him four guineas; from London to Hamburg he was charged five guineas, the skipper giving as a reason that the provisions which he had to buy in London were dearer than in Hamburg. Moritz's *Reisen eines Deutschen in England* is in the form of letters, written to Gedike, the German humanist and educationist, and was first published, in Berlin, in 1785.

All these men, Holberg, Goldsmith, Smollett, Sterne, Moritz, and a host of others, were citizens each of their own country, and they only incidentally and without express purpose shared the cosmopolitan character of the age. There were others who were professed cosmopolitans, deliberately citizens of the world, such as Gibbon, Rousseau, and Voltaire. Gibbon learned to be a European by passing " the flexible period of youth, from the age of sixteen to twenty-one," in the home of a pastor at Lausanne. " I had ceased to be an Englishman," he wrote later, with some exaggeration. Previously to his time at Lausanne he had been an undergraduate at Magdalen College, Oxford, from which his father removed him, owing to a (temporary) conversion to Roman Catholicism. " If," he wrote in his *Autobiography*, " my childish revolt against the religion of my country had not stripped me in time of my academic gown, the five important years, so liberally improved in the studies and conversation of Lausanne, would have been steeped in port and prejudice among the monks of Oxford."

Rousseau's *Contrat social* is like More's *Utopia*; it is a political treatise on the State, which ignores nationality and frontiers, and reduces politics to universal principles. Rousseau himself, though he started out without a sou, went from country to country, spending years in each, and formed a social circle in each place as if he were born there. Voltaire wrote *Candide*, which is a picture of the world as it was then and of a philosopher's progress through it; and the novel ends with the serene advice to cease worrying about other people or peoples or yourself, and just to cultivate your own garden. Voltaire made it his aim to enfranchize himself and keep himself free from any one Government by having a footing in three states. Not exactly rich, but always spending somewhat less than he made, he accumulated enough money to buy land and a house in each; and thus, he wrote, " I so managed my destiny that I was independent in Switzerland, in the territories of Geneva, and in France. I have heard much of liberty, but do not believe there is an individual in Europe who has wrought his own freedom like me." [1] His friend, the philosopher Condorcet, wrote of him: " Such had ever been his secret design, in all the arrangements he had made of his fortune ; and it would have required a league among the Powers of Europe to have deprived him of independence and reduced him to want." [2]

These cosmopolitan gentry of the eighteenth century were not tepid people. They were fighters for most of their life in one cause or another. Even Voltaire, who had a hatred of war in general and a contempt for the alleged causes of nearly every conflict in his time, approved of the unending struggle of Russia against Turkey. The cosmopolitans of the end of the century—Metternich, Gentz, Alexander I, Wordsworth—were inflexible once they were roused to see the real tyranny of Bonapartism. A man could be a friend of humanity without sacrificing love of country. The career of Benjamin Thompson, Count Rumford, shows this.

Benjamin Thompson was born at Woburn, in Massachusetts, in 1753, of an old New England family. He received the sound education provided by the schools even of the villages and small towns of Massachusetts. At the age of sixteen he was apprenticed to a store or merchant's business at Salem; but, like his older contemporary, Benjamin Franklin, the ideal citizen of the world, he spent his spare time in improving his mind, and particularly in conducting experiments in physics; also in learning French and practising fencing. He became a student at Harvard, married a widow with a little money, served as an officer in the New Hampshire militia, but sold his property and sailed for England when the Revolutionary

---

[1] *Memoirs of the Life of Voltaire written by Himself* (trans. 1826), p. 84.
[2] *Ibid.*, p. 119.

War broke out in 1775. Lord George Germaine gave him
employment in the office of War and the Colonies, which left
him time to continue his experiments in matter and motion.
The great Sir Joseph Banks was attracted by these experiments,
and had him elected a Fellow of the Royal Society. Towards
the end of the American Revolutionary War Thompson was
given a commission of Lieutenant-Colonel in the King's
American Dragoons, and fought in North Carolina.

When the war was over Thompson returned from New
York to England, was knighted by George III, went for a trip
in the Rhineland, and after obtaining an introduction to the
Elector of Bavaria entered the Bavarian service. For eleven
years (1784–95) he was a Minister of State at Munich, and
was created a Count of the Holy Roman Empire. With the
quenchless reforming zeal of an enlightened man of the
eighteenth century he improved the military system (particularly easing the frightful condition of the private soldier),
cleaned the city of dirt and beggars, and made a public park
(the " English Garden ") out of a desolate waste. His monument, erected by grateful citizens when he left Munich in
1795, still adorns the English Garden.

Returning to England as Count Rumford (he took his title
from Rumford, now Concord, in Massachusetts), he pursued
his experiments in electricity, in heat, and on the prevention
of smoky chimneys, the improvement of cooking, the hygiene
of clothing; for, like Franklin, he was nothing if not practical,
and was the friend of the common man. The humane Lord
Pelham, who had a house in Dublin, invited Rumford to go
there on a visit; during his stay in Dublin he proposed, with
success, reforms in the hospitals and workhouses, carried on
his scientific experiments, and was made a member of the
Royal Irish Academy.

There was no end to Rumford's benevolence and the fertility
of his mind. He gave £1000 to the Royal Society and another
£1000 to the American Academy of Arts and Science, to
encourage research on light and heat; and in 1799 he founded,
by obtaining subscriptions and promises of support, the Royal

Institution of Great Britain, of which he was the first Secretary and architect. He revisited Bavaria. In 1805, now a widower, he married the widow of the great chemist Lavoisier. At the age of fifty-six he bought an estate at Auteuil (the fashionable suburb for men of letters and learning), two miles from Paris, and lived there till his death in 1814, although England and France were at war all this time. He was buried at Auteuil, but his fortune was left partly to his daughter, partly to the Royal Institution, and partly to maintain a professorship of physics at Harvard University.

Governments took talent into their service wherever they could find it. Another cosmopolitan, of the type of Count Rumford, was Sir John Acton, sixth baronet, of Aldenham Hall, Shropshire, who was Prime Minister of the Kingdom of Naples. His father had practised as a physician at Besançon and married a French lady; John Acton was born there in 1736. He entered the navy of the Grand Duchy of Tuscany, and rose to the rank of captain. Invited to join the Neapolitan navy in 1779, he became its head, or Minister of Marine, and by the end of his life was Prime Minister of the whole kingdom in the stormy times of the French Revolution and Napoleonic wars. His eldest son and heir married the heiress of the great German and international noble family of Dalberg; the second son, educated at Westminster School, became a cardinal.

Goethe, though he gave the greatest of impulses to German literature, is, like Shakespeare, a mind and spirit on the grand scale, the possession in common of all mankind. He conceived literature as an expression of universal culture, as *Weltliteratur*. " Hatred for foreign elements, or nationalism in poetry, seemed to him stupid, or at most antiquated; and his famous idea of *Weltliteratur*, of universal literature, of which he announced the coming, only meant opposition to every nationalistic idea."[1]

Perhaps the cosmopolitanism of the eighteenth century was due to the fact that it was a literary century. Comparing 1769 with 1700, Dr Johnson declared to Boswell: " There is now an elegance of style, universally diffused." Nearly everybody

[1] B. Croce, *Goethe* (trans. Ainslie, 1923), p. 11.

wrote well; and the majority of books which were published were worth reading. Men of letters of various countries freely consorted with one another, and were generous in their appreciation of each other. Rousseau, in his *Nouvelle Héloïse*, gave the great impulse to the European reputation of Samuel Richardson. The gentry had a speaking knowledge of the French tongue. It was the sign, Macaulay wrote in his essay on Horace Walpole, " by which the freemasons of fashion recognized each other in every capital from Petersburg to Naples." When the Academy of Berlin crowned Rivarol's work on the universality of the French language French writers were pointing out to the rest of Europe that it should not follow too closely " the age of Louis XIV " as a model of literary perfection. France, writes F. Brunetière, inaugurated literary cosmopolitanism. " If literary cosmopolitanism makes further gains, and succeeds in extinguishing the blood-hatreds which differences of race have kindled, I see there a great gain for civilization and for all humanity. . . . For the hatreds of races, more terrible than all others, have something animal about them, something therefore particularly *unhumane*." From 1726, when Voltaire ventured into what was then considered " the sacred horror of the Shakespearean forests," to 1810, when Madame de Staël published *De l'Allemagne*, France was steadily extending the free commerce of the republic of letters.[1]

---

[1] F. Brunetière, *Études critiques* (1905), 6ᵉ série, " Le Cosmopolitisme et la Littérature française."

CHAPTER III

GOETHE AND VOLTAIRE: THE WAR
AGAINST HATRED AND PREJUDICE

THERE is a European atmosphere," wrote Sorel in *L'Europe et la Révolution française*; "the same ideas are spread everywhere; they are all French, and find by nature in France their most perfect expression." [1] The claim that the common eighteenth-century ideas were all French is not, in fact, justified. It is true, however, that the same ideas were spread everywhere in Europe, and possibly also that they were expressed with the nearest approach to perfection in France; Adam Smith wrote in 1766 that it was "the peculiar talent of the French nation to arrange every subject in that natural and simple order which carries the attention without any effort along with it." [2]

Certainly the great ideas were the common intellectual currency of the whole of educated Europe. The scholars and men of letters absorbed them with avidity; they warmed both hands before the fire of life. Every year some thrilling event occurred, some new book or discourse, in the world of letters or science. The princes of Europe had correspondents, like the Abbé Raynal and Grimm, who wrote regular and voluminous letters about the literary life of Paris. The eighteenth-century scholars could cope with all the books that came out. "They lived in a continual intellectual feast, which the world will never see again." [3] The whole of existing knowledge could still be grasped by a single mind. The eighteenth-century scholars believed that they were living in the fullness of time, and at the moment

---

[1] A. Sorel, *L'Europe et la Révolution française* (1912), vol. i, p. 147.
[2] F. W. Hirst, *Adam Smith* (1904), p. 119.
[3] E. Lavisse, *La Jeunesse du Grand Frédéric* (1916), p. 12.

of the complete development of civilization. They and the ages before them had produced a body of thought and culture which gave to mankind the possibility of becoming perfect. In order to place this final and complete accumulation of culture, this means of perfection, at the disposal of all men, a group of humane French scholars, with the assistance of the Académie and royal Government, undertook to compile an encyclopædia. The prospectus came out in 1750, subscribers being offered the whole set for 280 livres (£56).[1] This great work, thirty-five volumes, beginning to appear from the year 1751, received an eloquent testimony from Voltaire, himself one of the contributors :

> The last age has put the present in a condition to assemble into one body and to transmit to posterity, to be by them delivered down to remoter ages, the sacred repository of all the arts and all the sciences, all of them pushed as far as human industry can go. This is what a society of learned men, fraught with genius and knowledge, are now labouring upon, an immense and immortal work, which accuses the shortness of human life.

Scholars and men of letters freely exchanged ideas with each other. They read each other's works, whether those works were in French, like the *Encyclopædia*, or in Latin, like the *Acta Eruditorum*, or in translations, such as the French translations of Adam Smith's *Theory of Moral Sentiments* and *Wealth of Nations*. The scholars and men of letters moved about in various countries. Hume and, for a time, Adam Smith were perfectly familiar in the Paris *salons*. Montesquieu, Voltaire, and Rousseau passed considerable periods of time in England, and knew many eminent men there. Even if some scholars or men of letters travelled little, like Kant, who never went outside Germany (living continuously for nearly fifty years in Königsberg), and Goethe, who, except in his younger days, kept closely to Weimar, yet they were perfectly familiar with the intellectual development of the neighbouring peoples. The ideas which made the common stock of such scholars came from every-

[1] F. M. Grimm, *Correspondance* (1877), vol. i, p. 486.

where: theories of crime and punishment from Count Beccaria in Italy; educational theories from Pestalozzi in Switzerland; ideas on political philosophy from Rousseau in Geneva or Paris; ideas on Parliamentary law and constitutions from Bolingbroke and Blackstone and Bentham in England, on economics from Quesnai in France, from Adam Smith in Scotland; metaphysics from Kant in Germany; botany from Linnæus in Sweden. There was no intellectual 'nationalism'; every scholar regarded himself as an exponent and developer of European culture, as a member of the republic of letters. Voltaire and Goethe were the complete cosmopolitans.

Goethe was born in Frankfort in 1749, of a burgher 'patrician' family. The German *bourgeoisie* of the eighteenth century were all cosmopolitan, and especially the *bourgeoisie* of the smaller states, which had no military power, and no pride in war or conquest. Frankfort was a free city within the Empire. Its quaint streets and houses were romantic souvenirs of the Middle Ages. Its bankers, its printing-press, its political independence, its geographical position in the Rhineland, its cultured, liberal *bourgeoisie*, made it a cosmopolitan centre in Western Europe. Goethe's *Autobiography* describes his early life in this congenial environment: the spacious old house of his family, the gardens of the well-to-do citizens, the ancient civic dignity, the French military occupation during the Seven Years War, the impressive medieval pomp of the Imperial coronation of Joseph II. After studies at the universities of Leipzig and Strasbourg, and a short period in practice as a young lawyer before the Imperial Law Court (*Reichskammergericht*) at Wetzlar, he settled down in the Duchy of Weimar, a model state under an enlightened, liberal prince. For ten years he was an industrious, conscientious official. Weimar became a kind of Athens, a beautiful little town of culture and of moderate politics, the home of literary men and artists, the centre of attraction for cultured visitors. When Duke Carl August went on the campaign against Revolutionary France in 1792 Goethe went too; and although never enlisted or gazetted as a soldier, he went under fire, and was present at the battle of Valmy. A year later he was at the siege of Mainz, which was held by a French garrison, and went under fire several times. After that he retired to Weimar, and there spent the rest of his long life (except for a memorable visit to Italy in 1786–88 and a few occasional journeys) until his death in 1832, being for part of the time a Minister of State of the Duchy. He was interested in administration and good government; but he simply detested war and the ' high politics ' of the time. War to him was just a cruel, devouring monster, the tragic burden of suffering humanity. For the warriors who bore a large part of this tragic burden in their own persons he had sympathy and admiration; for war itself only loathing. His loathing for it was increased all the more by the fact that war was unnecessary, avoidable, if only people would be sensible and would co-operate. " My children," says the good landlord to Rose and George, his tenant-farmers, in *Der Bürgergeneral*, " love each other and look after the land and your household. Let every one begin with himself and he will find plenty to do. Let him honourably seek the advantage of himself and those dependent on him, and he will thus contribute to the general welfare." A modern critic—not a German, but an Italian—sums up Goethe's personality as being " calm virtue, earnest goodness and justice, wisdom, balance, good sense, sanity, and, in a word, all those qualities which are generally laughed at as being *bourgeois*." [1] In *Hermann und Dorothea* Goethe writes: " To build and maintain one happy home serves mankind better than all the talk about the rights of man." What he had observed of the French campaign in 1792 and later convinced him that no revolution was ever worth the price which had to be paid for it. [2]

After his two campaigns, Valmy and Mainz, Goethe saw no more fighting. He remained at Weimar, occupied in long years of tranquil work at his books and in his official duties, and in conversation with his friends and distinguished visitors. He paid little attention to affairs outside the Duchy, though

[1] B. Croce, *Goethe* (trans. Ainslie, 1923), p. 3.
[2] See G. P. Gooch, *Studies in Modern History*, "Goethe" (1931), p. 163.

he read the journals and knew what was happening in the
' great world.' He met Napoleon at Erfurt in 1808 and conceived a deep admiration for the Emperor. Napoleon, on his
side, warmly admired Goethe, and always carried *Werther* with
him on campaigns, and was said to know long passages of it
by heart. It would be quite incorrect to conceive of Goethe
as indifferent to the Great War which was in progress. On
the contrary, like Kant, who too was digging his mine for peace
at Königsberg, Goethe was reflecting on the long-drawn-out
human tragedy, and expressed his passionate hatred of war and
his conception of its lack of reason in one work after another
—*Reise der Söhne Megaprazons; Der Bürgergeneral; Die Bela-
gerung von Mainz; Die Aufgeregten; Das Mädchen von Ober-
kirch; Hermann und Dorothea; Unterhaltungen,* a sort of new
Decameron, " the French armies playing the disruptive part
which in the distant days of Boccaccio had been taken by the
plague " : a group of French exiles on the German side of the
Rhine tell a series of tales to each other in order to distract
their minds from the evil of the times. *Hermann und Dorothea*
is ' a sermon on war.' Goethe had seen the horrors of a battlefield, the hopeless miseries of a siege, and the poignant sufferings of refugees flying before the devastating armies of invaders.
In *Hermann und Dorothea,* however, against the dark background of war stand out in sharp relief " the angels of love
and hope." [1]

When Frederick William III of Prussia made the Peace of
Bâle with France in 1795, and arranged a ' line of demarcation '
within which all the existing German states should be regarded
as neutral, Goethe (along with Kant) was one of the few men
who completely approved. Weimar was within the line of
demarcation which guaranteed peace and quiet for men to go
about their labour, and which made the beating of the drums
of war into a distant echo. This, in Goethe's view, was statesmanship. " We have all cause to be thankful," he wrote to
his master, the Duke Carl August, for neutrality meant that
the Duchy would not be ravaged. " For me it is a new spring,"

[1] G. P. Gooch, *op. cit.*, p. 170, *op.* 168.

he wrote to Schiller, who, as Professor of History in the University of Jena, had become a great friend; " everything in my nature bursts into joyful life." When ten years later Frederick William III took up arms again Goethe felt no enthusiasm; and soon the dreadful sight of Prussian soldiers, after the rout at Jena, fleeing through Weimar before the French pursuers only confirmed his horror of war and his belief in its tragic futility. Even the War of Liberation in 1813 stirred him not at all. In later years he seems to have been reproached for not taking up arms against the French. " How could I take up arms without hatred? " he said to Eckermann. " How could I, to whom culture and barbarism are alone of importance, hate a nation which is among the most cultured on earth, and to which I owe so great a part of my own possessions? There is a stage where national hatred vanishes altogether, and where one stands to a certain extent above the nations, and feels the weal or woe of a neighbouring people as if it were one's own." This, notes a philosophic historian, " is the voice of the last and greatest of the cosmopolitans whose spiritual home was in the eighteenth century." [1] About a hundred years later Benedetto Croce, during the maddening tragedy of the World War, reread Goethe's works. " I consider it singularly fortunate," he wrote, " that among all the sublime poets, perennial sources of deep consolation, there should yet be one who, possessing a knowledge of human nature in all its aspects such as no other poet ever possessed, nevertheless keeps his mind above and beyond political sympathies and the inevitable quarrels of nations." [2] But Goethe would have denied that they were inevitable.

Voltaire is the other great cosmopolitan of the eighteenth century. It would not be correct to say that he had no country, but rather that every country was his own. He had a home; indeed, he had several homes. He took root easily—in England, in Belgium, in Potsdam, in Lorraine (at that time an independent duchy), in Geneva; and in all his various travels

[1] G. P. Gooch, *op. cit.*, p. 179.
[2] See above, p. 33; B. Croce, *op. cit.*, p. xvii.

and residences he kept in touch with Paris; for the last twenty years of his life he was a country gentleman, an active resident squire, on French soil, in the Pays de Gex. He had an immense correspondence with men of the European 'republic of letters' and with statesmen, with kings even. He was thrifty, wealthy, had investments and houses in several states, and was the freest man in Europe.

Born in 1694 at Paris, of a prosperous legal family, educated at the famous Jesuit school, the Lycée Louis le Grand, Voltaire grew to manhood in the dissipated, free-thinking, mocking society of the Regency. He became an elegant, if rather dangerous, trifler, with a sharp tongue and a sharp pen. He was twice sent to the Bastille, where he employed the leisure of that commodious and not uncomfortable home in writing plays. A caustic retort to the Duc de Rohan procured him a beating by the Duc's lackeys; and a challenge to the Duc to fight a duel led only to his arrest and exile in England. This was the beginning of Voltaire's very leisurely wanderings, which provided him with homes and friends under so many flags. He became, the lordly Saint-Simon said, " a kind of personage in the republic of letters and even a kind of *important* in certain circles."

Voltaire was nearly three years (1726-29) in England, where he wrote plays and poems, knew Pope, Congreve, Bolingbroke, and other wits, and made a good deal of money. He gathered materials for a series of letters on the English, admiring descriptions of English life, really attacks upon French institutions, upon the despotic and interfering system of government which he abhorred; and he wrote the life of Charles XII of Sweden, about whom, by reading, and by talking with statesmen like Bolingbroke, he collected an extraordinary amount of valuable information.

For the next three years he was in France, in incessant literary activity. He always had many works on hand, but the great thing at the present moment was the publication (1731) of *L'Histoire de Charles XII*. His *Lettres philosophiques sur les Anglais*, however, published in 1734, was seized by the French authorities and burned, and a warrant was issued for his arrest, but with his unrivalled faculty for publishing things, yet keeping within the safety-line, he was already comfortably settled in the independent Duchy of Lorraine.

From this time he was the complete cosmopolitan and the recognized head of the republic of letters. Lorraine is a pleasant country. The Duchy was well governed under a line of benevolent princes about whom Voltaire has written with pleasing gratitude in his *Siècle de Louis Quatorze*. The Duke in 1734 was Francis, later Grand Duke of Tuscany, husband of Maria Theresa of Austria, Emperor, father of Joseph II, and founder of the house of Lorraine-Habsburg. After 1737 the Duke was Stanislaus, ex-King of Poland, for whom Duke Francis obligingly gave way, being compensated with the Grand Duchy of Tuscany. Voltaire had a friend in Lorraine, the Marquise du Châtelet-Lomont, whose husband had a pleasant country-house or *château* among the hills at Cirey. She was young, cultured, witty, not very happy with her husband, who lived apart from her but came on occasional visits. The Château of Cirey was old and ruinous, but Madame du Châtelet restored it and laid out pleasant gardens round it. Voltaire was wealthy —he had about 80,000 livres or £4000 a year—and generous; he took up his home in the Château and contributed handsomely to the expenses of the household. He discussed the Latin classics with Madame du Châtelet, taught her English, read Tasso and Ariosto in the original Italian with her, studied with her the mathematical works of Leibniz and Newton, and helped with a translation, on which she was engaged, of Newton's *Principia*. Men of learning and letters visited them. Voltaire wrote plays—*Alzire*, *Mérope*, *Mahomet*—and produced them on a private stage. He composed an *Essay on Universal History* from Charlemagne to his own time. The life at Cirey just suited Voltaire. " A man of letters," he wrote, " must live in a free country, or reconcile himself to being a slave." Lorraine was a free country, and it was a frontier country, wedged between France and Germany. Voltaire always preferred to live in a frontier zone, partly because he could slip over the line, if necessary to escape from an arbitrary Government, partly because frontiers have an international and cosmopolitan aspect. A *coterie* of free kindred spirits was the social circle that he liked. " What a delicious existence," he writes, " to find oneself lodged with three or four men of letters, with talent and without jealousy, loving each other, living greatly, cultivating their art, talking about it, clearing up difficulties in common [*de s'éclairer mutuellement*]." It was a little Paradise, he said. " I only ask to live, immured, among the mountains of Cirey." As a matter of fact, Voltaire never remained immured anywhere very long. During the Cirey period he paid two quite long visits to Brussels, and successfully terminated there an ancient lawsuit of the Marquis du Châtelet, gaining for him some 220,000 livres. This was in 1740, the year Frederick the Great mounted the throne of Prussia.

One of the first things that Frederick did as king was to set forth on a tour of his large and scattered dominions, which extended from the Baltic to Guelderland. When he came near Brussels he sent a message expressing his desire to meet Voltaire, who, the King suggested, might make the first advance. " We prepared elegant apartments for him," writes Voltaire, " in the little Château de Meuse, two leagues from Cleves." Voltaire went there, found a single soldier on guard at the door, and the King inside, not in one of the grand prepared rooms, but in a little bare closet, lying on a truckle-bed. Frederick had a fit of the ague. Voltaire, who thought that he knew medicine (and everything else), felt the King's pulse. The fit ceased; the King rose, dressed himself, and forthwith sat down to table with Voltaire, the Dutch ambassador, and two scholars who had come on the royal tour, Algarotti, a Venetian, and Maupertuis, a Frenchman, both eminent physicists. This was in September 1740, and was the beginning of Voltaire's long and sometimes stormy friendship with the great King. In the following month the Emperor Charles VI " died of an indigestion, occasioned by the eating of a dish of champignons which brought on an apoplexy, and this plate of champignons changed the destiny of Europe." [1] Frederick II of Prussia almost at once (December 1740) invaded Silesia, and so started the War of the Austrian Succession. In that fateful year, 1740, shortly before the campaign opened, Voltaire, on Frederick's invitation, had paid a visit to Berlin and Potsdam, and heard the King say to the French ambassador, à propos of the coming war, " I am going, I believe, to play your game; and if I gain the ace we will share."

The ban against his living in Paris had been lifted by the French Government since 1735, so Voltaire paid occasional and sometimes lengthy visits there, and even obtained an appointment at Court as one of the gentlemen of the royal chamber. He was a valued visitor also at Sceaux, the *château* and *salon* of the Duchesse de Maine. Paris, Brussels, Cirey, Potsdam, were his various places of residence; he continued his literary activity and output in all of them. If anybody suggested that he worked too much he replied that it was no effort, that indeed it was both a necessity and a pleasure to him. " When the spirit has been for long devoted to *belles-lettres* it gives itself up to them without trouble and without effort, as the hand of a musician travels without fatigue over the clavier." Once or twice Voltaire acted as semi-official diplomatic envoy between France and Prussia. In 1748 Madame du Châtelet and he went, on the invitation of Stanislaus, ex-King of Poland, at this time Duke of Lorraine, to Lunéville. It is a pleasant enough little town, and Stanislaus, who was something of a *roi philosophe*, kept a Court which Voltaire found to be tolerably agreeable. In 1749, however, Madame du Châtelet died. Voltaire felt that he could no longer bear to live in Lunéville. So he went to Paris, and later, in 1750, to Frederick the Great at Potsdam. He was treated with much honour, had a fine suite of rooms put at his disposal, could order his own meals and dine alone when he chose, could carry on his literary work and attend the King's witty supper-parties as he pleased. The society of the great King was even more Voltairean than Voltaire quite liked. Frederick was

[1] Voltaire, *Memoirs* (trans. 1826), p. 41.

married, but ignored and neglected his wife. Voltaire wrote:
" Neither women nor priests ever entered the palace; and
Frederick lived without religion, without a council, and without a Court." In the end Voltaire and the King had a quarrel
over a lampoon, *La Diatribe du Docteur Akakia*, which Voltaire
had written against Maupertuis, President of the Royal
Academy of Berlin. Voltaire left Potsdam in 1753, with his
niece, who kept house for him, and made a leisurely journey
through Germany. They were both arrested in the Free City
of Frankfort, and their baggage searched for unpublished poems
of Frederick's at the King's orders. Later he was able to proceed to the watering-place of the Vosges, Plombières, and from
there to Lyons; at last, as the French Government did not
encourage him to settle down in France, he bought a charming
country-house and about sixty acres on the bank of the Rhône,
in the territory of Geneva, just outside the gate of the city. The
district was healthy. In Théodore Tronchin, Bolingbroke's
protégé, Geneva possessed one of the finest physicians in
Europe. The house and land cost a great deal—twice what
they would have cost near Paris; but pleasure, wrote Voltaire,
is never too dear. The Rhône rushed by the foot of his garden.
In the distance the Alps terminated the horizon, covered with
eternal snow. He was, apparently, one of the first men to
appreciate mountain scenery. Just entering upon his sixtieth
year, escaped from kings and tyrant Governments, he found
a quiet refuge and lived happily, even, as he calls it, in that
" iron age." He watched with sardonic amusement and regret
the kings and emperors of the civilized world levy upon each
other the war which weighed upon their suffering people for
seven years. Inclined as he was to frontier zones, he bought
a few years later another estate at Ferney, in the Pays de Gex,
in French territory, on the shore of Lake Geneva; and gradually he came to spend most of his time there. He also bought
a house and land in canton Vaud. It was *à propos* of these
purchases that he wrote (as already quoted): " At last I so
managed my destiny that I was independent in Switzerland,
in the territories of Geneva, and in France. I have heard

much of liberty, but I do not believe there is an individual in Europe who has wrought his own freedom like me."

At Les Délices (his Geneva home) and at Ferney Voltaire entertained nobly, though he " never became the slave of his guests." Every eminent man who came to the neighbourhood was sure to visit the squire of Ferney. He was a good country gentleman, developed his estate, built a church for the inhabitants, planted trees, established a local craft or trade in watches. He had a private theatre in his own house for the performance of his plays. It was in the early years of his Geneva period that he wrote *Candide* (1758–59); and in one fiery pamphlet or letter after another he stood up for justice. The Duc de Choiseul, lately Prime Minister of France, in retirement at Chanteloup, was his friend. His greatest, but by no means his only, triumph in the cause of justice was the restoration of the good name, with compensation to the widow, of Jean Calas, a Protestant who had been condemned and broken on the wheel and burned (1762) by the Parliament of Toulouse on a charge of killing his son.[1] The advent to power of the philosophic statesman Turgot filled the old Voltaire (aged eighty-four) with hope and optimism. " We are now in the Age of Gold," he wrote.

Candide, which is very good reading simply as a tale, is a vivid description of the world in the eighteenth century, a travel novel, exposing and ridiculing prejudice, a cosmopolitan philosophy of life. The tale takes the reader pleasantly from Westphalia to Bulgaria, to Portugal. At Lisbon the travellers experience the great earthquake of 1750. Candide, Pangloss, and Cunégonde go into Spain and take ship from Cadiz and land in the Jesuit dominion of Paraguay. From here they go to the Inca territory of El Dorado, where children play with lumps of gold and leave them lying in the street. The travellers approach Surinam, the busy town of the Dutch island-colony. They find by the wayside a negro slave, half naked, with one leg and one arm, mutilated in a sugar-mill. " It is at this price that you eat sugar in Europe," says the slave. They take ship for France ; next

---

[1] For the Calas affair see below, pp. 83–84.

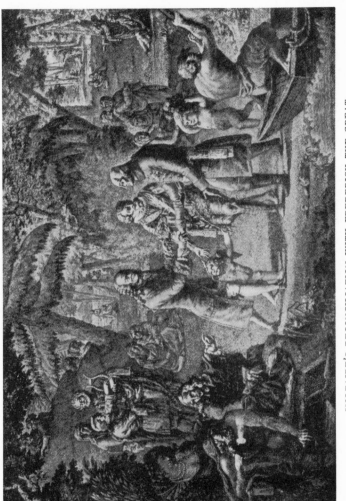

VOLTAIRE'S RECONCILIATION WITH FREDERICK THE GREAT

The scene depicts the Elysian Fields.

From a contemporary print

to England, where, at Portsmouth, they witness the execution of Admiral Byng. From England they go to Venice, where the famous incident of the six exile-kings takes place.[1] They complete the journey round the world at Constantinople. They have seen all nations and their prejudices. A " good Mussulman," who has excellent coffee and four or five children, tells them the secret of his happiness—" work, which keeps away the three great evils: tedium, vice, and want." The citizens of the world agree. " Grandeur is highly dangerous," says Pangloss. " To work without thinking [*travailler sans raisonner*]," says Martin; " this is the only way to make life bearable." Pangloss, the philosopher, points out that all their experiences, however painful, show that this is the best of all possible worlds. If they had not adventured round the world they would not now be eating sweetmeats and *pistachios* at Constantinople. " Well said," replies Candide, " *mais il faut cultiver notre jardin.*"

After Voltaire's death his friends the Marquis and Marquise de Villette, who became the proprietors of Ferney, made his bedroom into a museum. They deposited Voltaire's heart there in an urn, and placed pictures of his friends round the wall.[2] The pictures included those of three sovereigns, Catherine the Great of Russia, Frederick the Great of Prussia, and Stanislaus of Poland; of men of letters, Diderot, Helvétius, Condorcet; of statesmen, Benjamin Franklin, the Duc de Choiseul, the Duc de Richelieu, Turgot, Necker; of ladies of intellect and society, Madame du Châtelet, Madame du Deffand, Ninon de l'Enclos (who died when Voltaire was fourteen), and many others. Not even Dr Johnson or David Hume had such a circle of friends, such a world of friendship in his heart. In the eighteenth century the world of learning and the world of letters, though grand in its outlook, was small in its area. The eighteenth-century scholars were fortunate in being able

---

[1] For the Byng incident see below, p. 74; for the Venetian scene see p. 169.
[2] Picture of " La Chambre au cœur de Voltaire " in *Histoire de littérature française*, by Abry, Audic and Crouzet (1931), p. 372. In 1864 the heart and urn were presented to the French nation.

to know almost every one and everything. They had the best society of men and minds, and the joy of creativeness, an intellectual feast the like of which can scarcely occur again.

The characters of Goethe and Voltaire differed greatly from each other. Goethe was serene, ' Olympian,' indifferent to world politics, only interested in culture, in purely scientific inquiry, in art and letters. There was a classic calmness about his spirit, which showed his kinship with the Greeks, with the unruffled nature and simplicity of the expression, for instance, of the Venus of Milo. The classical spirit exists with difficulty to-day. " Antiquity will retain for some time yet for the initiated the grace of its arts and the charm of its eternal and simple wisdom; then it will vanish into night. A hundred years ago it was the light. All cultured men found in classical antiquity the life of their intelligence. They found there the perfection of form and thought." [1] Such, essentially, was Goethe's view. Voltaire, it is true, was, in a sense, classical, but with affinities to Latin rather than to Greek studies. The strong-minded men of the Roman Republic appealed to him, with their ideal of a universal and equal law, their passion for sane order and justice. But at this point the classical affinity of Voltaire ceased. There was nothing serene about him. He was never tranquil. Incessantly busy, active, unsettled; living amid conversations, recitations, dramatic performances, dramatic compositions; writing pamphlets, championing prisoners, attacking out-of-date institutions, exposing shams, thrusting at unchallenged forces of the Church and at the Christian religion itself; buying, selling, investing; generous, hospitable; overflowing with ideas, plans, and ambitions, Voltaire is a type of the restless genius for whom no task is too great, no avenue of human enterprise too remote. Yet he and Goethe had, at any rate, one great thing in common : they were above the prejudices that still persisted from the days of medieval darkness, and above other prejudices which post-Renaissance Europe had produced. They were open-minded men, not confined and warped by inhuman misconceptions drawn from

[1] E. Lavisse, *La Jeunesse du Grand Frédéric*, p. 42.

race, country, religion. " Nor will I rest now," wrote Goethe during his Italian journey, " until nothing is mere word and tradition to me any more." Goethe and Voltaire were both " without prejudice," and hated cant, hypocrisy, selfishness, and hatred itself. Goethe and Voltaire alike stood for, and won, the exercise of the single virtue which makes mankind share in the divine—freedom of mind and spirit, self-ordained, self-controlled.

Chapter IV

ARMIES

IF the eighteenth century failed to eliminate war from civilized Europe, at any rate it was sensible in its attitude towards soldiers. It regarded the military career as a profession or a trade; the men who chose that profession earned a living, like other people, and were entitled to no more and no less respect than other people on this account. Death or wounds were accidents or incidents of the profession or the services for which a soldier drew his pay. Nobody, theoretically at any rate, was forced to serve, except in Prussia, where about half the army could, according to the regulations of 1733, be recruited by conscription from the villagers, and in Russia. The hellish device of putting a whole nation into the army and making the common man, willy-nilly, go into battle to suffer and to die was never thought of by the aristocrats and despots of the *ancien régime*, who, with all their faults, were gentlemen. There were always young men ready to enter the military trade, just as there were young men ready to enter other trades. There were always time-expired soldiers, willing to be re-engaged. These men, the young and the experienced alike, knew or were supposed to know the conditions of service. They received wages and took the consequences.

War was merely a means of settling differences between states. Voluntary soldiers, drawing a daily wage, were expensive, but, serving for years at a stretch, they were highly trained. Therefore, partly because it required time to train men, partly because state revenues were not elastic, an army was a valuable thing, which could not easily be replaced. War was waged for the most part by means of these voluntary, professional armies; and when the army of one state had been destroyed (but it never quite came to that) or seriously diminished in size and strength by the action of the opposing army the game was finished, the war was over. The civilian populations were not supposed to be interested in the struggle, and were not asked to take part. On campaign it was understood that they were to be left severely alone, though in fact their villages were sometimes burned. It was like the wars of the Italian cities as carried on by *condottieri* in the fifteenth century, only in the eighteenth century more blood was shed. The mercenary soldiers fought and died, and when more had died on one side than on the other the dispute was finished by a treaty of peace. As each state used its professional army as a means of settling its political disputes with other states (failing settlement by negotiation), it did not care where the professional soldiers came from so long as they knew their business. The eighteenth-century autocratic Governments were not nationally minded. They had to recruit a certain number of soldiers. If young men of the nation offered themselves for service they were accepted and were put into training; if foreigners, especially when they were ' old soldiers '—that is, trained men who knew their business—they were accepted with alacrity. All the Continental armies of the eighteenth century contained numerous foreigners, whole regiments of them. As armies were composed of volunteers, Governments had ' enrollers ' or ' recruiters ' in various countries, whose business was to engage men for the forces. The monarchs of France, Prussia, and Russia all had recruiters, sometimes called ' crimps,' in the countries of Central Europe, who by fair means or foul enticed young men to leave their native land and to join the army of a neighbour or even of a very distant state. As Candide found, in Voltaire's spirited romance, the polite stranger at an inn who invited a lonely young man to share a meal was really an agent for *le roi des Bulgares* or some other almost unknown potentate requiring recruits for his grenadiers. " ' Drink to the health of the King of the Bulgars ! Your fortune is made, young man ! ' Almost before he knows where he is, he is turning to right, to left, pushing the ramrod, drawing out the ramrod, levelling the musket, firing, quick marching, and he is given thirty strokes with the cane." [1] The standing army of France before the Revolution often had as much as half its strength in men who were not born in France; the army of King Frederick William I of Prussia comprised over one-third foreigners. [2]

The rank and file of a Continental army served for small wages. The Austrian infantryman was paid six kreutzer, about three-halfpence, a day, with an extra kreutzer daily as field allowance during war. The corporal had ten kreutzer. Privates in special corps—sappers, miners, artillerymen—had eight to ten kreutzer daily. The commissariat was responsible for feeding them, or else they were entitled to a certain messing allowance. Private soldiers in the Prussian Army were paid about twopence a day. A Prussian captain was paid forty thaler (about £5) a month, a lieutenant twelve thaler (about £1 15s.) a month. [3]

The officers were not so ' mixed ' as the men. A large proportion of them were nationals of the country of the army in which they served. Foreign officers, however, were quite common. At the end of a campaign a large number of officers and men were inevitably paid off and sent back to civilian life. Naturally many of these preferred to look for service elsewhere, and they offered themselves where soldiers were wanted. The nobility of the Prussian county of Cleves generally sought a career, which for some of them would prove to be permanent, in the service of the Dutch, who were just over the Cleves border. Other Prussian officers would be found serving in a French regiment, on condition, naturally, that they were not employed against the King of Prussia; if there was a war between France and Prussia they would be posted to a garrison on the French or Sardinian frontier, or given an opportunity of service in Canada or India. The Russian and Turkish Armies had many foreign officers, particularly in the

---

[1] Voltaire, *Candide*, Chapter II.
[2] H. Tuttle, *History of Prussia* (1883), p. 386 *n*.
[3] Information supplied by Professor A. Dopsch, Seminar für Wirtschaft-und-Kulturgeschichte, Wien, from Bibliothek des Kriegsarchivs, Wien, and by Hans Snyckers, Leipzig.

artillery or engineering branches. The Comte de Bonneval, of the Turkish Army, rose to be a Pasha of three tails and Governor of Chios. He died at Constantinople in 1747. He had a fine mansion there, and passed his last years agreeably over books, philosophy, and wine, as Casanova says he found on visiting him. The Austrian Army had officers of almost every European nation; the Spanish Army, like the French, offered a particular welcome to Irish Roman Catholics or Scottish Jacobites, debarred from an active career under the British Crown. Marshal Keith, a Protestant Jacobite, friend of Frederick the Great, killed at Hochkirch in 1758, had served in the Spanish, Russian, and Prussian Armies. Younger sons and also ruling princes of small German states, like Anhalt-Dessau or Waldeck, or even of comparatively large states, like Baden and Brunswick, entered the Austrian or Prussian service, and might serve for their whole lifetime. Thus the military profession was really international. General Fink von Finkenstein, one of the tutors of Frederick the Great as Crown Prince, had served with the Dutch under William of Orange, with the French under Luxembourg, and in the Prussian Army under Frederick I and Frederick William I.

The Prince de Ligne draws a picture of one of these cosmopolitan knights-errant, the Prince of Nassau-Siegen. Ligne himself was an instance of the same kind; a Belgian, native of the " Austrian Netherlands," he spent his military career in the service of Maria Theresa and Joseph II, but as a courtier he was almost as familiar at Versailles and St Petersburg as at Vienna. On the voyage down the Dnieper in 1788 with Catherine II and Joseph II, reclining in his tent, " on the shore of the Black Sea," during a brilliant night which prevented him from sleeping, Ligne reviewed in his mind some of his recent extraordinary experiences : [1]

> I have just seen four naval battles won by a volunteer who, since the age of fifteen, has known how to acquire glory by brilliant adventures : a fine, good-looking little *aide-de-camp* attached

[1] Prince de Ligne, *Mémoires*, vol. i, pp. 186–187 (letter of August 1, 1788).

to a general who gave him plenty to do; as lieutenant of infantry, captain of dragoons, courtly knight avenging female wrongs, rectifying the ills of society; quitting, in order to go round the world, all the pleasures of society, for which he was compensated for an instant by the Queen of Otaité, in Asia. Killing monsters, like Hercules; back again in Europe, as colonel of a regiment of French infantry and of a regiment of German cavalry, without knowing German; chief of an expedition, captain of a vessel, almost buried and drowned in the service of Spain, major-general of the Spanish Army, officer-general in the service of three countries whose language he does not know, and the most brilliant vice-admiral Russia has ever had. They have refused him the position that is due to him, and he has made one for himself till such time as justice shall grant him the one that is properly his. By birth Nassau-Siegen, he has become Nassau-Sieger through his exploits. You know that *Sieger* in German means ' conqueror.' He was recognized at Madrid as an ancient nobleman of Spain without having the least idea of it; in Germany he is a Prince of the Empire, although his estates have been given to another. If injustice had not deprived him of them, he would have expended some of his fiery temper on wild boars or perhaps on poachers, but his taste for danger would soon have given him an idea of his value in war.

What then is his sorcery? His sword is his magic wand; his example is his conjuring book. And, again, his sword is also his interpreter, for he uses it to indicate the shortest line when it is a question of attack. His eyes, sometimes as terrible for friends as for enemies, complete the explanation. His tactics are in his glance; his talent lies in the experience which his zeal has caused him to seek; his science in the short, concise, clear orders which he gives on the day of battle and which are always easy to translate and to understand; his merit lies in the precision of his ideas; his resources in a great and strongly pronounced character, which one can read on his face; and his success in an unparalleled courage of body and mind.

The internationalism of eighteenth-century armies, the travelling propensities of the eighteenth-century soldiery, were reminiscent of the Age of Chivalry, of medieval knights and craftsmen:

The profession of arms did not yet know the frontiers between peoples. War was loved for itself, and the gentry sought it everywhere, as formerly the knights flocked to the Crusades or to adventures. The common soldier was a sort of workman of the military corporation, who toured the world and stopped wherever the trade was good—that is, where war, falling upon some fat country, could nourish its artisan. As soon as the country is exhausted the news is spread everywhere; the war is said to be ' crabbed,' has a bad name in Flanders, or on the Rhine, or in Lombardy. In that case the pay of the soldiers has to be raised.[1]

The old soldier, particularly the officer, had many tales to tell, not simply of one army or one commander, but of perhaps all the armies of Europe, and of all the great captains of the age under whom he had served—William of Orange, Luxembourg, Marlborough, Eugène, Villars. Like General Oglethorpe, who had served in the Austrian Army against the Turks and in the British Army against the French, and among the Georgian colonists against the Spaniards of Florida, the retired officer of many campaigns and many masters could be found in the social groups of the coffee-houses of London, Edinburgh, The Hague, Berlin, Vienna, and Paris, and in some of the most distinguished *salons*.

Scholar-soldiers were not uncommon. In those days no attempt was made to fill up all the time of a garrison officer. He had his parades, and, if he was a colonel, he had a little office work; but there were many hours each day for him with nothing to do. Some spent these hours in study. Few such officers became as celebrated scholars as Descartes, the seventeenth-century philosopher who was an officer in the Dutch and Austrian armies. Maupertuis, however, the scientist, who became President of the Academy of Berlin, is an instance.[2] Another is Vauvenargues, who was almost the most noted writer of maxims (at any rate, after La Rochefoucauld) in the eighteenth century, and to whom Sainte-Beuve has consecrated one of his fine studies.

---

[1] E. Lavisse, *La Jeunesse du Grand Frédéric*, p. 16.
[2] See *infra*, p. 259.

Luc de Clapiers, Marquis de Vauvenargues, was born at Aix, in Provence, on August 6, 1715. His father belonged to the official class, *noblesse de robe*. Owing to delicate health, he had a poor education; he stands alone among the famous French writers of the eighteenth century, as knowing neither Latin nor Greek. At the age of eighteen he obtained a commission in the army, and fought in 1734, the War of the Polish Succession, in Italy, and in 1742, the War of the Austrian Succession, in Bohemia; in Marshal Belleisle's retreat from Prague he had his feet frostbitten. Next he took part in the battle of Dettingen, in 1743. Vauvenargues was a just officer, beloved by his company. Dettingen was his last battle; he had to retire from the service with his health ruined.

While still a soldier, in the monotonous periods of barrack life, he had turned, like Descartes in the previous century, to the love of letters and philosophy and the practice of writing, and had corresponded on literature with the Marquis de Mirabeau, father of the more famous statesman of that name, and with Voltaire. On retiring from military service Vauvenargues, though his means were very small, took up residence at Paris and was received into the circle of Marmontel. In 1746 his important work appeared: *Introduction à la connaissance de l'esprit humain, suivie de réflexions et maximes*. In the same year he offered himself with his fellows, the gentlemen of Provence, for the army against the Austrians, who had invaded his native province; but his health made service impossible. He died of consumption on May 28, 1747, at the age of thirty-one. His literary and philosophical work is distinguished by grace, force and precision, sobriety and strictly controlled imagination; Sainte-Beuve has compared him to Xenophon.

Ewald von Kleist, the poet, was a professional soldier, and, like Vauvenargues, a fine instance of the type of scholar-officer. He was born in the same year as Vauvenargues, on March 3, 1715, at Zeblin, in Pomerania. He belonged to an old landed family. Although Protestant, he was educated at the Jesuit college at Deutsch-Krone, and later at the Danzig *Gymnasium*.

In 1731 he became a law student at the University of Königsberg, where he also studied theology, philosophy, and classical literature.

On completing his university studies Kleist entered the Danish Army, in which his grandfather had served as major. On the accession of Frederick II of Prussia he returned to Germany and obtained a commission in one of the newly formed Prussian regiments. During the first part of the War of the Austrian Succession his regiment was in garrison at Potsdam. Kleist had no sympathy with the amusements of his brother officers. He had made friends with a civil servant of about his own age, Gleim, a former student of the University of Halle and a gifted ' Anacreontic ' poet; with his friend he read poetry, and began himself to write. Campaigning in the latter part of the war, in Bohemia, he was impressed by its horrors. Retired to garrison life, he wrote poems on war and on country life—the life which he sighed after, in vain.

Kleist was unmarried, and inclined to melancholy. Poetry was his consolation, especially poetry of the countryside. In 1749 his great poem *Frühling* (*Spring*) was published, the year after the publication of the first part of Klopstock's *Messias*. Recognized as a work of genius, *Frühling* brought Kleist the friendship of Wieland and other poets, and opened the happiest period of his life.

When the Seven Years War came Kleist went on active service with his regiment. After the Prussian Army overran Saxony he was stationed for a time in Leipzig, at that time the most cultured city in Germany. Next he went on campaign during the Russian invasion of Prussia. Leading his company against a Russian battery at Kunersdorf on August 12, 1759, Kleist, now a major, was wounded in the right hand. Taking his sword in his left hand, he continued the fight along with his men until a ball shattered his right leg. Without medical attendance he lay all night on the battlefield; next morning he was taken to Frankfort-on-the-Oder, where he died on August 24.

The officers as well as the men were ' international,' because they depended upon their profession for their living; therefore they went where they could find employment. Something of the ' European ' ideal of chivalry lingered on, particularly in France. Smollett, visiting France in 1763, wrote :

> I respect the French officers in particular for their gallantry and valour; and especially for that generous humanity which they exercise towards their enemies, even amidst the horrors of war. This liberal spirit is the only circumstance of ancient chivalry which, I think, was worth preserving. It had formerly flourished in England, but was almost extinguished in a succession of civil wars, which are always productive of cruelty and rancour. It was Henry IV of France, a real knight-errant, who revived it in Europe.[1]

The *punctilio* of honour between the officers of opposing armies is expressed in the story related about the opening of the battle of Fontenoy, in Flanders, in 1745. The French and British lines were, of course, quite close to each other when musketry-firing became practicable. According to the story the British officers politely called across to the French, " *Messieurs des Gardes Français, tirez les premiers* "; and the gallant and chivalrous French officers called back, " *Non, non, nous ne tirons jamais les premiers.*" So each side bared its breast to receive the first shot.

Naturally, conditions of service were not the same in every country, but they approximated to a considerable extent to each other. The Prussian troops were recruited in regiments of three battalions, the battalion comprising 800 men. Most of the regiments, except Guards, and certain other special corps, were territorial, each recruited from its own district or canton, although only one-half or two-thirds of the total number could be recruited from the canton; the balance consisted of foreigners. The regiments had their territorial names, Baireuth Dragoons, Derschau Foot, and such. Recruits were taken exclusively from the peasantry, and none must be the

---

[1] Tobias Smollett, *Travels in France and Italy*, Letter XV, Nice (January 3, 1764).

only son of a peasant. For ten months of the year 10 per cent. of the effectives of each battalion were on leave, frequently in foreign countries, where they sought recruits for the regiment. The recruiting sergeants were not too scrupulous. A stranger who had lost his passport, or who was simply gullible and inexperienced, was in hourly danger of being crimped by them, especially if he were tall and well made. Count Pentenriedter, one of the best Austrian diplomatists, on his way to the Congress of Cambrai in 1726, had a breakdown in his carriage when he was near the Prussian city of Halberstadt. He was a tall, active man, so he left his lackeys to make the necessary repairs to the carriage while he walked on to the city. When he reached the town gate and guardhouse, without his papers or servants, the Prussian officer had him seized for a recruit to the King's Potsdam Guards. The ambassador protested, fruitlessly, but the ludicrous incident was closed by his anxious lackeys coming up with carriage and baggage and greeting him as " Excellency." Voltaire, in his novel *Candide*, has his hero crimped at an inn by the two polite strangers who offer to pay for Candide's supper. Thackeray's Barry Lyndon was a real man, crimped for Frederick the Great's army.[1] All the battalions or companies were employed as garrisons in towns. They had their work on the parade-ground and in the fort, but for the most part they (and certainly all the unmarried soldiers) lodged with private citizens. Each town had to pay a sum sufficient for the board and lodging of the soldiers; and this sum was used in providing quarters by private arrangement. By the regulations of Frederick the Great the soldiers must not sleep more than four in a room, and the room must not be a cellar in the ground nor an attic under the roof. The burgess provided only room. Each group of soldiers in a house formed their own mess and bought their food out of their pay and mess-allowance. Every member of the mess took his turn to cook for his companions with their own pots, but using the kitchen fire of the landlord. Good behaviour on the side of

[1] For Pentenriedter see Carlyle, *Frederick*, Book V, Chapter V ; also Mowat, *History of European Diplomacy, 1451–1789* (1928), p. 219.

the landlord and soldiers was strictly enforced. In a few important towns the King had barracks, where quarters were provided for the married men.[1]

Every summer the troops were concentrated in Silesia, for Austria was the most likely enemy, and in any case difficulty of communications made concentration elsewhere—for instance, in the Rhineland—practically impossible in Frederick's widespread dominions. This annual review was more for the purpose of inspection than of military exercises or grand-scale manœuvres. The regiments were inspected man by man, and every defect in equipment or in health was closely examined. Opportunity was then taken to weed out all the unfit, those whose old wounds had become putrid, or chests consumptive, or whose lack of teeth made them unfit for active service. Every two years grand manœuvres were held, and the soldiers were inured to war conditions. A small provision was made for discharged private soldiers; some received little pensions, others were given low positions in the excise or such office; the best of these petty employments under the Government were reserved for retired non-commissioned officers. For commissioned officers a number of pensions were secured on Silesian abbeys and on certain other funds which were at the disposal of the Crown. Frederick instituted the Order *pour le mérite*, but, as he said, it did not carry a sou with it. Successful generals after a war were not, as a rule, endowed with estates and a fortune, although Marlborough was given the magnificent house and lands of Blenheim by Queen Anne, Maurice de Saxe was made life tenant of Chambord by Louis XV, and the Emperor Joseph I made one of his field-marshals Sovereign Prince of Liechtenstein. Prussian generals, and most others, had to be content with their pay when in work; and they were fortunate if they drew a pension in retirement.

Discipline was exact and severe, for soldiers were to be taught to obey blindly, so that they could march steadily up

[1] *Das Politische Testament Friedrichs des Grossen von 1752* (ed. Kuntzel und Hass, 1920), pp. 86–87.

to the opposing line without firing a shot, and could change
direction or even change ranks under fire at the order of their
officers. Any soldier, whether officer or private, who refused
an order, or drew his weapon to defend himself against a
superior, was punished by death. A less serious offence might
be condoned by the soldier running the gauntlet; as he stag-
gered down the line he was beaten with the canes of the soldiers
from each side. Voltaire wrote that the philosophical Frederick
would stand at his window reasoning upon ethics with a companion while he watched condemned soldiers run the terrible
gauntlet, up and down, six-and-thirty times.[1] Conditions in
the British Army were said to be even worse. Foreign visitors
to an English camp or garrison fled in terror and astonishment
from the shrieks of the flogged soldiers; the men were strapped
to the halberds; "rows of bleeding bodies were the daily
feature of life in the British camps."[2] Naturally these conditions provoked frequent desertions. The Prince de Ligne,
writing from Peterwardein in the campaign against the Turks
on the Danube in 1788, said 15,000 deserters from the French
Army did splendid service in the Austrian ranks (*quinze
mille déserteurs français se battent à merveille dans nos rangs*).[3]

There was a certain amount of trafficking, wholesale, in
soldiers during the time of war. Neutral princes could hire
out their regiments to belligerents. The best-known instance
of this is the German regiments hired to the British Government for service in the American Revolutionary War. The
princes who entered into these contracts were the Duke of
Brunswick, the Landgrave of Hesse-Cassel, the Princes of
Hesse-Hanau, Waldeck, Ansbach-Baireuth, and Anhalt-Zerbst.
The total number of men supplied was 30,000. The princes
received a bonus of five shillings for every soldier, and in
addition an annual subsidy during the period of the war. The

---

[1] Voltaire, *Memoirs*, p. 55. The six-and-thirty times in which a soldier
had to run the gauntlet is probably an exaggeration, as Voltaire in *Candide*
has his hero sentenced to this, but Candide actually only did two turns,
and then broke down.

[2] See G. Costigan, *Sir Robert Wilson* (1932), p. 20.

[3] Prince de Ligne, *Mémoires*, vol. i, p. 170.

subsidy paid by the British Government to the Landgrave of Hesse was £110,000 a year. The men received English pay (sixpence a day for infantry privates), and were well fed. Twopence-halfpenny was deducted daily for rations from their pay; in return for this deduction they were given two and a half pounds of beef and one and a half pounds of flour. If a soldier drew only one pound of beef and one pound of flour he could have English peas, Irish butter and rice for the balance; and all this while campaigning in the forests of North America.[1] There were no special service uniforms in the eighteenth century. Men went into battle in their long gaiters and high hats, whether they were in Canada or in Europe. In India, however, they were allowed to adapt their clothes to the climate. The equipment which the European soldiers carried was unconscionably heavy, and seriously impeded their power of manœuvring. Only the Turks had the sense to fight armed and clothed in light order.[2]

Every army on campaign was almost a moving town, for it included, or was followed by, numerous small tradesmen and hangers-on, including many women. Generals took their mistresses with them. Maurice of Saxe, who had expensive tastes, always took a troupe of actors and actresses with his army, to perform before him on his campaigns. The soldiers and the swarm of camp-followers exhausted the country, although everything taken from the inhabitants was supposed to be paid for by requisition notes, which, when the war was over, could be presented for encashment to the Treasury of the requisitioning state. Frederick the Great said that he honoured every requisition note and met it punctually on demand.

France and Holland had ancient regiments composed partly or entirely of foreigners, on a practically hereditary basis. The French foreign units consisted of Swiss Guards, for which there was a regular recruiting system, both for officers and men. The sons of families of the old Swiss territorial nobility regularly

---

[1] Pettengill, *Letters from America, 1776–1779* (1924), pp. 41–42.
[2] Prince de Ligne, *Mémoires*, vol. i, p. 197.

took commissions in these units, which were recognized by treaty between the Swiss Confederation and France. There were also some Irish units, which formed a brigade at the battle of Fontenoy, in 1745; they were more difficult to keep up to strength than were the Swiss regiments, as they were naturally not recognized by the British Government, and French recruiting agents were not permitted to come to Ireland. The officers of the Scottish regiments in the Dutch service came generation after generation from certain Scottish clans; the rank and file, however, were no longer chiefly Scots in the eighteenth century. " Mackay's regiment " was originally in the Swedish Army, and served in the campaigns of Gustavus Adolphus in the Thirty Years War. After the Peace of Westphalia it was discharged from Sweden, and, like the White Company of the Hundred Years War, or the Italian *condottieri* of the later Middle Ages, it went off as a body under its own colonel and accepted service with the States-General of the United Netherlands.

Every sovereign was still actual commander of his troops, and was trained to arms. This military aspect of the ruler, however, was not unduly emphasized, because there was little difference between the normal dress of a gentleman and the uniform of an officer. The eighteenth-century monarchs, accordingly, had not anything like the self-conscious parade of militarism of the nineteenth- and twentieth-century monarchs, usually un-military men, who were seldom, if ever, seen without stiff military tunic, Orders, and medals. As a matter of fact, the advance of the military art, the hard necessities of aiming at success in the field, were tending to keep the monarchs away from active command of armies on campaign, and to leave the conduct of battle to proved, professional commanders. The truth is that monarchs in that age were becoming a little ' soft.' The fashion of building copies of Versailles, and of living in a round of banquets and plays, was not conducive to the maintenance of the military qualities. Augustus II, the Strong, Elector of Saxony and King of Poland, though he had been an active commander of Imperial troops in the Turkish wars, became merely dissolute and luxurious before he reached middle age. Louis XV, though he went on a campaign in the War of the Austrian Succession, was no soldier. Frederick the Great, who, though he had no moral principles, was by nature Spartan, deplored the withdrawal of the monarchs from active service. He held that every monarch should have a regiment of his own, which he should regularly train and exercise, so as to keep himself up to the mark in military affairs, and to acquaint himself continuously with conditions in the army. " If the sovereign does not concern himself with the soldiers, and if he does not himself set the example to them, all is over [*Si le souverain ne se mêle pas lui-même du militaire, et s'il n'en donne pas l'exemple, tout est fini*]." [1] Frederick, it is well known, slept upon a camp-bed, and even in his particular palace, Sans Souci, preferred a little bare chamber; in this way of life he was followed by his young contemporary, the Emperor Joseph II. King George II of Great Britain kept up the fighting tradition of English kings by actually leading the advance of the infantry at Dettingen on foot, into the fire and bayonets of the hostile line; but he is the last English monarch recorded by history as having done such a thing. The Emperor Joseph II, the finest character among eighteenth-century monarchs, the only unselfish one of the whole lot, was no soldier and no believer in war, but he insisted on exposing himself freely under fire at the capture of Shabatz in 1788. The monarchs probably realized that war was, of all forms of public activity, the most incalculable, the most ' chancy.' The great captain Charles William Ferdinand, Duke of Brunswick, said to Mirabeau in 1786, discussing the possibility of his engaging in further military service : " If it were necessary in an affair so important to consult nothing further than the despicable gratification of self-love, do I not know how much war is the sport of chance? I have formerly not been unfortunate. I might hereafter be a better general, and yet might not have the same

---

[1] " Exposé du Gouvernement Prussien von Friedrich dem Grossen," in Kuntzel und Hass, *Die Politischen Testamenten der Hohenzollern* (1920), p. 107.

success. No prudent man, especially one who is advanced in life, will risk his reputation in so hazardous a pursuit, if it may be avoided." [1]

The military profession was not held in especially high respect. It was considered to be quite an honourable profession, at any rate for officers; but it was just like any other profession or trade which a man, according to his choice, could enter or not. It was not considered to be a citizen's duty to join the army because his Government happened to be at war; it was the duty only of the soldiers who were paid for this purpose. Dr Johnson said that every man thought meanly of himself for not having been a soldier; [2] and the poet Collins, during the Austrian Succession War, felt drawn to volunteer for the active army, but contented himself instead with writing an ode on the men who lost their lives at Fontenoy. There was no public opinion, no social pressure, upon peaceful young citizens to sacrifice themselves in their country's war. Governments did not seize and intern the citizens of an enemy Government found within their frontier, but, on the contrary, tolerated them and gave them permits to pursue their studies or business, as the British Government gave to the American artist Trumbull, in 1777, during the American Revolutionary War. The army being purely professional, the regard in which it was held largely depended upon the kind of people who entered it. The officers were gentry, and carried social respect with them; the men, because service in the ranks was unskilled labour and because of the severe disciplinary conditions, and because service unfitted them for civil life, enjoyed no such respect. ' Scoundrels,' ' rascals,' ' thieves,' were words often applied to them. The ' old ' soldier, skilled in all the ways of shirking duty and an adept at deserting, was a recognized character:

Among the dupes whom they enticed and captured there were decent quiet men who made the best of their wretched lot, though they never became reconciled to it; and in war-time the

[1] Mirabeau, *The Secret History of the Court of Prussia* (trans. 1789), vol. i, p. 12.
[2] James Boswell, *Johnson, sub anno* 1778.

more wayward and turbulent natures found congenial excitement in the hazards of a campaign, and the hopes of plunder and promotion. But the greater number sank into moral ruin, and became worthless citizens, and dishonest and disreputable soldiers. Always, and especially during a long peace, Europe swarmed with a nomad population of mercenaries. The tramps and vagrants of military life, they would serve one month in Turin, and another at Munich, and the next at Stuttgart, taking to the fields at the first opportunity which offered itself as soon as they had secured a bounty. They played this game in France, in Austria, in Holland, and (much more cautiously, and only as a desperate resource) in Prussia. Whatever garrison town might be their temporary domicile, they were everywhere watched like convicts, and punished with frightful severity. Each in his time had ridden the wooden horse, with a couple of muskets strapped to either foot; or had lain in a mouldy dungeon, or dragged a cannon-ball at his ankle on the ramparts, for years together; or had run the gauntlet of a battalion armed with switches as far down the line as he could stagger before he fainted. Without honour, without patriotism, they were thieves and drunkards; seducers in time of peace, and something much worse when during an invasion they had a village or farmhouse at their mercy. Hardly able, some of them, to name a country where they could ever make a home, and settle down to a trade without the almost certain prospect of being shot as deserters, they lived for the passing moment, intent only on misusing it in some manner agreeable to themselves.[1]

The coarseness and licentiousness of the soldiery are frequently mentioned in current literature. The seducing of innocent young women by a soldier billeted in a citizen's house is the tragic theme of several German novels or plays. The best-known, the most terrible, of these is Heinrich Leopold Wagner's tragedy *Kindermörderin* (*Child Murderess*), 1776, the story of a butcher's daughter ruined by an officer quartered in her father's house.

In 1789 the Englishman John Howard visited the military hospital at St Nicholas, in Southern Russia. He found it in

---

[1] G. O. Trevelyan, *The American Revolution* (1913), vol. ii, pp. 39–40. Quoted by kind permission of Messrs Longmans, Green and Co. Ltd.

a horrible condition, recruits, many in the prime of life, dying on coarse reeds, with no linen, no coverlets, only a few remnants of their old clothes to cover them; their persons dirty beyond description; their shirts in rags. He turned to the attendant officers and said " that in none of the countries I had ever visited, had I found so little attention paid to the military as in Russia." He walked on, and saw recruits at work, carrying sand on their backs to fill a mole. Many looked very sickly, and tottered under their burden.

Let but a contemplative mind reflect a moment upon the condition of those poor destitute wretches, forced from their homes and all their dearest connexions, and compare them with those one has seen, cheerful, clean, and happy, at a wedding, or village festival; let them be viewed quitting their birthplace, with all their little wardrobe, and their pockets stored with rubles, the gifts of their relations, who never expect to see them more; now joining their corps in a long march of one or two thousand wersts; their money gone to the officer who conducts them and defrauds them of the Government allowance; arriving, fatigued and half naked, in a distant, dreary country, and exposed immediately to military hardships, with harassed bodies, and dejected spirits;—and who can wonder that so many droop and die in a short time, without any apparent illness? The devastations I have seen made by war among so many innocent people, and this in a country where there are such immense tracts of land unoccupied, are shocking to human nature! [1]

Battlefields in the eighteenth century were, as they are in any time or place, appalling and horrible, but the men of that age did not deliberately try to make them worse. It was the custom between contending armies to permit an armistice, in order that the wounded might be saved and the dead buried. Only the Turks had the reputation of mutilating the fallen. " Nevertheless," said the Prince de Ligne, " this custom of cutting off heads does no great harm to the dead, and is sometimes a great blessing to the wounded: it at least prevents

[1] John Howard, *An Account of the Principal Lazarettos in Europe* (1791), Appendix, p. 20.

them from being made prisoner." [1] The Turks had one habit as soldiers which rendered them almost popular in the opinion of the Christian armies: they never attacked before ten o'clock in the morning, when the sun was comfortably warming the air and after they had taken their morning coffee. They made none of those dismal attacks in the chill dawn which were (and are) the rule in European armies, and which seemed designed to add the last item of lugubriousness to a baleful sacrifice. The Prince de Ligne knew the Turks only to have made one night-attack in the campaign of 1788, and that was when they wanted (and obtained) a Russian general's head.

The steadiest element in the armies was the non-commissioned officer. Unlike his betters he neither gamed nor drank; he was brave, self-controlled, punctual, and tidy; otherwise he never could have risen from the ranks. After release from the service he was the backbone of his country's administration, collecting customs dues, checking passports, enforcing the excise; or else he kept an inn and acted as postmaster along the stagecoach routes; or finally, in the villages where no pious foundation kept a school, he was the local schoolmaster, whipping into the boys a meagre but accurate knowledge of reading and writing and of the elementary arithmetic which he had learned in keeping his company or regimental accounts.

Most of the officers were sons of small gentry, living on their pay, for the army was never ' fashionable ' in the eighteenth century. They fell into three classes. The majority, the plodding, workmanlike, unimaginative, and unambitious regimental officer, never rose above the rank of lieutenant or, at most, captain in command of a company, throughout the whole twenty or thirty years of service. When he became middle-aged and heavy, but still not old enough to be retired, he was posted to some small quiet garrison town, while a younger and more active man was given his majority. A second class, marked by *esprit*, by quickness of mind and aptitude for speaking, writing, and planning, were taken away from their regiments (which they would never see again) and were placed in the

[1] Prince de Ligne, *Mémoires*, vol. i, p. 203.

General Staff. They became specialists, and laboured incessantly in the central bureaux at the same task—one officer in charge of the problem of communications; another, commissariat; another, munitions; another, drawing and designing. Count Thorane, the French lieutenant who was quartered on Goethe's father at Frankfort in 1759, was one of this kind. Charged with the duty of settling disputes between the citizens and the foreign soldiery, he showed himself to be fair-minded, polite, and considerate. He was intellectual and inclined to melancholy, and took an intense interest in the pictures of modern artists which Goethe's father possessed.[1] The third class were the active, keen field officers, who never left their unit until they had been promoted to the rank of colonel and, endowed with despotic authority, had commanded the regiment for some years. These men were selected for promotion with the greatest care, for it was among them that the high commanders were ultimately to be found: " they are the school of generals," wrote Frederick the Great. The qualities which were looked for among them by the final selecting authority were " bravery, knowledge of the art of war, capacity, and, above all, the happy instinct which makes an officer take the right decision immediately and without effort, as well as potentialities in his spirit, and resources in his imagination." All this was asking for a good deal. If Turennes could have been found everywhere, no others would have been employed. But, as many general officers were required, and as it was impossible to find so large a number equally good, one should be careful, said Frederick, at least not to choose stupid men; and every effort should be made to select, for the position of general, officers " who, at any rate, have sufficient intelligence to carry out the orders given to them." [2] And thus the great Frederick, a little cynically, dismisses the subject of those great commanders who directed the serried masses of common folk to the fields of death, and, in the

[1] Goethe, *Autobiography*, Book III.
[2] *Das Politische Testament Friedrichs des Grossen*, in Kuntzel und Hass, *op. cit.*, pp. 72–73.

prevailing unscientific conditions of warfare, themselves went bravely into action too, and died in the *mêlée*.

All this was changed, like so many other things, in that somewhat artificial old Europe by the French Revolution. For then the *levée en masse*—that is, universal and compulsory military service—was enforced; war was developed on the grand scale; decisions were ultimately not reached by the rout of a single army, but by the overthrowing of a whole people; and war, which had been just an inconvenient and rather costly excrescence upon the body politic, became an all-devouring demon, which, unless ended, will end mankind.

CHAPTER V

THE PEACE MOVEMENT

THE eighteenth century in Europe was a comparatively peaceful age. There were, indeed, more wars in Europe then than there were in the nineteenth century. There were, however, fewer and less destructive wars in the eighteenth than in the seventeenth century.

Nevertheless, although wars were less destructive, they were frightful enough to excite the horror of reflective men. Lord Monboddo, writing in 1773, went so far as to declare that war, if not controlled, would destroy European peoples and their civilization:

> The destruction of modern war is so prodigious by the great armies brought into the field and which are likewise kept up in time of peace, and by the extraordinary waste of men, by fatigue, by disease and unwholesome provisions, more than by the sword, while the internal policy of Europe at present is so little fitted to supply such destruction that, unless the princes either fall upon some other way of deciding their quarrels or provide better for the multiplication of people, Europe is in the utmost hazard of being again depopulated, as it once was under the Romans, but without the resource which it then had of barbarous nations to repeople it.[1]

The great failure of the eighteenth century was the failure to prevent war. The fact that wars were fought by Governments with professional armies, and not by peoples, robbed war of many of its horrors, and, at any rate, shrouded them from popular view. The habit of fighting proved fatal. The

[1] James Burnet, Lord Monboddo, *Origin of Language* (1773), vol. i, p. 430.

eighteenth century ended in a European war. Its political system, to some extent its economic and social system, were threatened with ruin not merely by the general war, but by the rise of a violently propagandist state (the French Republic), which had a different ' system ' from the rest. The system of the eighteenth century, however, survived the catastrophe, and was restored, with modifications, after twenty-two years of warfare. The nineteenth century likewise (if we reckon it as coming down to 1914) ended in general war and the rise of a propagandist state, Russia, with a different system from the rest. The Restoration of 1919 was not as complete as that of 1815; and the survival of the old European system, based on classical culture, the Christian religion, and individual freedom, is still in doubt. Its survival probably depends on the same question as that which the eighteenth century failed to solve, the question whether it can eliminate war from Europe's civilization.

Voltaire was the great hater and derider of war; but derision, which is an appeal to reason, has little relation to war, which is an appeal from reason to force. Nevertheless, Voltaire's satire has been of weight in the peace movement. *Candide* is full of it.[1] The incident of the crimping of Candide for the service of the King of Bulgaria has been mentioned. The same incident shows Voltaire's view on the question of a soldier's interest in his master or in his enemy. War, Voltaire seems to say, is unreasonable, absurd, for many reasons, among others because those who have to bear the brunt of it seldom, if ever, know what they are fighting for. One of the crimps who sups with Candide in the tavern at Valdberghoff-trarbk-dikdorff inquires if he does not " tenderly love the King of the Bulgars." " Not at all," replies Candide, " for I have never seen him." " How? " says the crimp. " He is the most charming of kings." Candide enters the service, greeted enthusiastically by the crimp as " the support, the defender, the hero of the Bulgars." He goes off to the wars in Bulgaria, the eternal and incredibly tedious and fatiguing marching and

---

[1] Voltaire, *Candide*, Chapter III.

counter-marching. " Stupefied, he did not yet distinguish too clearly how he was a hero."

At last the opposing armies come together. There is a battle, which begins on a radiant day, with trumpets, fifes, hautbois, and then cannon making harmony. The cannon kill some six thousand on either side. Next the musketeers approach each other and " remove from the best of all worlds some nine or ten thousand rascals who infect its surface." Some additional thousands found their death on the point of the bayonet. Altogether perhaps thirty thousand men lost their lives. " Candide, who trembled like a philosopher, hid himself as well as he could during the heroic butchery." While after the battle the leaders on each side were chanting the *Te Deum* of victory Candide sped over the heaps of dead and escaped to a neighbouring village. It was, of course, in ruins, burned by the soldiery. " Here old men riddled with bullets watched their wives dying; the women, whose throats had been cut, held their children to their bleeding breasts. These girls, bayoneted after being ravished by the military heroes, gave up their last breath; others, half burned, cried to be killed. Brains were scattered upon the earth beside cut-off arms and legs." He goes from village to village, all in ruins. At last he passes beyond the theatre of war into a land of peace, into Holland, though even here he is disturbed for neglecting to answer off-hand that he believed the Pope to be anti-Christ.

Candide, Pangloss, and Martin fall in with a " charitable Anabaptist " called Jacques, to whom Pangloss opens his philosophical theory that all is for the best. Jacques doubts this. " It must certainly be," he objects, " these men have corrupted their nature a little, for they were not born wolves, and they have become wolves. God has not given them either twenty-four-pounder cannons, nor bayonets, and they have made bayonets and cannons to destroy themselves." Pangloss himself admits that the " honest mercenaries," well-brought-up men, are ravaged by secret diseases. Martin, the poor little scholar who worked for the booksellers of Amsterdam, has not a good word to say for them. Europe is given over to war. "A million of regimented assassins, rushing from one end of Europe to the other, practise murder and brigandage with discipline, to gain their bread, because they have no more honest means."[1] Further wanderings bring Pangloss, Candide, and Martin, after going round the world, to Dieppe, from which they take a Dutch ship for England. When just outside Portsmouth they see an extraordinary scene, the execution of Admiral Byng (March 14, 1757) on account of his unsuccessful action off Minorca.

"Ah, Pangloss! Pangloss! Ah, Martin, Martin! Ah, my dear Cunégonde! What is going on there?" said Candide on the Dutch vessel.

"Something very mad and very abominable," replied Martin. "You know England; are they as mad there as in France?"

"It is another sort of madness," said Martin. "You are aware that these two nations are at war for some acres of snow in Canada, and that they spend on that war far more than all Canada is worth. To tell you precisely whether there are more people to shut up in one country than in another, is what my feeble powers of perception do not permit me; I know only that in general the people whom we are going to see are very atrabiliar."

Thus speaking, they landed at Portsmouth. A multitude of people covered the shore, and looked attentively at a rather big man who was on his knees, blindfolded, on the deck of one of the vessels of the fleet. Four soldiers posted opposite this man each shot three bullets into his skull in the most peaceful manner imaginable; and the whole assembly went home extremely satisfied.

"What then is all this?" said Candide; "and what demon exercises his empire everywhere?" He inquired who was the big man who had just been so ceremoniously killed. "He is an admiral," somebody answered. "And why kill this admiral?" "It is," said one, "because he has not had enough people killed; he engaged in battle with a French admiral, and it has been found that he was not sufficiently close to him." "But," said Candide, "the French admiral was as far from the English admiral as

---

[1] Voltaire, *Candide*, Chapters IV, XX.

he from the French." " That is incontestable," some one replied ; " but in this country it is good from time to time to kill an admiral to encourage the others." [1]

Every great war produced its peace plan, but the statesmen would not listen. Just as the Thirty Years War moved the learned and practical Grotius to compose and publish his great treatise *On the Law of War and Peace* (1625), so the War of the Spanish Succession induced the Abbé de Saint-Pierre to frame his *Project for Perpetual Peace*.

Charles François Irénée Castel de Saint-Pierre deserves to be well known ; and indeed from time to time he has been almost famous, though something like oblivion has occasionally overwhelmed his reputation. He was born in 1658 of a noble though not rich Norman family in the Cotentin. Brought up for the priesthood, he studied philosophy at the Jesuit College at Caen. With a small independent income, and the position of titular (but not unpaid) Abbot of Tiron, procured for him by his powerful friends in 1702, the Abbé was able to live as a private gentleman in his house in the Faubourg Saint-Jacques at Paris. He frequented the *salons*, particularly Madame de Lambert's, and was greatly patronized by the Duchess of Orleans. In 1712 the Cardinal de Polignac, one of the French plenipotentiaries to the Peace Conference of Utrecht (which ended the War of the Spanish Succession), took the Abbé with him to Utrecht as secretary. Saint-Pierre had already sketched out his *Project for Perpetual Peace* ; he published a draft of it in 1712 at Cologne. The full edition was published at Utrecht in 1713, in two volumes. An *Abrégé du Projet de paix perpétuelle* came out in 1729. Saint-Pierre's scheme and arguments attracted considerable attention, for he was very much the man of his century ; he was a *philosophe*, a man who believed in the power of reason to remedy the ills of society, and who therefore, like all cultured Europeans in that age, was an optimist. Besides the *Projet*, many works of philosophy and political science and economy were composed by him, for his fertile

---

[1] Voltaire, *op. cit.*, Chapter XXIII.

mind produced schemes for every sort of reform. His long and laborious life came to an end in 1743, in the Faubourg Saint-Honoré.[1]

The *Projet* in many respects anticipated the Covenant of the League of Nations, which, though not deliberately modelled upon it, was undoubtedly influenced by Saint-Pierre's scheme. He limited the scope of his scheme to Europe, but looked forward to a time when Asia would have its own union or alliance, its ' regional agreement,' to use a modern expression. The twenty-four Christian states of Europe, within the frontiers assigned to them by the Treaty of Utrecht, were to constitute themselves into a permanent alliance. Each of those states, large and small alike, was to provide one delegate to the Alliance's Senate of Peace, sitting permanently at Utrecht. Each state was to contribute according to its revenue and liabilities to the expenses of the Alliance. In case of disputes between two states there must be resort to mediation of the other members of the Alliance. If mediation failed, the Senate of Peace, as a tribunal of arbitration, would consider the case in dispute, and would give a definite decision or award. If the disputing states would not accept the award, it would be enforced by an international army, comprising contingents from the member states. This international army was not to be a permanent force, but to come into existence only when required. No state would be permitted to conclude treaties incompatible with the conditions of the Alliance. The Alliance would maintain supervisors in each state, to survey negotiations in progress. Secret diplomacy was to be abolished. Existing treaties were to be maintained, unless the member states chose to negotiate new treaties—for instance, for exchanges of terri-tory—with the consent and under the guarantee of the Alliance, acting by a three-fourths majority. The fundamental articles of the Alliance could only be altered by unanimous consent of the members. Such is Saint-Pierre's project for perpetual peace through " a permanent system of arbitration of the

[1] See Grotius Society Publications, selections from the *Abrégé*, Intro-duction, p. 3.

Republic of Europe." Shortly before he died he sent a copy of his book to Frederick II of Prussia. It arrived amid the clash of arms in the War of the Austrian Succession. The King wrote to Voltaire (April 12, 1742): " The Abbé de Saint-Pierre, who distinguishes me so far as to honour me with his correspondence, has sent me a most excellent treatise on the means of restoring peace to all Europe, and on the manner of preserving it continually. The thing is exceedingly practicable, nor is anything except the consent of all Europe and some other such-like trifles wanting for its encouragement." [1] The great cynic who had deliberately provoked the war which he was waging was not likely to be a very favourable critic.

If the Abbé de Saint-Pierre had lived in a later age he would have been called a ' publicist '; he called himself a " counsel for the commonwealth." He believed that the best man was the most useful man, and his views had some influence on Bentham and the school of English Utilitarians. Rousseau was attracted too by the bold ideas and practical thinking of Saint-Pierre, and produced in 1761 a version of his own called *Extrait du " Projet de paix perpétuelle " de M. l'Abbé de Saint-Pierre*.[2] Jeremy Bentham, surveying the world at large from his own busy world of men and books and thought, brought out in 1786, after conversations with the statesman Lord Shelburne at Bowood, an essay on war and a project for peace, for the federation of Europe, and for a reduction of armaments obviously based on Saint-Pierre. " War is mischief on the largest scale " are his opening words.

The book on peace which attracted most attention in the eighteenth century appeared almost at the very end. This was Kant's *Zum ewigen Frieden : ein philosophischer Entwurf (On Perpetual Peace : a philosophical essay)*, published at Königsberg in 1795, the year in which Prussia withdrew from the French war by making the Treaty of Bâle. Kant believed in

---

[1] Quoted by N. Ausübel, *Superman : the Life of Frederick the Great* (trans. E. and C. Paul, 1932), p. 447.

[2] See C. E. Vaughan, *The Political Writings of J.-J. Rousseau* (1915), vol. i.

the efficacy of reason, the moral law, and liberty. He did not live simply upon the heights, for he paid close attention to current affairs, and regarded the French Revolution as the most momentous event of his lifetime. Although not unpractical, he held that it was for the philosophers to deal with principles and arguments, and for statesmen to put the philosophers' views into practice.

Reason, the moral law, the necessity of freedom—all required that violence between men and men should be absolutely prevented. This had been done within the state. It was of little use, however, to abolish the condition of violence between men inside the state if violence still remained the dominant condition between states. Though war is not a constant condition of state relations, there is no guarantee that it may not at any moment break out. Nevertheless, there can be no compulsion of states, for the sovereignty of each state is the condition and guarantee of the freedom without which the citizens cannot be rational and moral. Therefore, as we cannot aim at establishing a common authority over all states, peace must be ensured through a federation of states which is consistent with the freedom of each.

Such is the gist of Kant's reasoning, expressed in a style which is always hard to follow, though with occasional flashes of beauty, or occasional pungent remarks. " There used to be an inn in Holland," he writes in the opening of his essay, " with the sign of Perpetual Peace, and on the signboard was depicted a graveyard." Was mankind to attain peace only through the mutual massacre of the race? The alternative, which is a " categorical imperative," is a federation of free states. It is obvious that there is no justice in war; " for rights cannot be decided by war and its favourable result, victory; and a peace treaty, though ending the present war, does not end the state of war." Although there is no justice in war, no state has yet been frank enough " to expunge the word ' justice ' from the politics of war."

This verbal homage that every state pays to the moral law proves that there is a great moral disposition to be found in mankind, though dormant at present, some day in spite of all to master his evil genius.

This is to be done by the formation of a league of peace, a federation of states. " The guarantee is rendered by nothing less than that great artist, nature, whose mechanical course visibly demonstrates the purpose of harmonizing the discord of humanity—even against their will. . . . Nature wills irresistibly that justice shall triumph in the end."

When I say nature "wills" that this or that should be done, I do not mean that she imposes a duty on us to do it (for only practical reason, free from compulsion, can do that): she does it herself, whether we like it or not.

Zum ewigen Frieden was Kant's contribution to the great problem of humanity. He would not admit as valid the criticism, sure to be made by the practical politician, that his plan was merely ' general,' devoid of practical content. For the practical politician complacently maintains that the theorist is a pedant, incapable of grappling with the actual problems of states; it therefore lies with the scholar to produce the theories, and with the politician, in so far as they are valid, to put them into operation. Kant, at any rate, had done his part. " It is the moral duty of every man to assist in the solution of the supreme problem for the race." [1]

[1] Grotius Society publications (1927), *Kant's " Perpetual Peace,"* Introduction, p. 11.

CHAPTER VI

CRIME AND PUNISHMENT

UNDER the *ancien régime* people were, on the whole, law-abiding. Population was not greatly increasing. On the Continent there were neither great industrial nor agricultural developments. Most people were settled in their peasant holdings, or in trade or in a profession. There was much movement on the roads, but mainly of men and women who had something to do—strolling players, wandering craftsmen, students, soldiers on the way to a new depot. The legal profession, very old and highly respected, grew more powerful and more precise, while ' reason ' and scepticism were undermining clerical authority. Law was strictly enforced. Montesquieu, however, who examined so carefully the " spirit of the laws " in European countries, found that much of their development was the result of chance, of custom, of climate, of prejudice. And Beccaria, who modestly claimed only to follow in the " immortal President's " [1] steps, in the course of his own investigations came to the conclusion that laws were not dictated by the unimpassioned student of human nature, but by the passions of a few men or as the result of some accidental or temporary necessity. Yet laws ought, he declared, in a memorable sentence, to aim at " the greatest happiness divided by the greatest number [*la massima felicità divisa nel maggior numero*]." [2]

How few have sought, by a return to first principles, to dissipate the mistakes accumulated by many centuries, or to mitigate, with at least that force belonging only to ascertained truths,

[1] Montesquieu was for a time President of the *parlement* at Bordeaux. *Cf.* pp. 173–174, 175–176.
[2] Beccaria, *Dei Delitti e delle Pene* (ed. 1766), p. 11.

the excessive caprice of ill-directed power, which has presented down to this time only an example of lawful and cold-blooded atrocity! And yet the groans of the weak, sacrificed to the cruelty of the ignorant, or to the indolence of the rich; the barbarous tortures, multiplied with a severity as useless as it is prodigal, for crimes either not proved or chimerical; the disgusting horrors of a prison enhanced by that which is the cruellest executioner of the miserable—namely, uncertainty; these ought to startle those rulers whose function it is to guide the opinion of men's minds.

The immortal President Montesquieu has treated curiously of this matter; and truth, which is indivisible, has forced me to follow the luminous footsteps of this great man.[1]

The English judges were the most independent, having a guaranteed life tenure, *quam diu se bene gesserint*, under the Act of Settlement of 1701. Nobody could claim privilege by reason of his social position, and the fourth Earl of Ferrers was executed like a common felon in 1760 for killing his steward, though he was allowed to go from the Tower of London to Tyburn, the place of execution, in his own coach. The French high judiciary, which sat in regional courts called *parlements*, also enjoyed great independence, a curious result of the system of purchase; for a judge, having bought his office with good money, held it for life, and by another payment could ensure that his son should follow him. Learned, quasi-hereditary, independent, the French judiciary formed part of the *noblesse de robe*, the aristocracy of merit, which supplied all the ablest officials.

In Germany there was an Imperial Tribunal (*Reichskammergericht*), which could hear cases even against ruling princes. It does not appear, however, to have exercised criminal jurisdiction over them; on the whole, circumstances did not make ruling princes likely to commit ordinary crimes. It is true that King Frederick William I of Prussia frequently assaulted his subjects and beat them with his cane, but this does not appear to have made him unpopular.

[1] Beccaria, *op. cit.* I have used the translation of J. H. Farrer (1880), p. 119.

Punishment for crimes was quite merciless, for though the men of the Age of Reason were tolerant of many things they had absolutely no tolerance of murderers and assassins. A murderer was not merely to be put out of the way of doing further harm by being executed; the execution was to be public, and to be carried out in a sufficiently painful way to deter people from following in his steps. The wheel was in regular, though not frequent, use in most Continental countries, until it was abolished in France by the Revolution Government of 1793. The criminal was strapped to the spokes of a wheel, and the executioner, using an iron bar or mallet, broke a limb as the wheel slowly revolved. The executioner was held in universal detestation and loathing, yet he was defended by philosophers as the saviour of society:

Scarcely has Authority indicated his dwelling, scarcely has he taken possession of it, than the other habitations are withdrawn until they no longer see his. It is in the midst of this solitude and of this sort of emptiness formed around him that he lives alone with his wife and children. . . . A mournful signal is given: an abject servant of the Lord comes knocking at his door, warning him that he is needed. He goes; he arrives at a public square, filled with a dense and palpitating crowd. A poisoner, a parricide, or a sacrilegious criminal is cast to him. He seizes the criminal, extends him, binds him on a horizontal cross. He raises his arm to strike: then there is a horrible silence, and one hears only the crashing of the bones which break under the bar and the howls of the victim. He detaches the victim; places him upon the wheel; the broken limbs are laced on to the spokes, the head hangs, the hair erect, and from the mouth, open like a furnace, there issue at intervals only blood and a few words, calling for death.

It is finished. The executioner's heart beats, but it is with joy; he applauds himself and says in his heart, " Nobody can wheel better than I [*Nul ne roue mieux que moi*]." He descends, he holds out his bloodstained hand, and the magistrate throws into it from afar some pieces of gold, which he carries away between a double hedge of people, drawn back with horror. He sits down at table, and he eats; next, to bed, and he sleeps. On the morrow, awaking, he thinks of something quite different from what he has done the day before. Is he a man? Yes, God receives him in his temples and permits him to pray. . . . All grandeur, all power, all subordination, depend upon the executioner: he is the horror and the bond of human association. Take away from the world this incomprehensible agent; in an instant even, order gives place to chaos, thrones collapse, and society disappears.[1]

While ordinary murderers were broken on the wheel, assassins, or even those who attempted assassination, were treated with a cold fury and extremity of torture which are almost beyond belief. It is a fact, however, that political assassinations, which had been very common in the seventeenth century, were almost completely stamped out in the eighteenth. Robert François Damiens, a lackey, who conceived that Louis XV was an oppressor of the Paris *parlement*, attempted to stab the King at Versailles on January 5, 1757. He only managed to inflict a slight wound. After conviction Damiens had his right hand burned off; he was placed on an iron frame and racked; his flesh in places was torn off by red-hot pincers; finally he was tied to four horses and was pulled to pieces. Oliver Goldsmith in *The Traveller* (1764) said that the poor and unambitious in this world at least had the consolation of " rarely " experiencing such things. Referring to Damiens' punishment, and to a red-hot ring which had been put round the head of a Hungarian rebel, Goldsmith wrote:

> With secret course, which no loud storms annoy,
> Glides the smooth current of domestic joy.
> The lifted axe, the agonizing wheel,
> Luke's iron crown, and Damiens' bed of steel,
> To men remote from power but rarely known,
> Leave reason, faith, and conscience all our own.

The case of Jean Calas was noted and discussed all over Europe; but this was only because Voltaire took it up, and devoted to it the resources of his powerful pen and his purse.

[1] J. de Maistre, *Soirées de Saint-Petersbourg* (1822), *premier entretien*.

There were probably a good many similar cases which were never heard of. Jean Calas of Toulouse, a Huguenot, a substantial tradesman of good character, was accused in 1761 of hanging his son to prevent him from being converted to Catholicism. The *parlement* of Toulouse, by a decision of eight judges to five, condemned Calas to be broken on the wheel. The sentence was carried out. The unfortunate man died, protesting his innocence. His property was confiscated; the daughters were placed in a convent; the widow was allowed to leave the country. She went to Geneva; her terrible story came to Voltaire in his tranquil and happy retreat. He took up her cause, and immediately put into operation all his literary artillery, the engines of his wrath and sense of justice.

The case was reheard at the order of the King by the *parlement* of Paris, and in 1765 Calas was declared innocent. The Duc de Choiseul, Premier Ministre of France, to whom, after Voltaire, this tardy justice was due, obtained from the Royal Treasury a grant of 30,000 livres (about £1500) as compensation for loss of property to the Calas family.

Voltaire made similar, but in this case ineffectual, efforts to secure a retrial of the case of the Chevalier de la Barre, a youth of sixteen years of age, beheaded after having his tongue cut out, on a charge of having desecrated the crucifix on the bridge at Abbeville. The young d'Etallonde, the friend of de la Barre, had escaped from the country, and so avoided torture and death. Voltaire procured a commission for him in a Prussian regiment.

Torture was inflicted, partly as revenge upon a proved criminal, partly as a punishment sufficiently frightful to deter other possible criminals, and also, in many cases, as a part of the trial, as a means of examination, of obtaining evidence. ' Examination ' (*examinatio*) was a word regularly used in legal parlance to denote the infliction of torture. Beccaria, writing in 1764, denounced the use of torture for evidence as wholly barbarous and unreasonable, and completely out of date in an enlightened age: " This abuse ought not to be tolerated in the

THE CALAS FAMILY
From a contemporary print

eighteenth century [*questo abuso non dovrebbe esser tolerato nel decimottavo secolo*]."

It is to seek to confound all the relations of things to require a man to be at the same time accuser and accused, to make pain the crucible of truth, as if the test of it lay in the muscles and sinews of an unfortunate wretch. . . . This infamous crucible of truth [*Questo infame crociuolo della verità*] is a still-existing monument of that primitive and savage legal system which called trials by fire and boiling water, or the accidental decisions of combat, *judgments of God*, as if the rings of the eternal chain in the control of the First Cause must at every moment be disarranged and put out for the petty institutions of mankind. . . . This abuse ought not to be tolerated in the eighteenth century. . . . These truths have been adopted by England, a nation the glory of whose literature, the superiority of whose commerce and wealth, and consequently of whose power, and the example of whose virtue and courage, leave us no doubt of the goodness of her laws.

The use of torture was dying out; in most countries of Central and Western Europe it was abolished by the monarchs and governments of the *ancien régime* during the last forty or fifty years of the century. Besides England, Sweden, in the person of Gustavus III, abolished torture in 1780. Frederick II of Prussia had already abolished it in 1740, except in cases of high treason and treachery. The Elector Frederick III of Saxony (1763–1827) also abolished it. The Bishop of Osnabrück was still permitting infliction of torture in the Osnabrück prison when Howard visited him in 1781; in Brunswick-Luneburg torture, though not legally abolished, had not been employed for eighteen years. But in Vienna Howard, though he saw a torture-room and the terrible instruments of pain, could look at them only as curiosities, for the Emperor Joseph II had forbidden their use for ever. [1]

The punishments which Smollett found in use at Nice in 1764 for crimes less than capital (for which hanging was the

[1] John Howard, *Principal Lazarettos* (1791), Appendix 6, 9 ; Beccaria *op. cit.* (trans. Farrer), p. 119.

punishment) were whipping and the *strappado*. He described the *strappado* thus :

> This last is performed by hoisting up the criminal by his hands tied behind his back, on a pulley, about two stories high; from whence the rope being suddenly slackened, he falls to within a yard or two of the ground, where he is stopped with a violent shock, arising from the weight of his body and the velocity of his descent, which generally dislocates his shoulders, with incredible pain. This dreadful execution is sometimes repeated in a few minutes on the same delinquent; so that the very ligaments are torn from his joints, and his arms are rendered useless for life.

Convicts who were spared from the wheel could hope for nothing better than the galleys in the seventeenth century, and in the first half of the eighteenth. When Smollett went to Nice in 1764 he found that persons who illegally sold tobacco (which was a royal monopoly) were sentenced to the galleys for life. All the states in the Mediterranean kept war-galleys on that sea to fight the Turks and to keep down piracy. The oars were manned by slave labour, which, among the Christian states in the eighteenth century, was supplied by convicts. The galley was decked at the bow and stern, and was open in the middle. Here, in the open middle, were the benches for the galley-slaves. Six or seven convicts were at each oar. Between the opposite sets of oarsmen there was a gangway, or bridge, on which the boatswains paraded up and down, carrying long whips. The slaves at each oar were chained together. In winter, according to Smollett's account, the galleys did not put to sea, as they were only suitable for smooth water ; the slaves were employed ashore on public works. Nevertheless, they slept in the galleys all the year round. In summer their life was spent tugging at the oar. Even had the boatswains ceased to lash them with the whip, it was practically impossible for one slave or the slaves at one oar to pause, for all had to swing together to prevent their limbs or backs being broken by the oars behind or in front. When respited for a few hours from rowing the slaves, unable to lie or stretch, had to sleep on their benches. At night, wrote Smollett, " the slaves lie upon the naked banks, without any other covering than a tilt." They were given water mixed with vinegar and a little oil to drink and biscuit to eat and a handful of beans; twice a week a little rice and cheese. Naturally, ship and slaves alike were filthy, in spite of some sanitary precautions and of the severity of the discipline. Smollett, after his visit to the galleys at Nice in 1764, wrote:

It is impossible, they say, to keep such a number of desperate people under any regular command without exercising such severities as must shock humanity. It is almost equally impossible to maintain any tolerable degree of cleanliness where such a number of wretches are crowded together without conveniences, or even the necessaries of life. They are ordered twice a week to stop, clean, and bathe themselves in the sea; but notwithstanding all the precautions of discipline, they swarm with vermin, and the vessel smells like a hospital or crowded gaol.

People endured the inconceivable hardship of this life and survived. John Knox, the Scottish reformer, captured at the siege of St Andrews in 1547, was a galley-convict for some months on the Loire, where, it is true, conditions could not be quite so bad as on the Mediterranean. Nevertheless, Smollett at Nice found the galley-slaves apparently " quite insensible of their misery. Like so many convicts at Newgate, they laugh and sing and swear and get drunk when they can." They had a band on the galley which he visited, and they expected a " gratification " for playing on his arrival. As he walked forward he was accosted by slaves offering to black his shoes. If you submitted to have your shoes polished you had your pocket picked during the process. If you did not submit, but passed on, the galley-slaves maliciously transferred to you " a colony of vermin, which these fellows have a very dexterous method of conveying to strangers." [1]

In 1748 the French Government abolished (or rather began

---

[1] Tobias Smollett, *Travels through France and Italy* (1763–65), Letter XIII (Nice, January 15, 1764).

abolishing, as the process required time) galley sentences, and substituted penal service in *bagnes*, or land-prisons. At Nice in 1764 Smollett found that the King of Sardinia was beginning to abandon the use of galleys. Victor Hugo's hero, Jean Valjean, in *Les Misérables*, is represented as being a *forçat* in the early nineteenth century in the *bagnes*, where existence was just tolerable. Howard describes them in his *Account of the Principal Lazarettos of Europe*, published in 1791. He also shows that the galleys had become simply places of detention, or, in some countries, were nothing else than land-prisons under another name.

The description which Howard gives of European prisons during his last tour, 1785–86, leaves, on the whole, rather a good impression. At Marseilles he visited a prison called La Quarantaine, originally used for housing people who fled from the plague. It was now a prison for vagabonds and beggars. They were lodged in lofty, airy rooms; every room had a window at either end, giving free passage to the air. There was also plenty of water running constantly into stone troughs. At Marseilles the regular prison was crowded and the prisoners dirty. They lay on straw mattresses. Their bread was good, and their daily allowance of it was two pounds. A religious Order gave them soup every day and clean linen once a week.

The galleys at Toulon, five in number, had sixteen hundred prisoners—deserters, smugglers, and thieves. The thieves, after serving their sentence, were branded on the left shoulder with the letter " V " (for *voleur*) or with " Gal " (for *galérien*). The galley-slaves were kept below deck, but there was only one deck in each ship; the windows in the roofs were open; and the ship, being swept twice a day, was clean and not offensive. The galley-slaves also were clean, and their clothing neat. They were given a coat, waistcoat, and trousers, two shirts, and a pair of shoes every year, a greatcoat every two years. They had good brown bread, well baked, in loaves weighing a pound and three-quarters. They all had " some little allowance in money "; those who worked for the Government had an additional allowance of three sous a day for wine. There

was a canteen for the sale of " white bread, greens, etc." The
prisoners did not work at the oars, like ancient galley-slaves,
but were mainly employed at their own trades, such as shoe-
making, basket-making. Some worked at the Arsenal. When
employed outside the galleys they were chained two together.
All were loaded with chains of some kind. Protestant prisoners
were not compelled to go to Mass.

At Nice, in the Kingdom of Sardinia, Howard found the
prison well managed. It had three stories, with four or five
good rooms on each floor. Irons were never used, except when
prisoners were riotous or unruly, and then they were chained
to the wall. Their beds had mattresses and blankets, and they
were allowed two pounds of bread a day; other food came
from charitable contributions. The galley-slaves were kept at
work on pontoons, for dredging the harbour. They were
allowed two pounds of bread daily, with four ounces of dried
beans, without salt. They also had seven sous allowed them
in money on working-days; two and a half sous were deducted
for soup. Sundays and Thursdays were idle days.

At Florence, where Howard arrived in 1786, he found that
since he had been there, about seven years earlier, " a most
pleasing change had taken place, in consequence of the great
care and attention of the Grand Duke." This was Leopold
of Habsburg, brother of the Emperor Joseph II. The walls
of the Florentine prisons were whitewashed; debtors were
separated from felons; the number of prisoners was diminished.
A well-regulated house of correction had been lately built.
The Grand Duke had the rules copied out for Howard, and
also sent him a copy of the " excellent new code of criminal
laws." Howard was convinced of the Grand Duke's " great
attention to the happiness of his people."

In the new prison at Rome, in February 1786, Howard found
the infirmary clean, the sick, " as at the time of my former
visits," in clean wards and separate beds. The Hospital of
San Michele was not satisfactory; there, wrote Howard, " I
passed two mornings, and found it sadly neglected by the
cardinal and the inspectors, who never visit it."

At Malta, which belonged to the Knights of St John, the prison consisted of several dirty and offensive rooms in the *hôtel de ville*. There were nine prisoners in it when Howard arrived (April 1786). One of the prisoners, a Turk, had suffered the torture, " in consequence of which mortification had taken place." The surgeon was attending to him. Howard did not stay long enough on the island to know the result. The galley-slaves had many rooms. Some were employed in a woollen manufactory. Most of them were miserable ' blacks '— peasants, fishermen, or sailors carried off from the Barbary coasts by the Knights of St John, who were sworn to per-petual war with the Turks. " How dreadful! " comments Howard. " Do not these knights by such conduct make them-selves the worst enemies to the cross of Christ under the pretence of friendship? "

At Zante, in the Ionian Islands, which belonged to Venice, the prison consisted of two rooms on the ground floor. There were in it in May 1786 some five or six prisoners, very dirty, yet scarcely distinguished from the tattered Venetian soldiers.

At Smyrna, which was in the Turkish Empire, the prison was near the sea, and had two rooms and a court. The execu-tion of justice was very speedy, so that, on the three visits which Howard made, there were no more than seven prisoners there at a time. One of them had been bastinadoed so severely that he was swollen from head to foot. Howard advised him to bathe in the sea, and to apply plasters of salt and vinegar to the soles of his feet. " In the use of these means, with the addition of two doses of Glauber's salts, he recovered; and I acquired a credit which made the keepers, in my subsequent visits, *particularly* attentive to me." The debtors' prison had four or five rooms and a court for the prisoners to walk in. " In this populous city I found but fourteen prisoners at one time, and at another time not so many. Their subsistence depends chiefly on charity, and the collections made for them in the Greek and Roman Catholic Churches."

At Constantinople Howard noticed nothing remarkable in

the prisons, except that they were very still and quiet. " I
was at a loss to account for this, till I reflected that the only
beverage for the prisoners is water." In the prison at Galata
there were eighteen debtors. Their subsistence depended
partly on collections made for them in the churches; there
was also a bag hung in the middle of the street leading to the
prison, to receive contributions of bread, meat, and other food
from charitable persons. Prisoners of different sects—Greeks,
Armenians, Jews, and the rest—were kept in separate com-
partments. Howard observed that there were always fewer
prisoners of the Mohammedan than of other religions. The
prison for galley-slaves was large, but almost empty, as the
Captain-Pasha had taken most of them into his galleys. These,
accordingly, really were employed in rowing. The few who
remained in the prison were healthy; " a very humane attention was paid to them." The hospitals of Constantinople which
Howard visited were not clean, nor in other respects was much
attention shown to the patients. " In the midst, however, of
this neglect of human beings I saw an instance of attention to
cats, which astonished me; I mean an *asylum*, which has been
provided for them, and which is situated near the mosque of
San Sophia."

At Venice the galleys were clean and not offensive, in consequence of possessing easy access to water. At Trieste the
prisoners were free from irons, but they were kept confined
to their rooms, which consequently were offensive. The keeper
said that prisoners in constant confinement were more healthy
when fed on white than on brown bread; Howard thought
that this might be true if the brown were only coarse rye-
bread. The Trieste ' galley-slaves ' were not in galleys at all,
but in a house of correction, lately a convent (doubtless one
of those secularized by Joseph II). The men and women were
lodged separately, the men below-, the women above-stairs.
The men were in chains, and were employed in cleaning the
streets and bridges. The women were carding and spinning
in the house. Howard saw the prison dinner of wholesome
bread and soup. The prisoners looked healthy. " From the

placidness of their countenances, I inferred the humanity of
their keeper; and I was a witness of his showing them an
attention which in such houses is of particular importance."
The Great Prison of Vienna, visited by Howard in December
1786, was a place of dungeons, three prisoners in each. He saw
three horrid cells crowded with twelve women. The men
lived in total darkness, and were chained to the walls. No
priest or clergyman had been near them for eight or nine
months; the prisoners complained of this, in the presence of
the keepers, with tears. They had an allowance of four kreutzer
(a penny) a day, but were not permitted to spend any of this
upon lighting. There was a torture-room, nine steps deeper
than the dungeons, with instruments of torture; but they were
idle now, because the Emperor Joseph II had abolished the
shocking practice. Moreover, the Emperor had just completed
a new prison to which the prisoners were in process of removal.
" It consists of forty rooms, and also twenty dungeons at the
depth of twenty-two steps below the surface of the ground,
boarded with thick planks, in which are strong iron rings, for
the purpose of chaining the prisoners. These dungeons are
larger, and in other respects (though horrid enough) less horrid,
than those in the old prison."

The convicts in the *Grosse Caserne* of Vienna were eighty-
six men in one large room, with no windows except two holes
in the ceiling. In the daytime the convicts were taken out to
work on cleaning the streets. They slept in the same room,
in their clothes, chained to the floor. The atmosphere was
offensive beyond expression. In the house of correction there
were only women. They had one pound of bread and two
dishes of different kinds of soup every day. No bedding was
provided. Out of 153 prisoners 35 were ill—a high proportion; but the sick were well treated in clean rooms separated
from the rest.

Criminals sent off to Hungary had irons on their necks and
feet, besides a chain ten inches long between the feet of each,
and another chain, six feet long, fastening each convict to the
next. Their labour, drawing boats up the Danube, combined

with coarse fare, wore them out so fast that few lived more than four years.

Vagrancy and begging were forbidden. There was a house of correction for such people. It had 149 inmates, employed in carding, spinning, and weaving. The rooms and passages were airy and spacious, and the house well supplied with water from a constantly running stream. The officer in charge, Count Pergen, was humane and on the alert to make improvements. He kept a journal, containing carefully recorded statistics about the prisoners.

The tower for lunatics was kept clean, but owing to structural defects the passages had a very offensive atmosphere.

In the suburbs there was a general hospital; twenty beds in every ward, with three feet and a table between each bed. Every ward was furnished with basins and towels, and great attention was paid to cleanliness. Three nurses were assigned to each ward, along with a room of moderate size, with a fireplace, for washing and other purposes. The roof had corridors which, unfortunately, were glazed, so that the escape of foul air was prevented. There was a lying-in section of twelve neat rooms, furnished with child-bed linen, a toilet, and tea-things. All in this department was clean, calm, and quiet. " Women were admitted at any hour, through a private door, and no questions asked." The cheapest rooms were ten kreutzer a day (about twopence-halfpenny). The best rooms were a florin (two shillings).

The Frankfort house of correction was well managed. The inmates were kept hard at work, cement-making. Half of Saturday was given up to cleaning the apartments. There was an allowance of good bread and beer, soup twice a week, meat on Sundays and Wednesdays. There was a chapel, and a room in which the governors met twice a week. Ladies inspected the house, and its regulations were published.

At Aix-la-Chapelle the execution for citizens was by decollation with a broadsword. The execution was concealed from public view by a scaffolding round the spot where it was performed. In Holland criminals were still executed by being broken on the wheel, but in the eight years before 1783 only five had been executed in this way in Amsterdam, and from then to January 1787 only one.

The Dutch prisons were clean, the Prussian prisons not so clean, though otherwise well ordered, except at Königsberg, where even visitors soon found themselves covered with vermin. At Mittau, in Courland (annexed to Russia by Catherine II), Howard found in 1789 a reasonably well-managed prison. But in Riga the prison was dirty and offensive; here men and women were not, as a rule, kept separate. The house of correction was clean; the inmates had a cheerful and healthy look. Grinding corn and spinning were the chief kinds of work. The bread was good, and every prisoner had a warm bath once a fortnight. Prisoners condemned to imprisonment for long sentences or for life were kept about ten miles from the town in wooden houses, surrounded by a high wall. The rooms were clean; each man had a separate bed; but their food and clothing were not good. Those condemned to life sentences had a piece cut out of each nostril and a mark on the cheeks. They were always kept in irons, except when sick. There was no execution for crime, even for murder, in Russia; but in addition to imprisonment for life condemned men received up to 250 strokes of the knout, not continuously, for twenty to twenty-five strokes could kill a man. The Cronstadt old prison was very dirty; the prisoners (ninety-one in number) had no beds, and seemed sadly neglected. The Tver prison was dirty, and had not been whitewashed since Howard visited it eight years earlier, in 1781. The prisoners had as much bread as they chose, and for the rest lived on the proceeds of a box placed outside the prison for charitable contributions.

At Moscow a new prison (the Ostrog) had been built of brick since Howard's first visit in 1781. Men and women were separated. The rooms had stoves and barrack beds, but no bedding. The prison infirmary was very bad; men and women in the same room, little bedding, scant attention. The Russian public was good-natured and charitable, so that everywhere charity supplied all the necessaries of life that were required.

The city prison, which was different from the Ostrog, was " a disgrace to a civilized country." The Grand Duke's Hospital, however, " would do credit to any country."

On the whole, it may be said that Howard's picture of the European prisons is not too depressing, and shows that there was a considerable advance in humanitarianism over the century. Torture was abolished in most countries, and capital punishment was falling out of use except for murderers. France was the only great state, down to the Revolution, which still resorted to torture. Howard, visiting Avignon, nominally Papal territory, but administered by France since 1768, was shown the torture instruments by the gaoler, who said that " he had seen drops of blood mixed with the sweat on the breasts of some who had suffered the torture."

CHAPTER VII

ENLIGHTENED MONARCHS:
FREDERICK THE GREAT AND
CHARLES WILLIAM FERDINAND

THE phrase ' enlightened monarchs ' (sometimes ' benevolent despots ') is frequently, though vaguely, applied to the monarchs of the eighteenth century. As a matter of fact, ' enlightened monarchy ' was a well-understood thing, based upon a philosophic theory; but it was only applied to the monarchs of the latter half of the century. Previously to this time, in the first half of the century, monarchs had guided themselves simply by reason of State (*raison d'État*), the self-interest of the State, as they conceived it. And this self-interest simply was that the State should be as powerful as possible, and should always acquire more land if it could. Frederick the Great had nothing but contempt for the monarchs of the middle period of the century. " Except the Queen of Hungary and the King of Sardinia," he wrote in 1752, " whose genius has triumphed over their bad education, all the princes of Europe are only illustrious imbeciles." [1]

The publication of Montesquieu's *De l'Esprit des lois* (1748) and of Rousseau's *Contrat social* (1762) and the writings of Voltaire and the Encyclopædists, and the teachings of Wolff and other professors of philosophy, spread abroad a great belief in the efficiency of pure reason. No longer merely *raison d'État*, which was simply political, was to be the guiding principle of sovereigns, but *raison d'État* based on pure reason. Thus interpreted, the interest of the State comprised a great deal more than

---

[1] *Das Politische Testament Friedrichs des Grossen von 1752* (ed. Küntzel und Hass, 1920), p. 92. The Queen of Hungary was the Empress Maria Theresa, the King of Sardinia was Carlo Emmanuele I.

power and land; internal reform was an interest. Once reason saw clearly the need for reform nothing must stand in the way. But the task of reform was stupendous; only the unlimited power of the State, embodied in the monarch, could accomplish it. The autocratic monarch alone could cut his way through feudal abuses and antique customary complications, and, untouched by popular prejudices, impose complete, reasonable reform. This was ' enlightened despotism,' a revival of Plato's theory that states would never be well governed until philosophers were kings. The British Constitution, with its popular representation, controls, checks, and balances, was quite out of favour.

The philosophers who were so prominent in society of the late eighteenth century recognized their ideal in the enlightened sovereign; or, rather, they saw in him the agent through whom their ideal could be realized. It was not easy to persuade a whole people or a governing class; but it was comparatively easy to persuade one man. Therefore Voltaire (for a time) gave his confidence and support to Frederick II; Grimm found reason and power personified in Catherine II; Mirabeau recognized benevolence, wisdom, and executive authority in Charles William Ferdinand of Brunswick; and every *philosophe* was ready to make a plan for reforming a constitution, a legislative or commercial system, if only he could find the appropriate autocrat. An alliance took place which helped the sovereigns by its impression on public opinion, and which also increased the friendship of men of letters for monarchs, of Voltaire for Frederick II, of Grimm and Diderot for Catherine II, of Goethe for Carl August of Weimar, and naturally enhanced these monarchs' reputation. The effect of this alliance on legislation was considerable; the laws against the Jesuits, for instance, would have been impossible without it. Doubtless there was a certain amount of vanity on both sides. Practical men like the approval of scholars who may immortalize them in books; scholars, a little sensitive of being considered unpractical, are pleased when their ideas are taken up by the men of affairs. Actually there

was never a period in history when politicians attended so
carefully to the truths which the scholars placed before them
as in the late eighteenth and early nineteenth centuries. Adam
Smith, Beccaria, Bentham, are examples of three men of the
study who in their own time profoundly influenced the men
of affairs. The despotic and aristocratic Governments of those
years could frame their policies on scientific principles, instead
of allowing themselves to be swayed merely by considerations
of political expediency. Not all Governments of the *ancien
régime*—for instance, the French—had sufficient strength of
will to persist in carrying into effect policies which they knew
to be right, but those which did—for instance, Austria under
Joseph II—reformed their State in time and forestalled the
Revolution.

Power and riches carry temptation with them. High life in
the eighteenth century was rather sensual; and the monarchs
were not immune from the prevailing vices. Yet there were
virtuous people in high life as well as among the *bourgeoisie*
and country-people, and, on the whole, the monarchs of the
" Enlightenment," the *Aufklärung*, were a class distinguished
for private virtue as well as for public spirit. Peter the
Great and Frederick II and Catherine II cannot be reckoned
among the virtuous ones; but Maria Theresa (a kind of Queen
Victoria, a matron of Roman virtue), the Emperor Joseph II
and Charles III of Spain (Spartans both of them), Leopold
of Tuscany (the Emperor Leopold II), Louis XVI of France,
and, though he was not *philosophe*, George III of Great Britain
were among the most respectable characters of the age. Some
of the lesser German princes, who recognized simply power
without responsibility, were debauched, like the notorious
Augustus the Strong of Saxony, who, however, belongs to the
first half of the century, before the period of enlightened
monarchs. Charles Theodore (1742–99), Elector of the Palatinate and Bavaria, was, as a patron of the arts, something of
a German Mæcenas; but he was shockingly immoral, extravagant, greedy. Würtemberg under Eberhard Ludwig (1677–
1733) was given up to his mistress, Wilhelmina von Grävenitz,

for whom he built the huge palace, an imitation Versailles, of Ludwigsburg. Carl Eugen (1737–93) was even worse. " The ruler of a poor and tiny duchy lived like an Oriental potentate, adding palace to palace, and passing his time at Ludwigsburg in balls and operas, hunting and gambling." [1] Notwithstanding inaccuracies of fact, Feuchtwanger's novel *Jew Süss* represents truly enough the moral state of this minor eighteenth-century principality. Judged as a whole, however, it may be said that European monarchs had never been so respectable, hard-working, and public-spirited as they were in the half-century before the Revolution.

Public office as a public trust and the union of executive power with reason—these were the contributions of the enlightened monarchs to the theory and practice of Government. They might be compared to the Greek tyrants who, in the ancient Mediterranean world, displaced the aristocracies, and prepared the way for the advent of democracy in the city-states.

Frederick II of Prussia was regarded as the *beau idéal* of eighteenth-century monarchs. Frederick was a bad man, absolutely without moral scruple. He would just as soon wage a war and kill people as not, if it suited his policy. When the Emperor Charles VI died Frederick wrote to Voltaire (October 26, 1740): " The Emperor is dead; his death deranges all my pacific plans." And when his bewildered Minister of State Podewils discreetly suggested that the King's cause for making war upon Maria Theresa of Austria was doubtful, he answered decisively, " When one has the advantage, should one make use of it or not? " [2]

Frederick was a bad man, yet, as his tastes were simple and he had no passion, he stands forth as the Spartan of the age. His *Testament politique* is the handbook of enlightened monarchy. It was composed in the interval between the Austrian Succession War and the Seven Years War, forty-four

---

[1] G. P. Gooch, *Germany and the French Revolution* (1920), p. 11.

[2] Quoted by N. Ausübel, *Superman: the Life of Frederick the Great* (trans. E. and C. Paul, 1932), pp. 442–443.

years before his death. There is no religion or morality about it; the State is the be-all and end-all, something superior to all the citizenry, actuated by pure self-interest, without any hint of moral restraint. The power of the State, of course, is incorporated in the monarch.

The first duty of a citizen is to serve his country; it is an obligation which I have tried to fulfil in all the various conditions of my life. Entrusted as I am with the chief magistracy, I have had the opportunity and the means of making myself useful to my fellow-citizens. The affection which I have for them makes me desire to be able to render them some service after my death. I am not so misguided as to believe that my conduct should serve as the rule for those who shall fill my place; I know that the moment of death destroys man and his projects, and that everything in the universe is subject to the laws of change. I have no other intention in making this *Political Testament* than to communicate to posterity what I have learned by experience, as a pilot who knows the stormy passages of the political sea. I undertake to indicate to posterity the reefs [*écueils*] which they have to avoid, and the ports where they can find shelter. . . .

Government turns on four principal points [*Le Gouvernement roule sur quatre points principaux*]: the administration of justice; wise economy of the finances; the vigorous maintenance of military discipline; and, lastly, the art of taking the most suitable measures for furthering its interests—this we call policy.[1]

Prussia under Frederick II became the model state, with a Government-controlled commerce and industry (monopolistic, mercantilist), a tremendous army, a laborious, far-reaching, economical civil service. The rigour with which the officials, from the lowest to the highest, in whatever corner of the land they were stationed, were held to accountability for moneys, and were subject to controls, was ruthless and inflexible. Yet the system, in the long run, was not a success. It lacked the active collaboration of a free people, and it was shattered in

[1] " Testament politique," in Küntzel und Hass, *Die Politischen Testamenten der Hohenzollern* (1920), vol. ii, pp. 1–2.

the early years of the next century at the battle of Jena. Stein, a foreigner from Nassau, was required to regenerate it. The enlightened autocrats were genuinely interested in culture, and particularly fond of good music. Mozart owed a good deal to the suggestions of the Emperor Joseph II. Joseph himself played the violoncello in his orchestra. His mother, Maria Theresa, often sang in the operas produced in his private theatre at Schönbrunn or Laxenburg. Dr Burney at Munich visited the Electoral Court, and heard the Dowager Electress of Saxony sing and the Elector of Bavaria play the violin. Frederick the Great was a performer of merit on the flute, and used to console himself with it when dejected after an unsuccessful battle. There was no opera in Berlin when he succeeded to the throne in 1740. He built a theatre, and it was opened, with a company of " the most able German instrumental performers, Italian singers, and French dancers," in 1742. Thirty years later, on visiting Berlin, Dr Burney wrote : " The King always stands behind the *maestro di capella*, in sight of the score, which he frequently looks at, and, indeed, performs the part of director-general here, as much as of *generalissimo* in the field." [1] Monarchs when they unbend are always charming. Frederick, however, would have been noted as a remarkable man in any walk of life. " His conversation," wrote the Prince de Ligne, a good judge, " was encyclopædic : the fine arts, war, medicine, literature and religion, philosophy, morality, history, and legislation passed, turn by turn, in review."

After the titanic, and perfectly useless, struggle in which the European Continental states engaged, called the Seven Years War, the King of Prussia was accepted as the type of hero-king. His fortitude, his constancy in adversity, his resourcefulness and skill, his luck (all mankind admires luck), made him almost a legendary figure. Men of letters, like Dr Johnson, took him as their chosen hero, discussed his acts and magnified his qualities in coffee-house conversations. Protestants

[1] Charles Burney, *The Present State of Music in Germany, the Netherlands, and the United Provinces* (1773), vol. ii, p. 100.

regarded him as a defender of their faith. Philosophers considered him as the promoter of free thought and of the scientific spirit. They did not realize that the only difference between the Great Frederick before and after his period of wars was that whereas, before, he was a bad young man, after it he was a bad old one. There was the same complete lack of scruple, the same godlessness. He did just what he wanted; and if he worked assiduously to make government efficient and, according to the ideas of the age, progressive, this was because, like Napoleon, he liked work and liked efficiency; there was absolutely no spark of conscience or unselfishness about him.

After the war the Sultan of Turkey, with whom Frederick always had friendly relations, dispatched a deputation asking him to send three of the astrologers by whose aid he had been so magnificently successful. Frederick replied that his three astrologers were Diplomacy, the Army, and the Treasury. In effect, these were the pivots of his State and whole content of his statesmanship; and the greatest of them was the Treasury. Everything was taxed in Prussia under the great King; and, as if the old Prussian bureaucracy and the famous Department of Finance called the General Directory were not sufficient for the work, a horde of French officials was recruited to squeeze the last penny from the hated excise. No family was immune from the excisemen's visitations and exactions; and if a common article was not taxed for excise it was only because, as with tobacco and coffee, the great King preferred to make an exorbitant Government monopoly of it. Out of the over-taxation of his kingdom Frederick built at Potsdam a grand palace, called the Neues Palais, a sort of Versailles, though much smaller than the French palace. Its interior decoration is a gorgeous exhibition of eighteenth-century rococo-baroque, luxurious and opulent, though the King himself lived simply enough in it. The people naturally resented the financial exactions of Frederick, and some wits avenged themselves by hanging in front of the Fürstenhaus in Berlin a cartoon of the King grinding a coffee-mill between his knees and picking up every bean that fell to the ground. Frederick, riding up the Jägerstrasse, came upon it, with his horrified Staff. The cartoon was rather high up for anyone to see it clearly. " Hang it lower down," said the Grand Frederick.[1] Like many selfish men, he was good-natured when his self-interest was not particularly at stake. He submitted cheerfully when a Potsdam miller refused to sell his mill and land for the King's park at Sans Souci; he received a petition of a Thuringian student from whom the customs-house officers had extorted money, and by personal intervention he made them disgorge; and he went patiently into the voluminously documented case of Arnold, a miller in the Oder valley, whose land was being unjustly expropriated. This sort of intervention in the cause of justice under an absolute monarchy can only be casual and sporadic, and is no guarantee against miscarriages which, in a large country, must escape the eye of the most watchful autocrat.

The truth is that the great King was much less enlightened than his familiarity with the philosophers implied. Living almost on the eve of the French Revolution, he had not the slightest notion of democracy. He did everything that he could, and, indeed, successfully, to preserve and crystallize class distinctions. The nobles were not allowed to sell their lands or to engage in trade. He revived the old restrictive, privileged commercial guilds, and trade-guilds, which had been falling out of use; his object was to fix the *bourgeoisie* in their boundaries, to make them and them only the trading and commercial class. He left the peasants bound in serfdom to the noble landlords. The Prussian serf was in a worse legal situation than was the French peasant before the Revolution. In economics Frederick was purely medieval. He seems never to have even inquired into the principles of Adam Smith's *Wealth of Nations*, which was published in 1776, ten years before his death. Frederick's system was blindly protective. He believed that everything could be made in Prussia if only there was a prohibitive duty on imports; when the duty failed to produce the

[1] F. Kugler, *Life of Frederick the Great* (trans. 1877), p. 520.

result he subsidized the native industry. The soundest economic notion which he had was that land should be carefully developed, so he spent much capital on drainage; and he constructed a useful canal, the Bromberg canal, connecting the Vistula and the Oder. He did nothing for education, except that he allowed Jesuits to remain in Prussia even after the Society of Jesus had been dissolved by the Pope in 1773; the Jesuits were always good schoolmasters.

He posed as a defender of the Empire and of its constitution, but, as a matter of fact, he was one of the two men—Napoleon was the other—who between them broke it up. He had respect neither for the law of the Empire nor for the law of nations. He participated in the Partition of Poland in 1772 (indeed, he was the chief instigator of this), contrary to public law and morality. His assault upon Austria in 1740 was a breach of the peace of the Empire and a violent repudiation of its appellate courts. When he was able to keep Silesia as a result of piratical war the Imperial system was turned into a meaningless form. Against Austria, the head of the Empire, he fought three wars, the War of the Austrian Succession, 1740-48, the Seven Years War, 1756-63, the War of the Bavarian Succession, 1778-79, two of which were unprovoked. The last arose over Joseph II's plan, with the consent of the Elector, of incorporating Bavaria in Austria.

In 1785 Joseph II revived the plan, this time offering to make the Elector of Bavaria King of the (Austrian) Netherlands, in return for Bavaria, which was to be incorporated in Austria. Frederick prevented this by inducing certain other princes of the Empire to join with him in forming a Fürstenbund, a league of princes. The existence of such a league within the Empire was really incompatible with the maintenance of the Imperial constitution. It was as inimical to the Empire as was Mazarin's League of the Rhine (1659) or Napoleon's Confederation of the Rhine (1806).

Frederick's intense preoccupation with territorial annexation was not really in the interest of Prussia. If Silesia was a substantial gain the disintegration of Poland (which he

FREDERICK THE GREAT
From an engraving

started by the Partition of 1772) ruined the eastern frontier of Prussia.

The great King outlived all his friends; perhaps he never really had any [1]—the thoroughly selfish man seldom, if ever, has. " He was incapable of gratitude," Voltaire told the Prince de Ligne, " and never had any except for the horse on which he ran away at the battle of Mollwitz." [2] His wife, Princess Elizabeth Christina of Brunswick-Wolfenbüttel, to whom he had always been indifferent, was a lonely figure who outlived him, and died in 1797. He had no children, and he disliked the nephew who was to succeed him. He passed a loveless old age, without companions, without interests, without even the music that used to console and amuse him. The execution of the routine of government had become a habit with him which he could not abandon. In the last weeks of his life, overcome and dying of dropsy, he still mounted his horse at the regular hour, and trotted fifty paces with a man on each side of him. The physicians urged him in vain to forgo his labours or his pleasures. " He might drag on life," wrote Mirabeau from Berlin, " if he would take advice, Dr Baylies says, for another year, but I suspect he will never give up eel-pies." On August 15, 1786, Frederick, " though his feebleness was excessive," still transacted the Cabinet business; but on the 16th he was judged to be dead, because, for the first time in his reign, he did not remember that the day's business had not been done. " The conclusion was sagely drawn: dying only could he forget his duty." He expired on August 17, 1786, at twenty minutes past two in the morning. For whole decades he had been regarded as the greatest prince of his age, and was to be so regarded again. Yet on the day of his death, when all the talk was about him, two-thirds of the Berliners were " violently declaiming, in order to prove that Frederick II was a man of common, and almost mean, capacity." [3] The

---

[1] This is Herr Ludwig's view (*Genie und Charakter* (1932), p. 83).

[2] Prince de Ligne, *Mémoires*, vol. ii, p. 161.

[3] The citations in this paragraph are all from Mirabeau, *Secret History of the Court of Prussia* (trans. 1789), vol. i, pp. 6, 50, 198, 200.

only thing which ever daunted the great King was the approach
of death, and even this only for a few moments. Madame de
Staël has pointed out in *De l'Allemagne* that monarchs are (or
were) so omnipotent, so unresisted in every wish and action,
that they recognize no master but death, to which they all
must bow, and which alone therefore they fear, often to an
exaggerated degree. A modern biography, full, imaginative,
sympathetic, in dealing with the end of three generations of
Prussian kings—Frederick I, Frederick William I, Frederick II
—has three widely separated chapters with the same refrain :
" the King is afraid to die." [1] Louis XV of France could not
bear the mention of death ; and the tactless courtier who
referred to a *feu M. le Comte* had to explain *feu* away as " a
title that people took." But the great Frederick was of a
different mettle. " I no longer believe," wrote the Prince de
Ligne, " in the quaking of the earth and the eclipses at the
death of Cæsar, since none has been experienced at the death
of Frederick the Great." [2]

Perhaps the most remarkable thing about this many-sided
man who was so gifted though not lovable—a great captain,
a great statesman, diplomatist, administrator—is that he was a
great man of letters. " Frédéric II," writes a most competent
judge, " *est un grand écrivain.*"

At the school of Voltaire he formed himself ; stripped of his
Germanisms of spirit and tongue, he has found the form, at once
French and personal, suitable for his genius : a firm style, illumin-
ated by phrases vigorously neat or familiarly picturesque : a fund
of very serious philosophy, of thought free, active, penetrating,
the source of all his writings, but, above all, of his vast correspondence, one of the most interesting things to read that the
eighteenth century offers, even without taking account of its
historical value. [3]

This is from a critical history of French literature—Frederick

---

[1] N. Ausübel, *Superman: the Life of Frederick the Great* (trans. E. and
C. Paul, 1932).
[2] Prince de Ligne, *Mémoires*, vol. i, p. 40.
[3] G. Lanson, *Histoire de la littérature française* (1898), pp. 813–814.

the Great wrote in French. A French historian had previously declared, " He shared with Voltaire the intellectual supremacy of the eighteenth century."[1]

Apart from " Polish Prussia " and Silesia (the first of which has since been wholly lost, the second partially), Frederick's great contribution to the development of the Prussian State was the bureaucracy. He did not originate the famous Prussian bureaucracy; this was the work, substantially, of his father, Frederick William I, who in 1723 created the General Finance, War and Domains Directory, the supreme, co-ordinating ' college ' or board, controlling all the central and provincial officials.

Frederick the Great's kingdom was a ' managed state,' with a ' planned economy,' in which all industry, commerce, and even social relations were directed by the King. The sole object of this system was to produce the maximum possible revenue, so as to maintain the huge Prussian Army and ensure the greatness of the Prussian State. Everything was subordinated to the production of revenue, or, rather, to the King's ideas of the way in which revenue could be obtained. The officials were allowed no initiative at all; they were governed by inflexible regulations; they were driven ruthlessly and were paid little. *Travailler pour le roi de Prusse* was the phrase used in Europe for being treated with meanness and ingratitude.

The Prussian bureaucracy was conducted on the collegiate or ' board ' system, as contrasted with the French bureaucracy, which had the personal or *chef de bureau* system.[2] In the Prussian bureaucracy, down to about the year 1770, there was no genuine head of a department or chief of a section, with personal responsibility. There were officials with the title of Minister of Finance, Minister of War, and others, but they were merely agents of the King and of the official boards.

---

[1] C. Paganel, *Histoire de Joseph II* (1843), p. 344: "*Il partageait avec Voltaire la monarchie intellectuelle du dix-huitième siècle.*"

[2] The English Civil Service in the eighteenth century had both systems, but the *chef de bureau*, or permanent Under-Secretary of State, has now superseded all boards, except the Board of Customs and the Board of Inland Revenue.

Every department of state had its board, and the members controlled and checked each other and shared and divided responsibility. Every board was absolutely subject to the King. " Never did absolute monarchs take their autocracy more seriously than the Hohenzollerns of the eighteenth century. Mirabeau could truthfully say that the Prussian Government had become for the science of despotism what Egypt was to the ancients in search of knowledge." [1] The King seldom saw his Ministers, except for the regular ' annual review,' which he held of them every June. The rest of the time he was working with his private secretaries in the secrecy of his closet or ' cabinet,' reading the Ministers' and boards' reports, and issuing his decisions upon these.

The chief merit of the system was its rapidity. All matters were dispatched forthwith, if circumstances did not require a special investigation. Since everything was done by letter and the King's mind worked with extraordinary speed, there was no reason for delay. It should be remembered that the military order and preciseness of the King's life in Potsdam was conducive to hard work, that he had with him neither wife nor family, that there was neither Court nor French Court etiquette, that he never observed a religious holiday and never was distracted by undesired interruptions. There was something like Puritanical zeal in his unremitting application to work. His secretaries and Ministers testify to the tyrannical discipline which he exercised over his mind and body. With punctilious regularity he disposed of everything as soon as it came to him, sometimes issuing as many as thirty or forty Cabinet orders in a single day, and rarely did he postpone any matter from one day to another. Nowhere in the entire Prussian bureaucratic system was there such impeccable order as in the Cabinet of the King. Just as each hour of the day, each week and month, so the entire year was arranged in such a manner that no business crowded on the heels of another. A calendar on his table indicated not only the duties of each day and week, but informed him when all outstanding reports, replies, and other matters fell due. Even when in May,

[1] W. L. Dorn, "The Prussian Bureaucracy in the Eighteenth Century," in *The Political Science Quarterly* (1931), p. 408.

June, and August of every year the monarch regularly embarked on his inspection journeys through the provinces his secretaries and correspondence accompanied him. Any official who addressed himself to the King could expect an immediate answer. He could even calculate, according to his distance from the royal residence and the time required by the post, the very day when he was to receive his answer. If he did not receive his answer then none would be forthcoming at all.[1]

Only a man of extraordinary method, dispatch, and industry could have kept pace with all this mass of business and executed it efficiently. The system was certain to break down or to become torpid and inefficient under one or other of his successors. Nor did it work really well even under the great Frederick. In some respects it made for delay in business, in others for over-haste. Mirabeau, after his visit to Prussia, criticized " the mania of expediting the whole affairs of a kingdom in one hour and a half." [2] The extreme centralization killed initiative in the officials; and it led to a good deal of hypocrisy, cringing, and deceit on their part, for they found that business went forward best when they reported things that the King liked and suppressed the rest. " Of all the kings in Europe," wrote Mirabeau, " he was the most deceived."[3] Indeed, some suppression was inevitable. If everything had gone to the King delays would have become intolerable; for in those days it took as long for a letter to go from Königsberg to Berlin as it does now from London to New York—five days. The King was not always at Berlin. Correspondence might have to follow his carriage to Cleves in the extreme west, or to Ansbach in the extreme south. In the last fifteen years of his reign Frederick tended to rely more on single Ministers than on boards, but he never permitted his Ministers any real power of initiative or responsibility.

The fashion or movement for public service and for enlightenment among monarchs was not confined to the great states.

---

[1] W. L. Dorn, op. cit., pp. 412–413.
[2] Mirabeau, The Secret History of the Court of Prussia, vol. i, p. 111.
[3] Ibid., vol. i, p. 111.

The minor princes followed the great ones in this, as they did in other things—for instance, in building models of Versailles for themselves, or in maintaining a standing army, even though, like the Graf von Limburg-Styrum, they could only afford a colonel, six officers, and two privates.[1] Dresden owed much of its embellishment to Augustus the Strong of Saxony and Poland (1694–1733). He is considered to have been one of the most licentious monarchs of the age and the most luxurious. "When Augustus was taking wine," said Frederick the Great, "Poland was drunk" (*Quand Auguste buvait, la Pologne était ivre*).[2] Saxony-Poland was not exactly a minor Power. Among the minor, but not insignificant, principalities was one whose chief attained the height of fame, and was ranked as a peer of the great enlightened monarchs. This was Charles William Ferdinand, Duke of Brunswick-Wolfenbüttel, to whom Byron alludes in a famous passage of *Childe Harold* which celebrates the death of the Duke's heroic son.

The ancient family of Guelf had two branches; the elder ruled over the Electorate of Hanover and the younger over the Duchy of Brunswick. By one of those confusions of title, common in the complicated political system of the Holy Roman Empire, the Elector of Hanover (who after 1714 was King of England as well) had the title of Duke of Brunswick, though he possessed no territory there. To distinguish himself from the younger branch, the King of England, Elector of Hanover, took as his third title that of Duke of Brunswick-Luneburg. The head of the younger branch, usually indicated when the title ' Duke of Brunswick ' is employed, is called in genealogical tables Duke of Brunswick-Wolfenbüttel. His capital was the city of Brunswick. To put the confusing matter more shortly, in another way, George III of Great Britain was effective ruling Elector of Hanover, and was also titular Duke of Brunswick (-Luneburg). His distant cousin, Charles

---

[1] See " General Conditions of Taste," by W. H. Hadow, *Oxford History of Music*, vol. v, p. 3.

[2] Prince de Ligne, *Mémoires*, vol. ii, p. 68.

William Ferdinand, was effective ruling Duke of Brunswick (-Wolfenbüttel).

In the second half of the eighteenth century there were four famous members of the Wolfenbüttel Brunswickers. The first of these was Ferdinand, Frederick the Great's famous general, who won the battle of Minden in 1759. He was a younger son, and was never reigning Duke of Brunswick, though usually and correctly called Duke Ferdinand. This

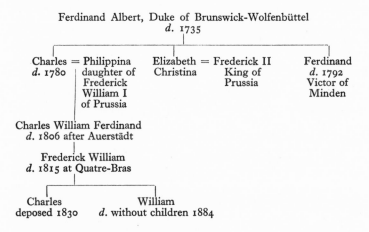

Ferdinand Albert, Duke of Brunswick-Wolfenbüttel
d. 1735

Charles = Philippina	Elizabeth = Frederick II	Ferdinand
d. 1780	daughter of	Christina	King of	*d.* 1792
	Frederick		Prussia	Victor of
	William I			Minden
	of Prussia			

Charles William Ferdinand
d. 1806 after Auerstädt

Frederick William
d. 1815 at Quatre-Bras

Charles   William
deposed 1830   *d.* without children 1884

great captain died in 1792. The second was Ludwig Ernst, Austrian field-marshal, and for a time practically ruler of Holland, Commander-in-Chief of the Dutch Army.[1] The third was Charles William Ferdinand, the most celebrated and the most remarkable of all the Brunswickers. He was Hereditary Prince (or heir apparent) and later reigning Duke of Brunswick-Wolfenbüttel, nephew of Duke Ferdinand, and, like his uncle, was a general of Frederick the Great. It was he who commanded the Allies in the invasion of France in 1792, the year in which his uncle, Duke Ferdinand, died. Charles William Ferdinand was mortally wounded at the battle of Jena-Auerstädt in 1806. The fourth was his son, Frederick William, reigning Duke of Brunswick. He was killed at

---

[1] See above, p. 24.

Quatre-Bras in 1815.[1] Byron's stanzas describe the hero's last night at Brussels:

> There was a sound of revelry by night,
> And Belgium's capital had gather'd then
> Her Beauty and her Chivalry, and bright
> The lamps shone o'er fair women and brave men;
> A thousand hearts beat happily; and when
> Music arose with its voluptuous swell,
> Soft eyes looked love to eyes which spake again,
> And all went merry as a marriage bell;
> But hush! hark! a deep sound strikes like a rising knell!
>
> .   .   .   .
>
> Within a window'd niche of that high hall
> Sate Brunswick's fated chieftain; he did hear
> That sound the first amidst the festival,
> And caught its tone with Death's prophetic ear;
> And when they smiled because he deem'd it near,
> His heart more truly knew that peal too well
> Which stretch'd his father on a bloody bier,
> And roused the vengeance blood alone could quell;
> He rush'd into the field, and, foremost fighting, fell.

Charles William Ferdinand was, like his uncle by marriage, the great Frederick, " one of the princely forerunners of the French Revolution,"[2] although his name is mainly associated with the campaign of 1792, the chief effort of the princes to defeat the Revolution. He was born in 1735, and was the eldest son of Charles, Duke of Brunswick-Wolfenbüttel and of Princess Philippina of Prussia, sister of Frederick, afterwards Frederick the Great. Charles William Ferdinand grew up as the great Frederick's favourite pupil in the art of war, schooled also in this art by his other uncle, Duke Ferdinand, general in the Prus-

[1] In 1884 the Wolfenbüttel line died out, and the rights of Brunswick (-Wolfenbüttel) passed to the head of the elder branch, George V, ex-King of Hanover, titular Duke of Brunswick (-Luneburg), Duke of Cumberland, grandson of King George III of England. George V had been defeated by Prussia in 1866. His kingdom, Hanover, was annexed to Prussia. The Duchy of Brunswick (-Wolfenbüttel) was not annexed, but placed under a regency.

[2] Lord E. Fitzmaurice, *Charles William Ferdinand, Duke of Brunswick: an Historical Study, 1735–1806* (London, 1901), p. 2.

sian service and Governor of Magdeburg. He received much, however, besides military education. His cultured mother, the Princess of Prussia, procured able tutors for him. The best known was Johann Friedrich Jerusalem (1709–89), called the Abbé Jerusalem, a Protestant theologian who was highly thought of in Germany and in England, a product of the Universities of Leipzig and Göttingen. He attended classes at the Collegium Carolinum, one of Germany's new ' Knights' Schools,' founded at Brunswick in 1735. Like Frederick, Charles William Ferdinand was going to be a *prince éclairé*, or a *prince philosophe*, but Fate was to cast his early years of manhood, again like those of Frederick, in the furnace of war. At the age of twenty-two he was serving with the Hanoverian forces under the command of the Duke of Cumberland in the opening stages of the Seven Years War. The Duke was disastrously defeated by the French at Hastenbeck, in Hanover, on July 26, 1757. The one bright spot in the battle, from the point of view of the vanquished, was the charge of the Hereditary Prince of Brunswick, who captured the central battery of the French, and would have turned defeat into victory if Cumberland had known how to exploit his success. It was after this defeat at Hastenbeck and the ensuing capitulation at Kloster-Zeven that the British Government requested Frederick the Great to select a new commander for the British-Hanoverian forces. Frederick chose Duke Ferdinand of Brunswick-Wolfenbüttel, brother of the reigning Duke and uncle of the Hereditary Prince. The selection of Duke Ferdinand proved to be a great success; and, along with Prince Henry of Prussia, the general who " made no mistake " (as Frederick the Great said), he was held to be one of the two finest commanders, after the King himself, in the war. The Hereditary Prince served under Duke Ferdinand's command, and had a share in the famous victories of Crefeld, in 1758, and Minden, in 1759. After the war Duke Ferdinand retired into private life at Brunswick, with an English pension and an annuity paid from Magdeburg Cathedral funds.

The Hereditary Prince emerged from the Seven Years War

with the reputation of being the most daring and dashing leader of his time. Chatham, writing to his wife, described the Prince's exploits in almost dithyrambic terms: " He pierced five times the French infantry, at the head of Elliott's; his horse wounded under him, and a led horse behind him killed."[1] In his last engagement he was seriously wounded. He recruited his health after the war with a leisurely tour round the great capitals of Europe, meeting and conversing with princes, artists, men of letters, and philosophers. Voltaire was enchanted with him, with his brilliancy, good fortune, modesty. On his visit to the English Court in 1764 he became engaged to the Princess Augusta, sister of George III. London received him with the wildest enthusiasm ; the people, Lady Chatham wrote, " almost pulled down the house in which he was [Somerset House] in order to see him." [2] As a marriage settlement, and in grati- tude for his military services, the British Government endowed him with a Parliamentary grant of £80,000 and an annuity of £5000 charged upon the revenues of Ireland.[3]

The marriage of the Hereditary Prince of Brunswick into the family of George III proved to be very unfortunate, for the King's madness was shared by his sister. Of the four sons born of the marriage the eldest is described as having been wellnigh imbecile, the second an idiot, the third blind; the fourth, who became a fine man, and succeeded to the duchy, was killed at Quatre-Bras. There were two daughters. One became Duchess of Würtemberg ; the other was Queen Caroline, the unfortunate and ill-used wife of George IV of England. " Only private persons," the Duke, Charles William Ferdinand, once said to a friend, " are happy in the married state. One of my class must marry according to certain conveniences, which is a most unhappy thing. The heart has nothing to do with these mar- riages, and the result is not only to embitter life, but also to bring the most disastrous experience on those who come after.

---

[1] *Correspondence of the Earl of Chatham* (1838), vol. ii, p. 55. Elliott's Light Dragoons are now the 15th Hussars. Their commander, Colonel Elliott, was later Lord Heathfield, the defender of Gibraltar.

[2] *Ibid.*, vol. ii, p. 271.   [3] Fitzmaurice, *op. cit.*, p. 15.

The children are mostly cripples in mind and body." [1] As in nearly every Court of the eighteenth century (though not at George III's), there was a recognized mistress, a *maîtresse titrée*, at the Court of even this virtuous prince. In 1780 Charles William Ferdinand succeeded to the ducal throne of Brunswick-Wolfenbüttel. For twenty-six years, until his death after Auerstädt and the annexation by Napoleon, the duchy was one of the two most happily governed states in the Empire (Baden was the other), the Duke (with Carl Friedrich of Baden) the most enlightened prince. The dashing cavalry general, the hero of Crefeld and Minden, showed no desire to maintain the parade of soldiery. He spared the depleted finances of his duchy by keeping only a small army. He attended to roads, common lands, and education, and in 1794 conceded to the Estates, the ancient representative Assembly, control of the public revenues. He had able men for his administration: Féronce, a member of the famous Leipzig family of French origin, as chief Minister; two Jews, Jacobson and Ephraim, for finance; his old tutor, the Abbé Jerusalem, for the headship of the Collegium Carolinum, the *Ritter-Akademie*, or school for sons of noblemen, at Brunswick; Lessing as his librarian at Wolfenbüttel. [2] His Court was well conducted. The Duke did not gamble, drank milk, and took his relaxation in a game of chess or in playing the violin, on which he was a skilful performer. Numbers of the cultured aristocracy and wealthy *bourgeoisie*, the international society which was the glory of the capitals of Europe, visited the Court of the famous Duke and admired his character and his reforms. He was equally at home in conversing with distinguished travellers in French or in speaking with his own subjects in the homely Brunswick *patois*. After the death of the great Frederick of Prussia, in 1786, Brunswick and Weimar were the most famous states in the Empire, their happiness unmarred until the French

---

[1] Fitzmaurice, *op. cit.*, p. 17.
[2] Lessing was appointed librarian at Wolfenbüttel in 1769, while Charles William was still only Hereditary Prince; his fruitful literary period at the ducal library lasted until his death, in 1781.

Revolution began to ruffle the tranquil waters of princely popular life. Mirabeau, who visited Brunswick in 1786, as it were on the eve of the French Revolution, left on record his impression of this eminent prince. " The Duke," he writes, " will certainly not be thought a common man, even among men of merit. His person bespeaks depth and penetration and a desire to please, tempered by fortitude, nay, by sternness. He is prodigiously laborious, well informed and perspicacious. However able his first Minister, Féronce, may be, the Duke superintends all affairs, and generally decides for himself. His correspondence is immense, and this he can only owe to his personal reputation, because he cannot be sufficiently wealthy to keep so many correspondents in pay. Few great Courts are so well informed as his." The keen French observer believed that the Duke, though still a Prussian general who took the military profession seriously, " appears effectually to have quitted military glory to betake himself to the cares of government." [1] Mirabeau was convinced that the Duke was " sincerely desirous of peace," and that he was " by much the most able prince of Germany." [2]

There are some men so universally trusted in respect of both their character and their capacity that in an emergency their services are sought upon all sides. It was so with the Duke of Brunswick. When the French Revolution had broken out, and France and Austria alike were believed to be in danger, each from the other, both offered the command of thei: military forces to the Duke.

At the time of the French Revolution the Holy Roman Empire was recognized as an outworn organism, with no life in it: it was just " an Emperor reigning over anarchy." In Goethe's *Faust*, at the drinking-scene in Auerbach's Cellar in Leipzig, Frosch sings:

> " *Das liebe heil'ge röm'sche Reich,*
> *Wie hält's nur noch zusammen?* "

---

[1] Mirabeau, *The Secret History of the Court of Prussia*, vol. i, pp. 18–21 ; Fitzmaurice, *op. cit.*, pp. 25–26.

[2] Mirabeau, *op. cit.*, vol. i, p. 17.

Brander replies: " A nasty song. Pfui! a political song. A poor song! Thank God each morning that you don't need to care anything for the Roman Empire!" [1] Frederick the Great already in 1752 called it *suranné et bizarre*. Thinking men had schemes for reforming it—the Duke himself is said to have had one. One plan, not his own, involved the creation of a new kingdom on the left bank of the Rhine, a buffer state to be made out of Limburg, Gueldres, and Luxemburg, and the Duke was to be made king of it. Poland, reduced in size by the Partition of 1772, but still a large kingdom, was trying to reform itself under its last Diet; there was a plan to have the reforming and universally respected Duke of Brunswick for King of Poland in the event of the death of the weak-willed King Stanislaus Poniatowski. Early in 1792 the French Government, which was now a constitutional monarchy under the Constitution of 1791, contemplated a war against Austria, a 'preventive war,' as it would have been called if the phrase had been in use at that time, but really an aggressive war, to divert the attention of the French people from domestic to foreign affairs. The French Ministry of War sent François de Custine (son of the general who was later executed) on mission to Brunswick to offer the Duke command of the French forces against Austria. The Duke, though repeatedly pressed to accept, declined. He was a Prussian general, he said, and it was his business to fight for Prussia in time of war, and in time of peace to administer his duchy; besides, if he took command of an invading army, he would not have the advantage of the enthusiasm which resistance to foreign attack always aroused. [2] Alas! almost immediately after this, with misgivings and against his better judgment, he accepted a command precisely under this disadvantage—invading a foreign country and so arousing an invincible national enthusiasm and resistance.

[1] Goethe, *Faust*, lines 2090–94:
" The dear Holy Roman Empire,
How does it still hold together ? "
The quotation from Frederick the Great is from *Das Politische Testament*, p. 61.

[2] *Revue historique*, vol. i, p. 167.

The offer of the command of the French army is an instance of the *naïve* cosmopolitanism of the eighteenth century. The offer of the command of the invading army of the Allies is another if less striking instance of this cosmopolitanism, which the defeat of that invasion at Valmy was to destroy, replacing it with an assertive nationalism. The Allied Army comprised Austrian as well as Prussian troops, and the Duke was in supreme command. He accepted the duty out of loyalty to the King of Prussia (Frederick William II, who had succeeded Frederick the Great in 1786), perhaps also owing to the influence of his uncle, the " Duke Ferdinand," who commanded the British Army at Minden and other battles of the Seven Years War. The aged Duke Ferdinand died on July 3, 1792, six years after the great Frederick. It was said that Charles William Ferdinand feared both his uncles, even when they were dead; hence his fatal acceptance of the offer of the German command in 1792. He took command of the army of the Allies and of the French Royalist *émigrés* at Coblenz, and signed the Manifesto of July 25, 1792, which bears his name. His mind saw things clearly, but he seemed to have lost his power of decision. The Brunswick Manifesto was drafted by Geoffrey de Limon, Secretary to the Comte de Provence, and it drove the Revolutionary elements in France to extremes. " That unlucky Manifesto! " observed the Duke to his biographer, Massenbach, later. " I shall repent it to the last day of my life. What would I give never to have signed it ! " The invasion of France was checked by the cannonade of Valmy on September 20. The September Massacres were already in progress. The proclamation of the Republic followed. " It puts a new face on the world," wrote Massenbach; " it is the most important day of the century." [1] It was also the anti-climax of a fine career: the Duke of Brunswick's great failure.

It was not the end, however, of the Duke, though it was the end of the invasion of France in 1792. He continued to command the Prussian troops, with a considerable degree of success, in the campaign of 1793, but resigned on January 10,

[1] Fitzmaurice, *op. cit.*, p. 70.

1794, on account of the intermeddling of King Frederick William II. He went back to his duchy, but came out to take command again of the Prussian " Army of Observation " after Prussia had made peace with France by the Treaty of Bâle in 1795. When Prussia went to war with Napoleon in 1806 the Duke once more was in command, although subject to interference by orders from King Frederick William III. Whenever the ordeal of battle approached the Duke became the hero : all indecision vanished ; he was confident, cheerful, active. At the age of seventy-one he shared all the fatigues of the private soldiers, slept in his clothes, rose at three in the morning, and in the heat of battle rode up to the critical points to supervise and encourage. In the terrible fight of Auerstädt, on October 14, he was blinded by a gunshot, yet managed to mount his horse and ride off the field. After this the defeat became a rout. The Duke, attended by only a few bearers, was carried on a litter towards Hamburg, uncomplaining, hopeful. " I shall be blind all my life," he remarked. " Well, at my age, that is not so bad after all." He died in a " miserable inn " at Ottensen, near Altona, on October 29, 1806. Napoleon overran his duchy and incorporated it in the Kingdom of Westphalia, and it remained under Jerome Napoleon's rule until the Restoration of 1814.

The big Courts of Germany were, on the whole, the best conducted. Their monarchs were the most exposed to public opinion ; they had the most command of talent for their advisers and civil servants. The monarchs of the little Courts could be good or bad, without much control from the public opinion of the localities over which they despotically ruled. The Zähringen house, the Dukes of Baden, were good; to the end of their time, to the great German revolution of 1919, they were models of liberal rulers. Carl Friedrich of Baden (1771–1811) " did all that could be done in a tiny state by a wise and unselfish ruler." [1] The Würtemberger princes— house of Bebenhausen—were about as bad as they could safely be. Duke Eberhard Ludwig (1677–1733), his mistress

[1] G. P. Gooch, *Germany and the French Revolution* (1920), p. 11.

Wilhelmina von Grävenitz, his brother and successor, Duke
Carl Alexander, an Austrian field-marshal (1733–37), and the
Finance Minister Joseph Süss Oppenheimer live and move in
Lion Feuchtwanger's crowded romance called *Jew Süss*. The
details of the novel have been shown to be not all accurate.
Joseph Süss Oppenheimer's origin was not mysterious; he
was the son of a collector of taxes in the Palatinate. He was a
loyal servant of Duke Carl Alexander, and was a capable and
efficient Minister of despotism. " He broke the power of the
guilds and civil officials and created absolute government."
His trial, after Duke Carl Alexander's death, was a travesty of
justice. Süss's private life appears to have been much like
that of the contemporary nobility, and not of the orgiastic
kind suggested in the novel.[1]

[1] See Selma Stern, *Jud Süss : ein Beitrag zur Deutschen und zur Jüdischen
Geschichte* (1929); reviewed by H. Loewe in *History*, July 1932, pp. 171–172.

CHAPTER VIII

ENLIGHTENED MONARCHS:
CATHERINE II

FREDERICK II was the Solomon of eighteenth-century monarchs. Catherine II was the Semiramis. The reputation of Russia for vast (largely because unknown) power, the romantic interest attaching to an empress who began as the dowerless daughter of the younger son of a petty German prince, the correspondence and intimacy of Catherine with the French philosophers and men of the *salons*, ensured her a place in the highest rank of *monarques éclairés*.

The father of Catherine II was Prince Charles Augustus, a younger son of the Anhalt-Zerbst family, who entered the Prussian Army and saw service in the Low Countries, in Italy, and in Pomerania. In 1727, at the age of twenty-seven, he married a princess of the Holstein-Gottorp family who was related to the royal family of Russia. Catherine was born in 1729 at Stettin, where her father was colonel of the garrison. He was a religious man, a Lutheran, and brought her up carefully, giving her a good education at the hands of governesses and tutors, chiefly French Protestant refugees. In 1743, when the family was spending Christmas with Catherine's uncle, the Prince of Anhalt-Zerbst, at Zerbst a messenger arrived from the Empress Elizabeth of Russia, bidding the mother and daughter set forth as soon as they could for St Petersburg; an order on a Berlin bank for ten thousand roubles was included to pay for the journey. After exciting and hasty preparations the party set off, with a few servants, in four lumbering carriages on January 12, 1744, from Zerbst for Berlin, Schwedt, Memel, Riga (where they were met and taken onward by Russian officials), St Petersburg, and then on to Moscow.

Catherine had been brought to Russia to be educated for marriage with the heir to the throne, the Grand Duke Peter of Holstein-Gottorp, nephew of the Empress Elizabeth. The girl of fifteen showed amazing adaptability, learned Russian, travelled in the country, accepted conversion, passionately, sincerely, as it seemed, to the Orthodox religion; made herself familiar with every side of Court life. She was left much alone, and read widely, chiefly in French: Voltaire, Madame de Sévigné, the novels of Mademoiselle de Scudéry. The marriage took place in 1745. Her husband, the Grand Duke Peter, was tall and clumsy, nearly always drunk, with one tremendous interest in life, soldiering, which to him meant simply drill and uniforms. Catherine was attractive-looking, vigorous, a lover of pleasure. Her intimate supper-parties and night excursions into St Petersburg soon made her independent of her boor of a husband, who became more and more given up to drink, to pet monkeys, and, curiously, to playing the violin. The Empress Elizabeth died in 1762, and Peter and Catherine succeeded to the throne. Probably Peter was half mad. His conduct was gross; but so was that of all the debauched Russian Court, including the conduct of Catherine. She was undoubtedly a party to the *coup d'État* which put Peter into a prison in 1762; a few days afterwards he came to a mysterious death, strangled in the prison. Catherine reigned alone. She was now thirty-four, the head of the largest, most unwieldy, worst-organized realm in Europe, with the most corrupt officials, the most debauched, immoral, and bloodthirsty Court nobility. Everybody agrees that she was a great woman. She made the Russian State work effectively; she gave it splendid renown in Europe; she improved it in many ways. But she only made worse the inner festering sore, the debauchery and immorality of the governing class, which ultimately—things move slowly in a great empire—brought it to ruin. Nevertheless, she was better than her neighbours. There was much that is reminiscent of Queen Elizabeth about her. Catherine was courageous, gay, serene. She worked hard, filled her day with the greatest exactitude, was temperate in eating, drank almost nothing, and performed the severe tasks of government with tact, intelligence, and firmness. She imposed the reputation of Russia upon Europe by her magnificent Court, her great armies. In public she was majestic, magnificent; the numerous strangers who visited the Court received the impression of meeting a great sovereign. She was tolerant of religions, and let the suppressed Jesuits come to Russia, where in subsequent years they are said to have made considerable investments. She set the example in her empire by being the first to submit to inoculation, in 1769, at the hands of the English physician Dimsdale. Had she found good statesmen to support her the improvement which she effected in the affairs of Russia would have been far greater. There was an astonishing dearth of political talent. The Empress alone was a statesman; the rest were greedy, corrupt courtiers, who wasted and exhausted the substance of Russia.

And yet, in a people as gifted and versatile as the Russians were, plenty of good material should have been found for making capable administrators, or even statesmen. Catherine's Court, however, did not provide the requisite schooling; she was not a Napoleon; and under her the Russian genius was allowed to lie waste or to run riot. Catherine, perhaps, with her Germanic thoroughness, gave the Russians up as being too mercurial. Yet the Prince de Ligne thought that they had great potentialities:

I have seen Russians to whom one has said: " Become this or that," and who do so; who acquire the liberal arts as the " Doctor in spite of himself " (*Médecin malgré lui*) took his degree, who have become foot-soldiers, sailors, hunters, priests, dragoons, musicians, engineers, actors, cuirassiers, painters, and surgeons.

I have seen Russians who sang and danced in trenches, where they were never relieved, and under gun-fire and cannon-shot, in snow and mud: quick, clean, attentive, respectful, obedient, and seeking to read in the eyes of their officers what orders they were about to give in order to anticipate them.[1]

Continually in correspondence with Voltaire and other

[1] Prince de Ligne, *Mémoires*, vol. i, p. 193.

philosophes, Catherine had the 'taste' for reform, and her genuine kindness to those around her naturally inclined her to benefit the people. Her reign, however, was troubled by frequent conspiracies and revolts. Two Emperors had died violent deaths in prison—her husband, Peter III, murdered in 1762, and a previous Emperor, Ivan VI (reigned 1740–41), dethroned at the age of two years by the Empress Elizabeth, and killed in the Schlüsselburg fortress-prison in 1764. From time to time 'pretenders' appeared, like those who in early Tudor England impersonated the princes murdered in the Tower. The most serious rebellion was that of Jemelian Pougatcheff, a Cossack who had served in the Seven Years War, and who pretended, apparently on the strength of some superficial resemblance, to be Peter III. The submerged misery of the Russian peasantry, as dreadful under Catherine as under any other Russian Emperor, broke forth in a long, devastating rebellion, which was only extinguished after four years of fire and bloodshed (1771–75). This prolonged and fearful crisis did not stimulate Catherine along the path of reform; it merely led to an intensified police system of suppression.

Catherine always had *velléités* for reform; and, indeed, her reign had begun with what seemed to be a notable instalment. Her husband, the Tsar Peter III, on his accession in 1762 had confiscated a large number of ecclesiastical estates, and had annexed them to the Crown. Catherine, on becoming sole ruler, had enfranchised the serfs on these estates, about 900,000 in all. The process of enfranchisement, however, was carried no further. In 1765 Catherine wrote to one of her philosopher correspondents in France, d'Alembert: "*J'ai pillé le président Montesquieu.*" She was referring to a long *Instruction* which she had drafted as a basis of legal reform, based on Montesquieu's *De l'Esprit des lois* and also on Beccaria's *Dei Delitti e delle Pene*. Two years later electoral colleges met throughout the empire and elected a 'Legislature.' This Legislature (or Diet) was convened in Moscow, and later in St Petersburg, and sat in the years 1767–68; but it could only discuss and recommend, and no action whatever was taken upon its deliberations. The prolonged revolt of Pougatcheff led Catherine to put aside all plans for reform, if she ever had any. The *Instruction*, published to the world in 1767 in Russian, French, and German, and in English in 1768, was hailed by Catherine's literary circle in Paris and elsewhere as a work of enlightenment, and secured her election to the Berlin Academy.[1] Serfs continued to be beaten with 5000 to 15,000 blows of the rod, from which they were allowed to recover by *not more* than one week in bed.[2]

Catherine's foreign policy was simply one of expansion, and was regarded as very glorious. The concrete results were only moderate. A large part of Poland was annexed in 1772, 1793, and 1795, but this never became a source of strength to Russia. Turkey had to cede Azov in 1774. The number of subjects of Catherine who lost their lives while they were being employed as instruments for her policy of expansion cannot be estimated. She also left a terrible legacy of ' Questions ' for Europe—the Polish Question, Eastern Question, Russo-Prussian Question, and many others.

The eighteenth century might almost be called a century of women sovereigns. There was Anne of England ; Elizabeth Farnese of Spain, who, although not queen in her own right, dominated the country; Ulrica Eleonora of Sweden, the last of the direct line of the Vasas ; Catherine I of Russia, wife and successor of Peter the Great ; Anna, Elizabeth, and Catherine II of Russia ; and Maria Theresa of Austria. Most of these great ladies were very warlike, but none so much as Catherine II. As with Elizabeth of England, so with these sovereigns, there is always a question whether policies were due to them or to their ministers. According to the judgment of history, when the monarchs are men they frame their own policies; when they are women the ministers are given credit for the

---

[1] The *Instruction* (or *Instructions*) is printed in the English text in Reddaway, *Documents of Catherine the Great* (1931), pp. 216–294.

[2] K. Waliszewski, *Le Roman d'une impératrice* (1894), pp. 345–346. On p. 350 the inconceivably brutal torture of the knout is minutely described.

decisions. There is not much doubt, however, that Catherine II made up her own mind.

She began well enough at the opening of her reign by declaring that she already had " a sufficient number of peoples to make happy "; a magnificent empress has, of course, entire *peoples*, not simply subjects or citizens, under her sway. Her pacific attitude lasted until 1768, when she embarked on Polish and Turkish adventures which proved to be endless. Simon Vorontzov, the eminent Russian diplomatist of the time of Catherine II and the Tsar Paul, placed on Frederick the Great the blame for this fatal deviation of Catherine from the way of peace :

> It is Prussia who engaged Count Panin to reverse the improvements which had just been introduced into the constitution of Poland, so as easily to take possession of that country. It is Prussia which persuaded the same minister to require that all the Polish ' dissidents ' be admitted to all offices of the State, which was impossible without employing against the Poles the greatest violence. . . . Our troops entered Poland, sacked everything, pursued the confederate Poles into the Turkish provinces ; and this violation produced the war which the Turks declared against us. . . . It is from this time that the debts of the State abroad date, and the creation of paper-money at home, the two calamities from which Russia is groaning.[1]

Frederick the Great was a wicked man, but he should not be made to bear the responsibility for Catherine's policy of expansion and blood. Her adventurous character, the artificial circumstances in which she lived, wholly unaware of the horrors of misgovernment and war, her passion for magnificence—all would, in the disturbed conditions of the time, have brought on the wars of annexation which she waged.

The large and extravagant and corrupt Court of the Empress deceived her, and helped to disguise from her the miseries of the people. In the famous journey down the Dnieper in 1787, with the Emperor Joseph II, the Prince de Ligne, the Marquis

---

[1] Quoted by Waliszewski, *Le Roman d'une impératrice*, p. 368. ' Dissidents ' were dissenters (Protestants or Orthodox Greeks) from the prevailing Polish religion, which was Roman Catholic.

de Ségur ("the first Frenchman to know Russia," wrote de Ligne), Prince Potemkin, and other brilliant men in her company, she was deceived on every side. The spectacles presented were magnificent, but there was hollowness everywhere. "As far as Kherson," wrote the Prince de Ligne in a letter to a friend, "we have found encampments, marvellous for their Asiatic magnificence, in the midst of deserts; I no longer know where I am, nor in what century." At Stare Crim a palace had been erected for one night's entertainment. The Empress had liberally dispensed money for building and developing towns; but the towns were unfinished, many of them without streets; and where there were streets many of them had no houses. The Empress was shown only finished parts—" well-built shops and the colonnades of the palaces of governors." The Prince de Ligne sometimes left the royal company and made expeditions off the main route, and discovered all this for himself.[1]

Vergennes, the French Minister of Foreign Affairs, whose department administered from year to year a whole order of inherited instructions, rules, and policies, said that Catherine had no 'system.' The criticism is not quite justified. Catherine was flamboyant and sometimes incalculable in her aims and actions, but as an adopted Russian she had, after 1770, a fairly steady ' Byzantine ' policy as regards Turkey, and as a German of Stettin she had a " Système du Nord " for the Baltic lands.

Peter III had succeeded to the throne of the Empress Elizabeth on January 5, 1762, when Russia, in alliance with Austria, seemed on the point of overwhelming Frederick of Prussia. Peter was really a drill-sergeant with immense admiration for the military King of Prussia, the greatest captain of the age. He at once made a truce and, some weeks later, a definitive peace with Prussia. Catherine II became Empress in her own right, after the murder of her husband, on July 9, 1762.

Next year (October 5, 1763) Augustus III, King of Poland, died. Catherine, without much difficulty, secured the election of one of her favourite courtiers, a Pole, Stanislaus Poniatowski;

[1] Prince de Ligne, *Mémoires*, vol. i, pp. 60, 94; vol. ii, p. 402.

she had, however, as it were, to admit into partnership, in her plan for dominating Poland, the vigilant King of Prussia. On April 11, 1764, a Russo-Prussian treaty of alliance was signed. The two monarchs guaranteed each other's territories; and they undertook, with regard to Poland, that they would maintain there the elective monarchy and " that it be permitted to nobody to make the said kingdom hereditary." The outcome of this unholy compact for interference with the domestic affairs of a neighbour state was the Partition and eventual extinction of Poland, and political unrest in Eastern Europe for the next hundred and fifty years.

Though the Russo-Prussian alliance of 1764 secured to Frederick equal power with Catherine over Poland, it was the interfering and ambitious Empress who gained and took all the advantage. By the year 1768 she had practically won complete control of Poland; Russian troops were in Warsaw, supporting Russia's puppet, Stanislaus. Catherine, though once a German Lutheran, was now more Russian than her own subjects; she demanded that Polish ' dissidents '—that is, Orthodox Poles—should have the same political privileges as the predominant majority of Roman Catholic Poles. King Stanislaus Poniatowski could not resist the demand, but a ' confederation ' of opposition Polish nobles did. They obtained Turkish support, and thus began, October 6, 1768, Catherine's First Turkish War. The Russian army and navy were beating the Turks; the Turkish fleet was destroyed by the Russian Admiral Greig in 1770 off Tchesmé, in the Ægean. Joseph II of Austria began to decide that he must intervene against Russia, or the conquering Catherine would advance the Russian standards up to his frontier. An Austro-Russian war would have brought in Frederick of Prussia on the side of Russia, under the alliance of 1764. War is always risky; and Frederick, having twice fought Austria for Silesia, and having narrowly escaped destruction and the loss of the precious province both times, did not wish to try a third throw. As a way of composing the differences between Catherine and Joseph, and gaining, what every monarch in those days liked, a little more territory for himself, he adopted the suggestion of a retired Danish diplomatist, Count Lynar, and proposed a three-handed partition of Poland. The idea was accepted, and after necessarily complicated negotiations among the three Courts Poland, by Treaty of July 25, 1772, was sacrificed to secure Russo-Austro-Prussian peace, or, more specifically, to ensure that Frederick should keep Silesia. Catherine obtained 42,000 square miles (" White Russia "); Maria Theresa and Joseph II obtained 27,000 square miles (Galicia); Frederick 13,000 square miles (West Prussia). This left a truncated Poland of 200,000 square miles. Actually Catherine lost; for she had formerly controlled a large and potentially powerful Poland, a ' buffer state,' or, as she called it, ' doormat ' to the west; now she had Prussia and Austria almost on her doorstep. The First Partition of 1772 made practically certain the Second Partition of 1792, for *l'appétit vient en mangeant*; and the Second made certain the Third Partition of 1795 and the extinction of the Polish State. With the final partition of Poland the frontiers of Prussia, Russia, and Austria met together. On that flat and open Polish *terrain* the state which can only mobilize its forces slowly is at a disadvantage in any war. Russia, by reason of her vast extent, was bound always to be slower at mobilizing than were Austria or Prussia. Catherine's policy of magnificence and the Partitions of Poland presented Russia with her most difficult military problem, as well as with a constant source of political weakness in the chronic unrest among the Poles.

Freed by the Partition of 1772 from the prospect of an Austrian war, Catherine was able to finish off the Turkish war in a fairly satisfactory way and to conclude the Treaty of Kutchuk Kainardji, July 10, 1774. By this Catherine obtained Azov and practical control of the Crimea, and advanced her standards to the Dnieper.

After this ' Byzantinism,' or the ' Oriental system,' cast a spell upon the great Empress. Mirabeau wrote that it was her " ruling passion," and that it equally fascinated Joseph II.[1]

---

[1] Mirabeau, *Secret History of the Court of Prussia*, vol. i, p. xvi.

In 1780, when the Emperor came to visit her at Mohilev, on the Upper Dnieper, she explained to him her views on the Eastern Question. Two years later Joseph sent to her a scheme for a partition of Turkey-in-Europe. In 1787 Joseph paid his second visit to Catherine, at Kherson, on the Lower Dnieper, and journeyed with her Court to the Crimea. Naturally the Turk was alarmed, and in the course of a diplomatic dispute threw the Russian Ambassador at Constantinople into prison. This brought on the impending Second Turkish War of Catherine, now in alliance with Joseph II. The doom of Turkey seemed to be approaching. In 1788 Suvárov captured Oczakov, and in 1790 Ismail, at the mouth of the Danube; in the same year the " Austrian army, awfully arrayed, boldly by battery besieged [and took] Belgrade." Perhaps Constantinople might have fallen after a joint invasion of Thrace by Russian and Austrian Armies, but such an invasion never took place.

As has so often happened since, Turkey was saved by the dissensions of Europe. The British and Prussian Governments, and the French Government too (so far as it could exert itself during the Revolution), were using diplomacy in favour of Turkey; Great Britain even mobilized an " Oczakov Fleet " in 1790, though it never proceeded to the scene of action. Joseph II died in February 1790, and the new Emperor, Leopold II, felt that he had enough trouble on his hands with the French Revolution, and also revolution and rebellion in some of his own dominions. He made the Peace of Sistova with Turkey, restoring Belgrade, August 4, 1791. Catherine's treasury was long since exhausted; the farther forward her armies marched the more costly in men and money was the effort to maintain them and replenish them from the interior of her empire. She too had to bow to necessity. She made the Peace of Jassy, January 9, 1792, with her frontier advanced to the Dniester. The ' historic mission ' to take Constantinople seemed nearer realization; but she was never to see this, nor were her successors either. The bleaching bones of Russian soldiers marked the ' Constantinople route ' from Siberia to the Danube, while the great Empress, verging on the age of seventy, continued her task of "making her peoples happy" by signing orders for her generals, and turning night into day with her dissolute supper-parties.

Catherine's project for a "Système du Nord" never progressed very far. If it meant anything definite, it involved some kind of alliance between Russia, Sweden, Denmark, and Prussia (all having Baltic provinces). The nearest that Catherine came to achieving this was in 1780 when, in the course of the war between Great Britain on the one hand and the American Colonies, France, and Spain on the other, she headed "the Armed Neutrality of the North." This was an association of neutrals, which eventually included Russia, Denmark, Sweden, the United Netherlands, Prussia, Portugal, the Two Sicilies and the Empire—to uphold the principle that "free ships make free goods." The Armed Neutrality served its immediate purpose, and passed out of existence when the Anglo-American-Franco-Spanish war came to an end in 1782, though it was revived again, after Catherine was dead, in the Napoleonic war in 1800. Catherine herself, far from achieving a permanent "Système du Nord," was faced with a great Swedish war in 1788, just when she required every soldier for the campaign in Turkey, and when St Petersburg was left almost without defence.

Every annexation seems to lead to a war of disannexation. In the seventeenth century the Swedes had annexed Livonia, Ingria, and Carelia, Baltic provinces belonging to Russia or claimed by Russia. In 1721 Peter the Great had taken these provinces back. In 1788 Gustavus III of Sweden seized the occasion of the Russo-Turkish war to recover them. The Swedish fleet defeated the Russian at Svenskund. Catherine at St Petersburg could hear the Swedish cannon, and she fortified her spirit by reading Plutarch's heroic *Lives*. Luckily for her the power of Gustavus III was not too secure at home, and he found it advisable to end the war. He made peace by the Treaty of Verela, August 14, 1790, on the basis of the *status quo ante bellum*, after wasting many lives and the slender resources of his kingdom; the war might just as well (or, rather,

much better) never have been fought. The autocrat Gustavus
—he had suspended the Swedish Constitution in 1789—went
from the extreme of hostility to the extreme of friendship. On
October 19, 1791, he made an alliance with the Empress
Catherine, whom he hoped to bring into a grand European
coalition against the French Revolution. While feverishly pushing forward his widespread plans for directing Europe the
restless despot could not command the allegiance of his own
people. The nobility conspired to dethrone him, and on
March 16, 1791, he was shot in the Stockholm Opera House.
He died a fortnight later. Beccaria called Gustavus, perhaps
on account of his abolition of torture, " one of the wisest
monarchs of Europe, who, taking philosophy with him to the
throne, has made himself the friend and legislator of his subjects." [1] He was, like Catherine, an enlightened monarch,
marred by the besetting political vice of despotism.

The last years of the great Empress were troubled by the
French Revolution and by a revolt (1794) in the Polish provinces which she had annexed. She continued to be busy with
politics, family affairs, balls, and entertainments almost to her
last day. On November 15, 1796, after rising at her usual
early hour to begin the day's administrative duties, she had
an apoplectic stroke. She died on November 17, 1796, at the
age of sixty-seven.

Catherine II has often been blamed for her favourites; and,
as the Prince de Ligne wrote on his journey through Russia in
1788, there were millions of abuses in the empire. Nevertheless, she selected capable men to be her friends and Ministers,
and though they deceived her about the condition of her
empire, they served her, in their way, faithfully too. The Prince
de Ligne describes Potemkin with genuine enthusiasm : [2]

> I see a commander of the army who appears idle but works
> unceasingly; who has no other writing-table but his knees, no
> other comb but his fingers; always lying down, but sleeping
> neither by day nor by night, because his zeal for his sovereign,

---

[1] Beccaria, *Dei Delitti e Delle Pene* (trans. Farrar), p. 119.
[2] Prince de Ligne, *Mémoires*, vol. i, pp. 188–191.

whom he worships, is ever active, and because a cannon-shot, which he is not exposed to, disquiets him with the thought that it has cost the life of some of his soldiers. Fearful for others, brave where he himself is concerned; halting under the heaviest battery fire to give his orders, yet more of a Ulysses than an Achilles; agitated on the eve of danger, and gay in the midst of it; sad in his pleasures, unhappy because he is happy, bored by everything, easily surfeited; morose, changeable; a profound philosopher, an able Minister, a sublime politician or a mere child of ten; never vindictive, asking pardon for any pain he has caused, quickly repairing an injustice; believing in a loving God, fearing the devil whom he believes to be greater and bigger than Prince Potemkin; with one hand beckoning to women whom he likes, with the other making the sign of the Cross; now with his arms in the shape of a crucifix at the feet of a statue of the Virgin, now with them round the marble neck of his mistress; receiving numberless presents from his sovereign, and giving them away directly afterwards; accepting estates from the Empress, and then giving them back to her, or paying what she owes, without telling her; selling and purchasing immense domains in order to set up a grand colonnade or make an English garden and then disposing of them soon after; always at play—or never playing; preferring to forgive debts rather than to pay them; prodigiously rich without having a sou; at one moment a prey to suspicion, at another full of trustfulness, now jealous, then full of gratitude, now indulging in bad temper, the next in joking; quickly prejudiced for or against a thing, as soon changing his mind; talking theology to his generals, and war to his bishops; never reading, but sounding all those to whom he speaks and contradicting them in order to find out more; putting on now the angriest, now the most agreeable face; showing now the most repulsive manners, now the most attractive; having, in short, the bearing of the proudest satrap of the East, turn about with that of the most charming courtier of Louis XIV; being in reality very soft at the bottom of his heart under an outward appearance of great sternness; freakish about the hours he keeps, about his food, his rest, his tastes; wanting to have everything like a child, knowing how to do without everything like a grown man; abstemious, but appearing to be fond of good-living; gnawing his nails or an apple or a turnip; scolding or laughing, mimicking or swearing, playing the fool or praying, singing or meditating; summoning, sending away, recalling twenty *aides-de-camp* without saying anything to them; enduring heat better than anyone while appearing to be thinking only of the most sought-after baths; making light of the cold while appearing not to be able to do without furs; never wearing drawers, always dressed in a shirt or a uniform embroidered on all the edges; without shoes or in slippers with embroidered lappets; without cap or hat, as I saw him once under fire; sometimes in a shabby dressing-gown, sometimes in a superb tunic with his three stars, his ribbons and diamonds as large as your thumb surrounding a portrait of the Empress: these diamonds seemed placed there to attract bullets; bent, huddled up when at home, but straight, his nose in the air, proud, fine, noble, majestic or seductive when he showed himself to his army, like an Agamemnon among the Kings of Greece.

What then was his magic? It was genius, more genius, and still more genius, and it was native wit, an excellent memory, a nobleness of soul, mischievousness without malice, subtlety without astuteness; a happy mixture of whims which occurring at just the right moment won him hearts; great generosity, graciousness and justness in his rewards; much tact, the gift of divining what he did not know, and a great knowledge of men.

Notwithstanding Catherine's overwhelming political duties as autocrat of a vast empire—and she performed her duties with unremitting industry—the remarkable woman found time to maintain a long and elaborate correspondence with Voltaire and Grimm, to write a scientific treatise on Siberia, a history of the Roman Emperors, several dramas, and the *libretto* of an opera, set to music by Padre Martini. She wrote in French, German, and Russian, and was a member of the Academy of Berlin and a doctor of the University of Wittenberg.

The long correspondence between Catherine II and Grimm is a touching instance of fidelity and friendship. Grimm visited St Petersburg in 1773 in the suite of the Landgravine of Hesse-Darmstadt. He was presented to Catherine, and was received with great kindness. Catherine wished to keep him at her Court; but the modest Grimm put aside the brilliant prospect, and after an argument of an hour and a half with the Empress succeeded in maintaining his decision to retain his " peaceable and happy obscurity." When he was taking leave of the Empress at St Petersburg after a joyous winter there Catherine asked him to send her his news from time to time, promising to answer punctually. " I calculated," wrote Grimm, years later, after the death of the great Empress, " that this excess of favour could not last more than a few months. The correspondence continued, nevertheless, always equally lively and warm, on one side and the other, from 1774 to 1796 [the death of the Empress], and was never interrupted except during my second visit to St Petersburg." [1] At first the ordinary post was used for transmission of the letters; but after a time the Empress arranged that every three months a courier should carry her letters from St Petersburg to Paris, or wherever Grimm should be, and bring his letters in return. " In this way she contracted the habit, fortunate for me, of writing to me almost daily, always carefully putting the date at the head of the sheet of paper; and when the packet had grown in two or three months into a volume sufficiently large, or when some pressing object required it, Her Majesty sent it off. I followed the same method, and did not remain behindhand in respect of the size of my volume." The Empress did not allow her cares and activities to interrupt the correspondence. Even during her journey by water down the Dnieper and into the Crimea her couriers arrived with more punctuality and with larger packets of letters than when she was living quietly at St Petersburg. No wonder that Grimm, a good cosmopolitan German *bourgeois*, considered the correspondence the " unique ornament " of his life.[2] Catherine's last letter, dated October 31, 1796, arrived with Grimm on November 22. It concluded with the words : " *Adieu*, keep well. I have said everything that came to the point of my pen. It is good that you should know what I think and how I look at things." Five days before the letter was in Grimm's hands the great Empress had died.

---

[1] F. M. Grimm, " Mémoire historique sur l'origine et les suites de mon attachement pour l'Impératrice Catherine II," in *Correspondance par Grimm, Diderot, etc.* (1877), vol. i, p. 21.

[2] *Ibid.*, vol. i, pp. 24, 25, 28.

CHAPTER IX

ENLIGHTENED MONARCHS: JOSEPH II

ALTHOUGH, like the maker of the medieval Papacy, Gregory VII, Joseph II died with the sense of failure, his life was not wasted. The impulse which he gave to the State, the ability (imperfect enough) to reform itself which he imparted to it, carried Austria through the Revolution at the end of the eighteenth century and into the new age. Although Metternich, so far as he showed an interest in domestic affairs, departed from the reforming spirit of Joseph, it was taken up again after 1852, and lasted, not unsatisfactorily for Austria, until the State was rushed to its ruin in 1914. In the eighteenth century the Habsburg monarchy looked solid enough. Gibbon thought that he was looking ages ahead when he wrote: " The romance of *Tom Jones*, that exquisite picture of human manners, will outlive the palace of the Escurial, and the imperial eagle of the House of Austria." [1]

Joseph had a favouring environment to work upon. Austria, the whole Habsburg monarchy, was growing prosperous in the eighteenth century. There was a large, comfortable, increasing *bourgeoisie*. Life was sweet. Madame de Staël, visiting Austria just after the close of the eighteenth century, was struck with the general air of comfort, affluence, repose, happiness. She found the country fertile, the climate mild, the people polite, pleasant, tranquil. The Prater, the magnificent park of Vienna (opened to the public by Joseph II), stretching down to the Danube, attracted her enormously. All the Viennese went there, walking or driving, after five o'clock. It was a sort of Italian habit, like the promenades on the Pincio at Rome. Madame de Staël loved to watch the good *bourgeois* and citizen

[1] Edward Gibbon, *Autobiography* (ed. 1907), p. 4.

families, eating their ample suppers in the open air, of a fine summer evening, on the Prater. It was said that Vienna consumed more food than any other city of its size.[1]

It was upon this tolerant, easy-going people (easy-going in Austria, not in Hungary) that Joseph had to work. Moreover, the way had been prepared for him by his mother, the Empress Maria Theresa. She had been mildly, judiciously reformative; she had even consented to the dissolution of the Jesuit Order. The Austrian nobility, a cosmopolitan body drawn from half the nations of Europe, had become very strongly attached to the Habsburg family in the reign of Maria Theresa. At the same time the failure of Austria in the two great wars with Prussia had shown that reforms were necessary. During Maria Theresa's reign, however, little of eighteenth-century ' enlightenment ' was visible in Austria; but " Joseph II came and scattered prodigally all his lights upon a state which was prepared neither for the good nor for the ill which they could do." [2]

Joseph II was born at Vienna on March 13, 1741, during the first year of the War of the Austrian Succession. His early education was chiefly in history and geography. He took great pleasure in Cæsar's *Commentaries*, that attractive handbook for all energetic spirits, "until pedagogues and ecclesiastics made study odious to him by over-insistence upon *minutiæ*. His naturally happy temperament sank into an excessive timidity." [3]

The benevolent Maria Theresa appears a little to have neglected her eldest son, spending most of her care, it is said, upon his younger brother, the Archduke Charles, who died at the age of sixteen. She went on with her work of founding hospitals, schools, academies, military cadet colleges, camps of soldiers. She authorized Prince Kaunitz to go to Versailles and to obtain the good offices of the mistress of Louis XV, Madame de Pompadour, for the proposed Franco-Austrian

---

[1] Madame de Staël, *De l'Allemagne*, Chapters VI–VIII.
[2] *Ibid.* (ed. 1879), Chapter VI, p. 39.
[3] C. Paganel, *Histoire de Joseph II* (1843), p. 231.

alliance. Against the protests of the Emperor Francis, the Archduke Joseph (aged fifteen), and of his governor, the Hungarian count Field-Marshal Batthyány, the alliance was made in 1756. Madame de Pompadour triumphed: *une courtisane détruit l'œuvre de Richelieu*.[1]

In 1760 Joseph made a happy marriage with the Infanta Isabella of Parma. His only regret, he said, was that he had not two hearts to give her. Within three years she died of smallpox. Two years later Maria Theresa arranged a political marriage between Joseph and the Princess Joséphine of Bavaria, daughter of a former antagonist of Austria, the late Emperor Charles VII. The marriage was completely loveless; Joséphine died of smallpox in 1767. Joseph married no more. He lived a disciplined bachelor life, worked hard, dined off a slice of meat and a glass of wine, devoted wholly to the public good and to his ideas of social improvement, allowing himself only one relaxation, a constant interest in music, and particularly in the opera.

On April 3, 1764, Joseph was elected " King of the Romans," and was therefore certain, if crowned by the Pope, to become Holy Roman Emperor. For weeks Frankfort was given over to Imperial officials, grand noblemen, and their festivities. Goethe, aged fourteen, witnessed much of the ceremonial of the great occasion, and has described it in *Dichtung und Wahrheit* (Part I, Book 5). In 1765 the Emperor Francis, husband of Maria Theresa, died suddenly. The good man, who had taken little part in politics, and had simply attended to his large investments, was universally regretted. Good-natured, kindly, approachable, and indolent, he was, in a sense, a man of the people, at any rate of the Viennese *bourgeoisie*.

" Joseph," wrote the Prince de Ligne, " did not know how to eat, drink, or amuse himself ; or to read anything except State papers. He governed too much, without reigning enough. He played some music every day." For a Habsburg he rose rather late—at seven o'clock ; and while dressing he was gay, and made his gentlemen and body-servants, who adored him, laugh. On

---

[1] C. Paganel, *Histoire de Joseph II* (1843), p. 237.

leaving his bedroom for his office or cabinet he always found some twenty or thirty, or even as many as a hundred, persons who had obtained admission to the antechamber with grievances and petitions. He talked with them, comforted them, and carried off their memoranda to read. Next morning at the same hour he gave them their answer and settled their complaints.

His memory, which he exercised as a young man, became even better as he grew older. He could talk with all kinds of people. " He knew four languages marvellously well, and two others passably." He never forgot a word, a person, or a thing. When he gave audience to anybody he walked up and down the room with him, talking effusively and with a jocular manner, taking the other's arm; next he would seem to remember himself, and would become serious. Often, as he continued walking and talking, he would stoop to put a block of wood on the fire, or would take up the tongs, or go and look out of the window. He was never at a loss for a word, and cared nothing what people said of him, and he was quite willing to defy the Pope, the Grand Turk, the Empire, Hungary, Prussia, and the Low Countries. His only fear was of being unjust and causing misfortune to innocent people; and this made him stop before pushing his designs to a conclusion by main force.

" The disquietude of his reign," concludes the Prince de Ligne, " is to be attributed to the agitation in his blood. He never finished nor polished any of his works. His only fault lay in sketching everything, the good as well as the bad." [1]

On the death of his father Joseph assumed the title of Emperor, and was wisely associated with the Empress Maria Theresa as co-regent of the Austrian dominions. He at once began a series of tours, travelling with no parade of state, and attending to all business personally, punctually, indefatigably. His first long tour as Emperor, however, had much of pleasure and relaxation in it, for he went through the smiling country of Italy, to Rome (where he studied the ancient monuments), Naples (climbing Vesuvius), Florence, and Milan.

---

[1] Prince de Ligne, *Mémoires*, vol. i, pp. 241–243.

There was no Pope to crown him at Rome, for (after the death of Clement XIII) the tedious process of election was going on.

The personality of Frederick II of Prussia threw its glamour over Joseph as over all the men of the latter half of the eighteenth century. Joseph had a picture of the great King above his bed, and, like Frederick, he lived a Spartan life, military, business-like, loveless. In 1766 Russia and Turkey were at war; the Russian eagles were approaching the Danube, and Maria Theresa had said they must never cross that stream. Frederick of Prussia was an ally of Russia, but he did not wish to be drawn into another ' Seven Years War ' with Austria; he did not wish to risk the loss of Silesia again. So he proposed to Joseph II a meeting at the fortress of Neisse, in Silesia. The sovereigns met, and established agreement. Next year they met again at Neustadt, in Moravia. The Prince de Ligne, who was present in Joseph's suite, wrote: " The Emperor took the opportunity of abandoning himself to the personal admiration which he had conceived for the King of Prussia." Frederick, with the ironical hypocrisy that was natural to him, wore the white uniform of the Austrian Army, and was polite and deferential. He was a great snuffer. The snuff fell down and stained the white tunic. The Prince de Ligne's explanation that Frederick wore the white tunic of the Emperor so as not to remind the Austrians of the Prussian blue, which they had too often seen on the field of battle, will scarcely obtain credit. The Emperor was more at his ease with the King than the King was with the Emperor. At supper, however, they became natural and cheerful. " This was one of the gayest and most agreeable suppers at which I was ever present," wrote the Prince de Ligne. " The amiability of two so superior men, both frequently experiencing astonishment at finding themselves together, was one of the most agreeable things that could be imagined." [1]

The conference resulted in Turkey accepting, through Frederick's pressure, the mediation of Austria in the Russo-

[1] Prince de Ligne, *Mémoires*, vol. i, pp. 4-19.

Turkish War. Frederick had helped the young Emperor, but this was his one and only act of complaisance.

Shortly after this the three Courts, Russia, Prussia, and Austria, found a means of avoiding mutual friction for a time by partitioning Poland, each taking a proportionate amount of territory, and explicitly renouncing any claims they might have on the rest of the Republic.[1] For this act, which ultimately had a ruinous effect upon Austro-Prusso-Russian relations, Joseph must share responsibility with Frederick and Catherine. It is only fair to say, however, that the Austrian Cabinet informed France, the ally of both Austria and Poland, of the proposed partition, and offered to oppose the design if France objected; but Louis XV, " occupied with his pleasures," gave no definite reply.[2] Years later King Stanislaus Poniatowski, becoming anxious lest something like the partition of 1772 might be carried out, asked for an assurance from Joseph II. " I promise you," replied the Emperor; " not a tree "—*pas un arbre*. " Give me your hand," said Stanislaus, deeply moved by the Emperor's frankness. " Here it is," said Joseph, holding out his hand; " and something which is stronger, *foi de gentilhomme*." [3] For the rest of the Emperor's life Poland was safe.

Joseph's activity was excessive. He had vast designs for modernizing the internal economy of the cumbrous Austrian State, although, as a matter of fact, it was in good condition during the last years of Maria Theresa, and actually had an annual balance of receipts over expenditure. He had the mania for rounding off territory, and for adding province to province, though none of his schemes for acquiring Serbia, Bosnia, Bavaria, Alsace, Lorraine, or Silesia came to anything. He was a most active traveller, and this is greatly to his credit, for the more heads of states see of each other the better it is for

---

[1] " . . . *renonçant à tous les droits . . . qu'elles pouvaient avoir sur les autres possessions et sujets de la République*." Declaration of Count Stackelberg, Russian Minister at Warsaw, September 2, 1772.

[2] The Comte de Ségur says that he had this information from Kaunitz, Cobenzl, and from Vergennes himself. Ségur, *Politique de tous les Cabinets de l'Europe*, in Paganel, p. 284 *n*.

[3] Prince de Ligne, *op. cit.*, vol. ii, p. 56.

international relations. Joseph travelled simply, under the title of Count of Falckenstein, attended by a couple of servants, sleeping at wayside inns. When he went to the gorgeous Court of Versailles in 1777 to visit his sister, Queen Marie Antoinette, and his brother-in-law, Louis XVI, he stayed, as Count of Falckenstein, not in the palace, but in a modest lodging in the town, and, instead of attending ceremonies and amusements at Court, spent his time visiting historical monuments, military schools, and hospitals. He considered the condition of one of the hospitals, at least, to be intolerable. Buffon and Buffon's great Jardin des Plantes received Joseph's warm attention. He advised his brother-in-law to visit the chief cities of France rather than spend his time flying through the woods after deer; and he remarked to his sister, in her gorgeous and elaborate Court, " How many things we are able to do without at Vienna ! " When the courtiers celebrated with enthusiasm the rebellion of the American colonists Joseph was silent; questioned on his attitude, he said simply, " I confess I am inclined to be royalist." Travelling *incognito*, he was often asked rather absurd questions by the common people, and he always replied with good nature. The woman who kept an inn at which he was staying saw him shaving himself, and asked what his position was at the Emperor's Court. " I sometimes have the honour of shaving him," said Joseph. After touring through Normandy, Brittany, Languedoc, Provence, and Burgundy Joseph left France, returning to Austria by way of Switzerland. He passed by Voltaire, who was anxious to meet the enlightened prince (but Joseph kept away, by desire of the devout Maria Theresa), and visited the celebrated Albrecht von Haller at Bern. Haller, distinguished in botany, surgery, and letters, was a native of Bern who held a chair at Göttingen from 1736 to 1753, and then retired to his native city. He was in his eightieth year when Joseph visited him. The Emperor found him, enfeebled by age, but still at work, surrounded with books. Haller died on December 12 of the same year (1777).

Shortly after returning home Joseph met the opportunity for which he had been waiting, in order to round off his dominions by the acquisition of the magnificent domain of Bavaria. The Elector Maximilian Joseph died on December 30, 1777. His heir presumptive, Charles Theodore, Elector Palatine (debauched, extravagant, careless, a sort of Louis XV), signed away his rights in favour of the house of Austria, thus disinheriting his heir presumptive, the Duke of Zweibrücken. Joseph's design would have gone forward to completion had not Frederick II of Prussia, now the upholder of the law and custom of the Empire, which he had previously flouted for his own purposes, intervened with a ' defensive war.' He marched with one hundred thousand men into Bohemia, and entrenched himself. Joseph did the same; and throughout the summer of 1778 there was a war with no battles, no sieges, but heavy casualties from disease. The under-nourished soldiers called it the " Potato War " (*Kartoffelkrieg*). France refused to give help to Austria, pointing out that there was no obligation under the Treaty of Alliance of 1756 to assist in acquisition of new territory. Maria Theresa managed to restrain her son, the fiery Emperor, and her most famous captains, Laudon and Lacy. She appealed to Frederick the Great himself, by the secret mission of Thugut, not to disturb two great nations whose monarchs were now grey-haired. It is unlikely that the appeal of his old adversary touched the stony heart of the cynic of Sans Souci; but he was willing to make peace if Joseph would give up his Bavarian design. Joseph, who never failed in dutifulness to his mother, yielded, and peace was made at Teschen, May 13, 1779.

Joseph, unassuming and simple though he was, liked the company of great monarchs. In the summer of 1780 he arranged to meet Catherine II at Mohilev, in Lithuania; and from there he accompanied her to St Petersburg. Shortly afterwards he returned to Vienna. Maria Theresa, the beloved mother of the Austrians, died with Christian resignation, and firm in the faith which always had supported her, on November 29, 1780. Joseph, who had always deferred to her moderate, if unenterprising, counsels, now entered into the plenitude of power. He was still a young man, thirty-nine years old, but was already accepted by the great European *intelligentsia*, the philosophers (although Joseph had no liking for the *philosophes* himself) and the reading public, as one of the grand *souverains éclairés*, as a peer of Frederick II and Catherine II. The Austrians took him to their heart, to fill the place left by the death of Maria Theresa. He kept his mother's experienced counsellor, the Chancellor, Prince Kaunitz, to whom the Prince de Ligne declared, " *Votre grande politique est la vérité.*" [1] The Austrian aristocracy found Joseph II too simple, too ascetic, and a little too firm-willed for them; but the growing *bourgeoisie* loved him for his unaffected manners, his family affection, his frankness, approachability, and simple way of life. If he was tolerant in religion, though Catholic, so were they; if he interfered with the opera and gave famous musicians instructions and advice, they were pleased with this genuine interest in Vienna's chief art.

The proper method of governing Austria was an enigma which only two or three statesmen made serious efforts to solve—Joseph II in the late eighteenth century, Schwarzenberg and Bach in the middle nineteenth, Beust in the seventh decade of the nineteenth, and in the twentieth century the unfortunate Franz Ferdinand d'Este, who was assassinated at Sarajevo. Joseph's plan was to abolish all the old feudal differences between the various Austrian states, and to convert them into simple provinces, with uniform local administrations, controlled centrally from Vienna. It was the system which the pre-Revolution monarchy endeavoured to achieve in France, and (as in Joseph's scheme also) without the help of any representative assembly or Parliament. Joseph carried his scheme into effect, amid strong opposition; and although modified after his death, it remained, substantially, the system as administered by the Viennese bureaucracy down to 1848. A permanent addition to the Austrian system was the successful completion of a code of law for all the Austrian Crown lands (not Hungary), begun in the early years of the eighteenth century, finished and published under Joseph II in 1786.

[1] Prince de Ligne, *op. cit.*, vol. i, p. 143.

Joseph also curtailed the powers and privileges of the Church in the Austrian lands. He refused to permit the entry of Papal Bulls, except on his express licence. Out of a total of 2046 monasteries and convents he suppressed 1143; " they were replaced by hospitals, schools, and barracks." [1] Pope Pius VI took the unprecedented step of making a journey to Vienna in 1782 to dissuade Joseph from his secularist policies —without success. Joseph freed the serfs from being bound to the soil, although their liability to labour rents and services for their land-holdings remained. On October 13, 1781, appeared his celebrated edict of religious toleration. He had a new translation of the Bible made into German. A later edict of the Emperor abolished the legal use of torture. The English philanthropist and prison reformer Howard when he visited the Vienna prisons in 1786 found that the edict was observed. [2]

In economics Joseph II was an inveterate protectionist. Under Maria Theresa a strict protective *régime* had been developed; Joseph in 1782 increased the customs duties on manufactured goods to 60 per cent. of the goods' value. This tariff, practically prohibitive, had to be modified later, in order to introduce, for the benefit of the Austrian consumer, a measure of foreign competition.

Joseph's reforms and measures, in spite of opposition at the outset, were accepted or enforced, and for a time the Austrian dominions enjoyed calm. All Central and Western Europe, indeed, was calm; the peoples of the *ancien régime* everywhere, under a perfect constellation of enlightened monarchs, were enjoying an Indian summer, before the bitter winter of revolutions and discontents which was to open in 1789. The great States had their *rois éclairés*—Frederick II of Prussia, Joseph II of Austria—or else, as in the case of France and Necker, they had at least a benevolent monarch and an efficient, public-spirited Minister. The lesser States had sovereigns who regarded government as a trust and duty:

---

[1] C. Paganel, *Histoire de Joseph II* (1843), p. 327.
[2] John Howard, *An Account of the Principal Lazarettos of Europe* (1791), p. 66.

Charles III of Spain, Gustavus III of Sweden, Charles William Ferdinand of Brunswick, Leopold of Tuscany (brother of Joseph II). The republics were rich and reposeful—Holland, Venice, Genoa, the Hanseatic cities. The monarchs of the great States were determined to keep the peace. It was one of Europe's halcyon periods.

In spite of a peaceful surface, however, Western Europe was threatened with war through projects of the restless Joseph. In 1784 he determined to free the Austrian Netherlands from the ' servitude ' imposed upon them through the Treaties of Westphalia and Utrecht, by which the port of Antwerp was closed against all commerce from the side of the sea. The Dutch possessed then, as they still do, both sides of the estuary of the Scheldt, below Antwerp. To make good his claim to open Antwerp to seaborne commerce Joseph dispatched an Austrian ship up the Scheldt from the sea, and another from Antwerp downward. " *Ils ne tireront pas*," he maintained to Kaunitz, who suggested that the Dutch would resist. The Dutch ports opened fire, and stopped the ship. " *Ils ont tiré*," said Kaunitz laconically when the news arrived from Brussels. Both sides prepared for war. The French Government, declining to consider this case as being within the guarantee of the Alliance Treaty of 1756, refused military aid to Austria, but offered mediation. Joseph, isolated, accepted mediation, claiming 10,000,000 Dutch florins indemnity. The Dutch Government offered 8,000,000 ; Joseph countered with an ultimatum, and war seemed certain. France, the mediating Power, paid the balance of 2,000,000 for the sake of peace. The *status quo* was then affirmed by a new Austro-Dutch Treaty, signed at Fontainebleau under the guarantee of France, November 8, 1786. This was almost the last piece of diplomacy of the eminent French Minister of Foreign Affairs, Vergennes. The cynic Frederick II had foreseen this result. " *Vous verrez*," he said to the French Ambassador at Berlin, " *que Vergennes finira par forcer la sérénissime République à s'accommoder avec mon frère Joseph, en lui donnant pour boire*." [" You will see that Vergennes will end by compelling the Most

Serene Republic to make terms with my brother Joseph, by giving him a tip."]

The great Frederick was approaching his end, but he had one more piece of active work soon in hand. In 1785 Joseph returned to his old project, the acquisition of Bavaria. This time it was to be accomplished by exchange: the Elector of Bavaria to have the Austrian Netherlands with the title of king—" King of Burgundy " probably. The exchange might have been completed had not the aged Frederick, protesting that it would be an infraction of the laws of the Empire, organized a league of princes among his satellites, nine minor German states, of which only Saxony, Brunswick-Luneburg, and Baden were of any consequence. A few months later the great Frederick was dead, his fatal work accomplished. He had sacrificed Austria to his own ambitions, and finally to his Prussian egotism. At the beginning of his reign he had seized Silesia from her, one of her finest provinces, German and Protestant. Now, at the end of his life, he had prevented Austria from acquiring a neighbouring territory, inhabited by a kindred German population. Thus Austria was driven more and more to depend on heterogeneous elements—Magyars, Croats, Czechs, Serbs—and so, growing more unstable under the disruptive influences of nationalism, ultimately fell to pieces and created a problem for Europe which probably only a future union with Bavaria or with the whole of Germany can solve.

In 1787 Joseph paid his second visit to Catherine II, meeting her at Kaidech and continuing with her in the gorgeous State barges down the Dnieper to Kherson, and farther to Kisikerman. Maintaining inflexibly his *incognito* as Count Falckenstein, Joseph was accompanied only by a general officer, the Prince de Ligne, and two valets. He insisted on being addressed as " Monsieur le Comte," and thus was able to engage in informal conversations with the courtiers, and to satisfy his curiosity, his interest in human beings, and his taste for unofficial political discussions. The ambassadors from St Petersburg were in Catherine's party—Cobenzl for Austria, Ségur for France, Fitzherbert for Great Britain. Joseph found

it very difficult to keep up the kind of numerous and high-flown
compliments which the enthusiastic ambassadors showered
upon the delighted Empress. "My own dear ambassador
sometimes takes up the censer," said Joseph to the Prince de
Ligne. "You throw grains into it very often, God be thanked,
for us all. Monsieur de Ségur makes very spirited and very
French compliments; and your Englishman discharges from
time to time, as it were in spite of himself, a little shaft of
flattery, with an epigrammatic turn that makes it all the more
piquant." Divested of the cares of empire Joseph enjoyed the
trip enormously, and enchanted his friends with his good
humour. An incorrigible reformer, however, he kept his eyes
on the future. When the Prince de Ligne tried to talk to
him about Lycurgus and Alcibiades Joseph answered, "Yes,
but what the devil are we to do about Constantinople?" [1]

The visit to the Chersonese over, Russia—and consequently Joseph, through his alliance with Catherine—was
involved in war with Turkey.[2] The campaign of 1788 was for
Austria a costly failure. "The Austrian Army," wrote the
Prince de Ligne, who commanded a corps in this campaign,
"ought to be invincible. If there is an inconvenience in not
being all of the same nation, there is one advantage resulting
from it, that is, the emulation which prevails between the
Hungarians, Poles, Bohemians, Tyrolese, Germans, Walloons,
and Italians." [3] Joseph, though his Spartan habits made him a
good campaigner, was no general; he took part, however, in the
capture of Shabatz, exposing himself freely to the fire of the
enemy.[4] He returned to Vienna towards the end of the year
1788, unsuccessful in war, with a rebellion brewing against
his reforms in the Austrian Netherlands. The campaign on the
Danube continued. "Patience and self-confidence in the face
of almost constant reverses were the outstanding virtues of
the Austrian Armies," wrote the Prince de Ligne. In October

---

[1] Prince de Ligne, *Mémoires*, vol. i, p. 64.
[2] For Russia's part in the war see above, p. 130.
[3] Prince de Ligne, *op. cit.*, vol. i, p. 169.
[4] *Ibid.*, vol. i, p. 224, letter of October 18, 1789.

1789 their virtues were rewarded when the Austrian Field-Marshal Laudon stormed Belgrade. " Here we are, on the rampart of the Orient," wrote the Prince de Ligne, who had command of a corps. It was the reign's success, and found Joseph on a bed of sickness, a victim of dropsy. There was acute trouble in Hungary, where, in order to escape the shackles of the coronation oath, he had refused to be crowned. His edict converting the states of the Austrian Netherlands into a uniform province provoked a rebellion. The news came as a last intolerable blow to Joseph II. " *Votre pays m'a tué,*" he said to the Prince de Ligne.[1] " He died firmly," wrote the Prince to Catherine II, " as he had lived." Knowing that his end was quite near, he fought against pain and weakness to the last, and concerned himself with details of State, especially with promotions of individual officers and with the pay of the soldiers. On the evening before his death he is said to have signed eighty documents. He expired on February 20, 1790, at the age of forty-nine. " If in order to be called great," wrote the Prince de Ligne of his friend, " it is sufficient to be incapable of littleness, he would be called Joseph the Great." Recognized then as a splendid failure, a young man in a hurry to reform an intractable state, Joseph was later acknowledged as the man who saved Austria from the great Revolution which was already breaking out in France. He gave to his country the " salutary germ which preserved it for long from all revolutions." [2] His cautious successor, his brother Leopold II, Grand Duke of Tuscany, by prudent concessions dissipated the frictions which Joseph's over-drastic policies had aroused. The spirit of the devoted Joseph remained to animate his country, " thou grand old Austria." [3]

[1] The Prince de Ligne was born in Brussels.
[2] See remarks of C. Paganel, *Histoire de Joseph II*, *ad fin.*
[3] See G. Meredith, *Vittoria*, Chapter XXVI, *ad fin.*

CHAPTER X

ITALY

IN the Middle Ages Italy was frequented by pilgrims from all the countries of Western and Central Europe; from the opening of modern history it was frequented by travellers who came for pleasure and education. It was the pleasure-ground of cultured Europe.

Italy in particular is beloved of Europe, and holds a unique place in its affections. Rome, which had made the first Europe, lured the barbarians to Italy, and Catholicism, which made the second Europe, is as much inheritor of the Imperial Roman as of the Christian tradition. To Italy were drawn all the German Emperors; Italy was the ideal of the Europe of the Renaissance which rediscovered the Mediterranean past; the Latin language cemented European culture. Again, late in the eighteenth century, Italy became the highway to the world of the antique cultures, and the great men of all nations were in love with Italy: Goethe and Winckelmann, later Keats and Shelley and Stendhal—to mention only a few out of a long and well-known list. In the nineteenth century Italy was the refuge from a Northern Europe getting ever more utilitarian, especially for the English. There was Ruskin and the Pre-Raphaelite movement, there were colonies of English settlers everywhere, from the *grands seigneurs* with Renaissance villas at Fiesole or on Posilippo to pathetic old maids in *pensions de famille*. Germans escaped to Italy, and Scandinavians and Europeanized Russians, even Frenchmen, least in need of it; and to all of them Italy stood for Paradise on earth.[1]

Joseph Addison had already said something like this, after his travels in 1700–3 : " There is certainly no place in the world

[1] P. Cohen-Portheim, *The Discovery of Europe* (1932), p. 288.

where a man may travel with greater pleasure and advantage than in Italy."

Everybody, even though they had not been to Italy, knew something about it; there was a conventional, but not improbable, picture of the sunny classical land in people's minds. Goldsmith's *Traveller* (1764) fairly represents this:

> Far to the right, where Apennine ascends,
> Bright as the summer, Italy extends:
> Its uplands sloping deck the mountain's side,
> Woods over woods in gay theatric pride;
> While oft some temple's mouldering tops between
> With venerable grandeur mark the scene.
>
> Could nature's beauty satisfy the breast,
> The sons of Italy were surely blest.
> Whatever fruits in different climes are found,
> That proudly rise or humbly court the ground;
> Whatever blooms in torrid tracts appear,
> Whose bright succession decks the varied year;
> Whatever sweets salute the northern sky
> With vernal lives, that blossom but to die;
> These, here disporting, own the kindred soil,
> Nor ask luxuriance from the planter's toil;
> While sea-born gales their gelid wings expand
> To winnow fragrance round the smiling land.

All who could visited Italy, and, in those days of slow locomotion, visited it fairly thoroughly, whether they were nobles on the Grand Tour or simple scholars, clergy, professional men, like Addison, Gray, Smollett. There were moral dangers in the Grand Tour; it was not all sheer gain. The grave and lofty Milton in the seventeenth, the serene and gentle Addison in the early eighteenth century, could travel leisurely through Europe, unspoiled; but Pope was doubtless right when he made the tutor in *The Dunciad* (iv, 311) relate the sheer loss to the soul which the Grand Tour could be for the pupil:

> Led by my hand, he sauntered Europe round,
> And gathered every vice on Christian ground . . .
> Dropped the dull lumber of the Latin store,
> Spoiled his own language, and acquired no more;

All classic learning lost on classic ground;
And last turned air, the echo of a sound!

Oddly enough, some people only had their national prejudice intensified by foreign travel. Addison's " Freeholder " roundly declared that a man had to travel in France if he were really to understand the bad qualities of the French and to learn to dislike them. Nobody, however, seemed to acquire an anti-Italian bias by travelling in Italy. As a matter of fact, there was little nationalism anywhere in Europe, except in England, in the eighteenth century. In any case, Italy was not a state; the Italians were not a nation. They were a quiet, friendly, cheerful people, living under placid, despotic Governments. Italy was a spiritual home for cultured cosmopolitan travellers.

Although there was popular religious pageantry everywhere, there was, at any rate according to the Protestant Smollett's experience, not the least hint of fanaticism. So good-natured were the men that it was the custom for a married woman to have a male friend (called a *cicisbeo*) in addition to her husband, and jealousy—on the side of the men—was absolutely unknown. Nevertheless, adds Smollett, " I would rather be condemned for life to the galleys than exercise the office of a *cicisbeo*, exposed to the intolerable caprices and dangerous resentment of an Italian virago." [1]

Addison's itinerary, on which he set out in the year 1700, is an example of the sort of tour made in Italy by people of the eighteenth century. It covered about the same places as people would wish to see to-day. After going through France he went to Monaco. This beautiful principality is just outside the County of Nice, which was part of the Duchy of Savoy, later the Kingdom of Sardinia. From Monaco, which was in sight of Italy, Addison went to Genoa, Pavia, Milan, Brescia, Verona, Padua, Ferrara, Ravenna, Rimini, San Marino, Pesaro, Fano, Sinigaglia, Ancona, Loreto, Rome, Naples, and Capri. On the return journey he went to Rome, Siena, Leghorn, Pisa,

[1] Tobias Smollett, *Travels through France and Italy*, Letter XXVII (January 28, 1765).

Lucca, Florence, Bologna, Modena, Parma, and Turin.[1] He
was twenty-eight years old when he set forth, with a Government pension of £300 a year and an Oxford Fellowship (Magdalen College) worth about £200, and he passed altogether
twelve months in Italy. This was meant as part of the pre-
paration for a political-literary career in the service of the
Whigs, who then dominated English politics. Addison's interest in Italy was mainly classical. Most of the visitors to
Italy, if they did not go simply for the pleasure of the Carnival
of Venice, went to review and make more vivid their acquaintance with ancient classical art and literature. Gibbon at the
age of twenty-six set forth to visit Italy, but he stopped on
the way at Lausanne (1763) and spent nearly a year there going
over his classical studies, and compiling an elaborate treatise
on the peoples, provinces, and towns of ancient Italy, with
numerous illustrative citations from Latin authors—his scholar's
guide-book to the fascinating land of bygone literature and
learning. He later went onward to Italy, and conceived the
idea of writing *The Decline and Fall of the Roman Empire*,
an historic episode which he calls " the greatest, perhaps the
most awful, scene in the history of mankind ": " It was at
Rome on the fifteenth of October, 1764, as I sat musing
among the ruins of the Capitol, while the barefooted friars
were singing vespers in the temple of Jupiter, that the idea
of writing the decline and fall of the city first started into
my mind." " This work," he wrote, when it was completed,
in 1787, " amused and exercised nearly twenty years of my
life."

Nobody, probably, ever went with a better mental and
spiritual equipment to Italy than Goethe—young (he was thirty-
seven years old), ardent, replete with a generous store of classical
learning, gained at the Gymnasium of Frankfort, with an
absorbing (and lifelong) devotion to culture, already the author
of great works, and with the ambition—and the power—to compose greater. " The principal object of my journey," he later
told the Duke of Weimar, " was to cure myself of the physical

[1] Joseph Addison, *Remarks on Italy* (*Works*, ed. 1856, pp. 357-358).

and moral maladies which tortured me in Germany and ultimately made me useless, and to quench my ardent thirst after true art." With all the passionate yearning of the old Teutonic North for the Italian South, Goethe set forth in 1786 for the land of his dreams—and found it.

In his wonderful two years in Italy (September 1786 to June 1788) Goethe came to the conclusion that the Italians knew the art of living. At Naples, among the children of the world, he felt " one can do nothing but live." From Rome he wrote : " How morally wholesome it is for me to live among a wholly sensuous people! " Nevertheless, while he could understand them and admire, he had no illusion that they should be copied by the people of the North. " They stand too far apart from us " was his verdict. " The fashion of this world passeth away, and I would fain occupy myself only with the abiding."

As described in a gazetteer of 1773, Italy, the geographical unity comprehended between the Alps and the Mediterranean and Adriatic Seas, also included, politically, the Duchy of Savoy and the County of Nice (each belonging to the Kingdom of Sardinia), to the west of the Alps. The Kingdom of Sardinia, though partly on the west side of the Alps, had its capital in Piedmont, at Turin, which, according to Gibbon, then (as now) " presented the same aspect of tame and tiresome uniformity; but the Court," he adds, " was regulated with decent and splendid economy." [1] The states comprised in Italy were the Republic of Venice, with dominions on both sides of the Adriatic; Austria, which had the Duchy of Milan (or " Lombardy "); the Kingdom of Sardinia (Piedmont, Savoy, the island of Sardinia), with its capital at Turin; the republic of Genoa, which until 1768 had Corsica; [2] the republic of

---

[1] Edward Gibbon, *Autobiography* (ed. 1907), pp. 143–144.

[2] Genoa, unable to hold Corsica against rebellions of the inhabitants, permitted France to occupy that island in 1768. Baron Theodore de Neuhoff, a Westphalian adventurer, led the inhabitants and called himself King of Corsica between 1736 and 1743. He died after imprisonment for debt in London, in 1756. See Voltaire, *Candide*, Chapter XVI, and also p. 170 of the present work.

Lucca, called in this age Lucca the Industrious, the home of olive oil; the Duchy of Parma; the Duchy of Modena; the Grand Duchy of Tuscany; the States of the Church (or the Pope's Temporal Dominion), which nearly surrounded Tuscany, and extended from the Venetian frontier on the north to the Neapolitan frontier on the south; lastly, the Kingdom of Naples, including the ' boot ' of Italy and the island of Sicily, the whole often called " the Kingdom of the Two Sicilies." In the sixteenth century a battleground for the rivalry of Valois and Habsburg, and in the first half of the eighteenth of Bourbon and Habsburg, Italy after 1750 was tranquil under the divided protectorate of the Spanish and Austrian branches of those two families. The Austrian Emperor held Lombardy, and his brother was Grand Duke of Tuscany; cadet branches of the Spanish Bourbons had the Duchy of Parma and the Kingdom of Naples. The Pope's slumberous territories were the greater part of the middle of Italy, and had the advantage of large revenues coming in from the rest of the Roman Catholic world until 1773. With the fall of the Jesuit Order in that year many of the external sources of Papal revenue are said to have stopped. Taken as a whole, Italy was probably the happiest country on the continent of Europe in the eighteenth century. The home of Harlequin and Columbine, of the innocent marionettes Punch and Judy, of the light comedy and the care-free opera, Italy was to the people of the late eighteenth century what the French Riviera was to the people of the late nineteenth. The gazetteer concludes:

It is a fine, fruitful country, producing the comforts and luxuries of life in great abundance; and, with great justice, is called the Garden of Europe. The religion of the Italians is Roman Catholic; but persons of all religions live unmolested in Italy, provided no gross insult is offered to their worship. Italy has produced some very great men, in literature and the fine arts, but at present the genius of Italy, with respect to arts and sciences, seems to have migrated to other countries.[1]

Rousseau noticed one drawback to the attractiveness of Italy

[1] Salmon, *The Modern Gazetteer* (London, 1773), *s.v.* " Italy."

—the absence of women as servers in shops and stalls. This work was done by men. " And," adds Rousseau (in *Émile*), " one can imagine nothing more dismal than a glance at the streets of this country for persons who are accustomed to those of France and England. When I saw tradesmen of fashion goods selling to women ribbons, top-knots, netting, trimmings, I found this delicate finery highly ridiculous in big hands, made for blowing the forge or striking the anvil."

The invocation of the fifteenth-century German humanist Conrad Celtes to Apollo, *that he would come to us from Italy, bringing his lyre with him*, seemed in the eighteenth century to have been fulfilled.[1]

The best route into Italy was from South Germany, by way of Innsbruck, the Brenner, Trent, and on to Verona; it was by this way that Goethe travelled in 1786. The Riviera route, Nice–Antibes–Genoa, was only a mule-track between mountain and sea. Hardy travellers often preferred to make the journey in a felucca, a large open boat, rowed by ten or twelve stout mariners. The journey, ninety miles on the map, was a hundred and twenty if the felucca followed round the capes and bays; the normal duration of the voyage was two and a half days, passengers sleeping on mattresses in the open boat; naturally, if, as often happened, the passengers preferred to be landed each night and to sleep ashore, the voyage took much longer. Smollett in 1764 went by gondola, rowed by four men; stress of weather made him land each night.

Rome, of course, bulked largely in the mind of everybody who thought about Italy. " My temper is not very susceptible of enthusiasm," wrote Gibbon, " and the enthusiasm which I do not feel I have ever scorned to affect. But, at the distance of twenty-five years, I can neither forget nor express the strong emotions which agitated my mind as I first approached and entered the *eternal* city. After a sleepless night, I trod, with a lofty step, the ruins of the Forum; each memorable spot where Romulus stood, or Tully spoke, or Cæsar fell, was at once present to my eye; and several days of intoxication were

[1] See Walter Pater, *The Renaissance* (1901), p. 123.

lost and enjoyed before I could descend to a cool and minute investigation." [1] At the time of the fall of the Jesuits (1773) Rome was a vast city, about twelve miles in circumference, including many huge and stately palaces, some 300 churches, triumphal arches, fountains, amphitheatres, circuses, obelisks, open spaces. It was a romantic, entrancing city of the Middle Ages and Renaissance, but less classical in appearance than it is now, for the Forum had not yet been uncovered. Among the cities of Europe it was unique, as Smollett noted, for the " prodigious quantities of cool delicious water, brought in acqueducts from different lakes, rivers, and sources." " These works," the observant physician continued, " are the remains of the munificence and industry of the ancient Romans, who were extremely delicate in the article of water; but, however, great applause is also due to those beneficent Popes who have been at the expense of restoring and repairing those noble channels of health, pleasure, and convenience."

In spite of all this the city was not well kept. " This great plenty of water," wrote Smollett, " has not induced the Romans to be cleanly." He is here referring to the place, not the people. " Their streets, and even their palaces, are disgraced with filth. The noble Piazza Navona is adorned with three or four fountains, one of which is perhaps the most magnificent that Europe can produce, and all of them discharge vast streams of water; but notwithstanding this provision, the piazza is almost as dirty as West Smithfield, where the cattle are sold in London. The corridors, arcades, and even staircases belonging to their most elegant palaces are depositories of nastiness, and indeed in summer smell as strong as hartshorn." [2] Horace Walpole wrote to his friend Richard West in 1740:

I am very glad that I see Rome while yet it exists; before a great number of years have elapsed I question whether it will be worth seeing. Between the ignorance and poverty of the present Romans, everything is neglected and falling to decay; the villas are entirely

---

[1] Edward Gibbon, *Autobiography* (ed. 1907), pp. 158–159.
[2] Tobias Smollett, *Travels through France and Italy*, Letter XXX (February 28, 1765).

out of repair, and the palaces so ill kept that half the pictures are spoiled by damp. . . . The Cardinal Corsini has so thoroughly pushed on the misery of Rome by impoverishing it that there is no money but paper to be seen. He is reckoned to have amassed three millions of crowns. You may judge of the affluence the nobility live in when I assure you that what the chief princes allow for their own eating is a testoon a day—eighteen pence: there are some extend their expense to five pauls, or half a crown; Cardinal Albani is called extravagant for laying out ten pauls for his dinner and supper.

The population of Rome was only about 170,000. The people made their living chiefly from pilgrims and tourists, and from the spendings of the Papal Court. The Romans had the reputation of being the most obliging people in Europe; " a universal civility reigns there." [1] Many distinguished citizens of Europe settled down in Rome, finding cultured and agreeable society. Christina of Sweden spent her last years there, until her death in 1689. James III, the Old Pretender, compelled to leave France according to the terms of the Treaty of Utrecht (1713), lived for the most part at Rome, in the Villa Albano, placed at his disposal by Pope Clement XI. He died at Rome in 1766, and is buried in St Peter's. Charles Edward Stuart, the Young Pretender, was born at Rome in 1720, and after a wandering and rather irregular life died at Frascati in 1788. Henry Stuart, younger brother of Charles, became a priest, and was made a cardinal by Pope Benedict XIV in 1747. He was the generous and much-respected Bishop of Frascati (fifteen miles from Rome); and he had the Villa Albano at Rome. Having lost his revenues in the French Revolutionary wars, he was given a pension by King George III, and died at Rome in 1807 at the age of eighty-two.

Winckelmann, whom Goethe regarded as his master (though they had never met each other), lived at Rome from 1755 as librarian to Cardinal Passionei, and afterwards as librarian to Cardinal Albani. He was murdered at Trieste, on his way back to Rome, in 1768. It was at Rome that he wrote the

---

[1] Salmon, *Gazetteer* (1773), *s.v.* " Rome."

History of Ancient Art, " that shrine of grave and mellow light for the mute Olympian family."

Alexander Pope, who had never seen Rome, was unfair to the Eternal City when he wrote:

> See the wild waste of all-devouring years !
> How Rome her own sad sepulchre appears.[1]

It was, in fact, an interesting, delightful, stimulating city. Goethe spent five months in Rome in the winter of 1786–87, lodging with some German artists in a house, Number 18, of the Corso, near the Porta del Popolo. There he met and was intimately associated with Moritz, who later travelled in England,[2] and with Angelica Kauffmann, one of the earliest Royal Academicians of England. She and her husband, the painter Zucchi, were very sociable, and had a distinguished circle of poets, artists, and scholars. During the same Italian journey Goethe, after a visit to Naples, came back and had a second period of residence in Rome, from June 6, 1787, to April 23, 1788. He spent most of this time sketching, writing, botanizing, and sightseeing. This life suited him excellently. " I have grown steadily happier during my stay in Rome," he wrote home to Weimar; and when he left the Eternal City he said that he would never know another day's happiness.

The dissolution of the Order of Jesuits, and the accompanying anti-clerical policies of the ' enlightened monarchs,' produced a serious diminution in the revenues which flowed into the Papal treasury at Rome. Pope Pius VI (1775–1800) had to increase the domestic taxes, among others that on the corn monopoly. The loaf went down to half its former size. Pius VI was generous in his care of neglected monuments, which, after restoration, he usually had inscribed " through the munificence of Pius VI " (*munificentia Pii Sexti*). Pasquino, the generic name for anonymous Roman wit, left in a public place one of the half-size loaves one morning, with " *Munificentia Pii Sexti* " attached on a piece of paper.

---

[1] Alexander Pope, *Moral Essays*, Epistle V, line 1.
[2] See above, p. 29.

The condition of Rome and the Campagna was described by Gibbon in 1787:

The clouds of barbarism were gradually dispelled; and the peaceful authority of Martin the Fifth and his successors restored the ornaments of the city as well as the order of the ecclesiastical State. The improvements of Rome, since the fifteenth century, have not been the spontaneous produce of freedom and industry. The first and most natural root of a great city is the labour and populousness of the adjacent country, which supplies the materials of subsistence, of manufactures, and of foreign trade. But the greater part of the Campagna of Rome is reduced to a dreary and desolate wilderness; the overgrown estates of the princes and the clergy are cultivated by the lazy hands of indigent and hopeless vassals; and the scanty harvests are confined or exported for the benefit of a monopoly. A second and more artificial cause of the growth of a metropolis is the residence of a monarch, the expense of a luxurious Court, and the tributes of dependent provinces. Those provinces and tributes had been lost in the fall of the Empire; and if some streams of the silver of Peru and the gold of Brazil have been attracted by the Vatican, the revenues of the cardinals, the fees of office, the oblations of pilgrims and clients, and the remnant of ecclesiastical taxes afford a poor and precarious supply, which maintains, however, the idleness of the Court and city. The population of Rome, far below the measure of the great capitals of Europe, does not exceed one hundred and seventy thousand inhabitants; and within the spacious enclosure of the walls, the largest portion of the seven hills is overspread with vineyards and ruins. The beauty and splendour of the modern city may be ascribed to the abuses of the Government, to the influence of superstition. Each reign (the exceptions are rare) has been marked by the rapid elevation of a new family, enriched by the childless pontiff, at the expense of the Church and country. The palaces of these fortunate nephews are the most costly monuments of elegance and servitude; the perfect arts of architecture, painting and sculpture, have been prostituted in their service and their galleries and gardens are decorated with the most precious works of antiquity, which taste or vanity has prompted them to collect. The ecclesiastical revenues were more decently employed by the Popes themselves in the pomp of the Catholic worship; but it is superfluous to enumerate their pious foundations of altars, chapels, and churches, since these lesser stars are eclipsed by the sun of the Vatican, by the dome of St Peter's, the most glorious structure that ever has been applied to the use of religion. The fame of Julius the Second, Leo the Tenth, and Sixtus the Fifth is accompanied by the superior merit of Bramante and Fontana, of Raphael and Michel Angelo; and the same munificence which had been displayed in palaces and temples was directed with equal zeal to revive and emulate the labours of antiquity. Prostrate obelisks were raised from the ground, and erected in the most conspicuous places; of the eleven aqueducts of the Cæsars and consuls, three were restored; the artificial rivers were conducted over a long series of old, or of new, arches, to discharge into marble basins a flood of salubrious and refreshing waters; and the spectator, impatient to ascend the steps of St Peter's, is detained by a column of Egyptian granite, which rises between two lofty and perpetual fountains, to the height of 120 feet. The map, the description, the monuments, of ancient Rome, have been elucidated by the diligence of the antiquarian and the student; and the footsteps of heroes, the relics, not of superstition, but of empire, are devoutly visited by a new race of pilgrims, from the remote, and once savage, countries of the North.[1]

Naples was a kingdom with one great city—the city of Naples, a home of *dilettanti*. Goethe visited it twice in his Italian journey, on the first occasion for five weeks, on the second for a fortnight. Not from an artistic or educational point of view, but for sheer joy in living, he gave Naples the primacy. " People may talk, describe, paint, as they will—to be here is more than all," he wrote. " Naples is a Paradise; every one lives in a kind of dreamless self-oblivion. That is just how I feel. I hardly recognize myself; I seem to myself an entirely different being." In Naples he saw Lady Hamilton, wife of the English Ambassador, later the friend of Nelson. He found the gardens and plants of unceasing interest. A journey across the Strait of Messina and over Sicily was a great success. At Palermo he visited the home of Cagliostro and made careful inquiries into the famous charlatan's origin.

---

[1] Edward Gibbon, *Decline and Fall of the Roman Empire, ad fin.*

Every one went to Venice, though some only because of the Carnival; but there were many things which appealed to people besides that.

Venetia, Venetia,
Chi non ti vede non ti pretia,

says the schoolmaster in *Love's Labour's Lost*.[1] The ancient State was in decline, but it still had a certain political grandeur on account of its extent and solidarity, as well as on account of its historic past. It had grown up, in adverse circumstances, through the vigour and enterprise of its inhabitants,

From dirt and seaweed as proud Venice rose.[2]

A prudent Government still maintained the State in position.

The Republic of Venice covered the north-east plain of Italy as far westward as the river Adige, and southward to the river Po, containing the provinces of Padua, Vicenza, Verona, Brescia, Bergamo, Crema, with the sub-Alpine districts of Rovigo, Friuli, Trevigiana, Feltre, Belluno, and Cadore. To the east, on the Adriatic littoral, it had Istria (but not Trieste, which was Austrian) and Dalmatia; Cattaro, Butrintò, Praga, Prevesa, and Vonizza, in Albania; the Ionian islands Corfu, Paxo, Santa Maura; also the Ægean islands of Cephalonia, Zante, the Strophades, and Cerigo. At the end of the seventeenth century down to the great Turkish War of 1715–18 the Republic had also held the whole of the Morea or Peloponnese, but it lost this at the Peace of Passarowitz, in 1718. The total population of the Republic in the eighteenth century was about three million; the exact figure in 1797 at the extinction of the Republic was 2,921,011.[3] The population of the city of Venice remained throughout the century fairly uniformly about the figure of 137,000.

Politically the Republic was well managed, in an old-fashioned way, completely aristocratic. The electorate was the Great Council, consisting of the whole Patriciate, or body of nobles. The list or book of the nobility, called the *Libro*

---

[1] Act iv, Scene 2.   [2] Alexander Pope, *Essay on Man*, line 292.
[3] P. Molmenti, *Venice* (trans. Horatio Brown, 1908), Part III, vol. i, p. 12.

d'Oro (*Golden Book*), was ' closed ' in 1297, but in point of fact new names were admitted from time to time, according as certain men or families had done well for their country. In the eighteenth century the Treasury was exhausted in consequence of the expenses and debts of the Turkish wars, and the revenue was declining. To help the finances admissions were made to the *Golden Book* for money. In 1775 no less than forty new families were thus admitted to the Patriciate. The names of new entrants of various dates show that the Republic was commercial and cosmopolitan in its outlook; it welcomed capable strangers within its citizenry. Signor Molmenti, extracting names from the Republic's muniments, found among others the following names of new nobles: Van Axel and Gheltof, from Holland; Widmann, a German merchant; Fonseca, from Spain, in the sugar trade; Cotoni, Greek bankers; besides a large number of natives from the Venetian country provinces, who had come into the city and made fortunes as sausage-makers, wool merchants, corn chandlers, silk merchants, dyers, glass-makers, cattle-dealers, jewellers. The old nobility, however, who were rather arrogant and proud in the wrong sense, kept the *Golden Book*, on principle, closed; they refused to treat the new nobles as their social equals, and tried to reserve all political influence to themselves.[1]

The Great Council, or corporation of nobles, numbering over 600, appointed the Senate, which was the legislative body of the Republic, and the Council of Ten, which was a kind of permanent Committee of Public Safety, and was, in effect, the real executive power of the State. At the head of the Republic was the Doge, elected for life by the Great Council, and assisted by a Cabinet. The Government (generally called the Signiory) was shrouded in secrecy; no inkling of its debates or intentions was given to the people, the large, unenfranchised portion of the State. This secrecy was part of the political art of the Venetian governing class. The State was awful, and must be obeyed; terror haunted the evil-doer. Actually justice, which was in the hands of paid judges, independent of the

[1] P. Molmenti, *op. cit.*, Part III, vol. i, pp. 25–26.

executive power, was well administered; and the English prison reformer and investigator Howard found the Venetian prisons, even the terrible Piombi (" the Leads "), to compare favourably with those of the rest of Europe. Legally, the Roman Catholic Church was the only recognized religious body (the State keeping a very firm control of it), but in practice there was complete toleration. The administration was economical. In the eighteenth century the total revenue of the Republic was about 5,000,000 ducats annually (£625,000); approximately half of this was earmarked for payment of the public debt. The principal of the debt was large. The rate of interest was not high. In 1754 the Republic was able to convert the interest on the public debt from 4 per cent. to 3½. In that aristocratic age the Venetian Constitution and Government were generally regarded as models. As Lord Beaconsfield pointed out later (in *Sybil*), the much-admired English Constitution and governing class of the eighteenth century had many of the characteristics of the " Venetian oligarchy."

The Venetian Army was, like most eighteenth-century armies, a volunteer and mercenary force, recruited from natives and foreigners. It was used chiefly for garrisons of the outlying dependencies in Dalmatia and Albania, where ' little wars ' with the frontier tribesmen were frequent. Casanova for a time served in such a garrison (at Corfu, in 1744), and describes the tough soldiery he lived with, officers with many scars on their bodies, unknown heroes who protected this frontier of Western civilization. The navy, which was originally a native and obligatory service, had now also become voluntary. The Government tried to keep up to date. The Arsenal, which was the naval office and dockyard, maintained a professor of pure mathematics and a professor of applied mathematics. In 1751 the Government established a military college at Verona for training army officers. The Republic did not aspire to play a part in the great politics of Europe. The army was a police army, to protect the frontier from savage tribes; the navy was for protection of sea-borne commerce from Mediterranean pirates.

The Republic still upheld its dignity in foreign affairs. Although the officials at home were paid only small salaries, the ambassadors whom the Republic maintained abroad had large incomes. The Venetian Ambassador at Vienna had over 11,700 ducats (about £2300) a year. The Resident in England was paid about £1100. As in the previous centuries, the Venetian diplomatists abroad sent very interesting full accounts (*Relazioni*) to the Signiory about the countries to which they were accredited.

The decline of the Republic, which was obvious to everybody, including the Venetians themselves, was primarily commercial, and was largely caused by the shifting of the great sea-routes from the Mediterranean to the Atlantic and Pacific. It was Vasco da Gama, by discovering the ocean-route to India, and Christopher Columbus, by sailing to America, who struck the fatal blows at the prosperity of Venice, although Adam Smith said that Italy as a whole had not suffered from the discovery of America.[1] " This famous market," an official Venetian report of 1600 declared, " has almost entirely lost its important trade, which has now definitely taken other routes." [2]   In addition, however, to causes like the discovery of America, over which the Signiory could have no control, there were other factors, to some extent preventible, in the decline. The Turkish wars loaded the Republic with a heavy public debt; but it is difficult to see how these wars could have been altogether avoided. The Republic's commercial policy was its own affair, and was bad. The Signiory was obstinately and narrowly protectionist; as the decline in commerce proceeded government became only more timid and more protective. In the eighteenth century, for instance, the import of manufactured silk was prohibited, to protect the Venetian manufacturer, while in order that he might have his raw material cheaper the export of raw silk produced in the Republic was forbidden. Thus a valuable import and export

---

[1] *Wealth of Nations* (ed. Cannan), vol. i, p. 202.
[2] P. Molmenti, *op. cit.*, Part II, vol. i, pp. 36–37, quoting Marin, *Storia di Commercio*, vol. viii, p. 103.

trade was suppressed. There was an enlightened science of political economy being thought out in the eighteenth century, about the time Adam Smith wrote his *Wealth of Nations,* but the Venetian oligarchy, whose great fault was its rigid adherence to tradition, took no cognizance of the new science. The rigidity, the unprogressive course to which the Venetian Patriciate adhered, in politics as in economics, is the real cause of the steady decline and ultimate extinction of the Republic. Had the Signiory adapted the political constitution to the times, and given the Republic a representative Government, Bonaparte could scarcely have extinguished it in 1797. Representative institutions saved Switzerland from annexation.

The glory of eighteenth-century Venice was its art and artistic treasures and the tasteful skill of its people. The Venetians still produced excellent glass, delicately tinted, beautifully shaped, though Bohemian glass was becoming even better. They still made beautiful silk altar-cloths and beautiful jewels; and Venetian architects could still rear stately palaces in baroque style, and dignified churches, though in that age of decline few new buildings were required.

Painting offered a lucrative, steady career for men of talent and industry. The great school of colour had passed away, but the Venetian artists of the eighteenth century maintained a fine tradition, and were nobly patronized by the native nobility and the rich strangers. The licentiousness, the gambling, the intriguing, imputed to high life in Venice, made no appeal to the artists, whose gorgeous and sometimes riotous imaginations were compatible with a tranquil and almost humdrum existence. Married, domestic, bringing up large families, living in substantial houses, well fed, occupied incessantly with their pleasant art and industry, the Venetian artists lived long, placid lives, covering the walls of Academy and palaces with large canvases representing the people and the buildings of their inexhaustibly beautiful city, until death called them away from the sunlit canals and coloured palaces at the age of seventy, eighty, or ninety. The Venice of the eighteenth century, its canals, palaces, churches, exists for everybody to see, in almost

every gallery of Europe, on the honest canvases of Antonio
Canale (1697–1768), called Canaletto to distinguish him from
his father, for painting, like music, frequently went in families.
Rosalba Carnera (1676–1758) was a painter of portraits of
aristocratic Venetian ladies. She married a painter, and was
devoted to her family and friends. The genius of the Venetian
school in the eighteenth century was Giovanni Battista Tiepolo
(1692–1769), who revived the glories of the Cinquecento by
his magnificent and gorgeously coloured canvases. He was the
son of a Venetian merchant skipper, who made money and
provided his son with good masters. At the age of twenty-two
Tiepolo married the sister of Guardi, a painter whose pictures
of Venice rival those of Canaletto. He bought a substantial villa
near Murano, where he lived with his wife and brought up his
nine children. When he was over seventy he was invited to
Madrid by Charles III of Spain to paint frescoes in the royal
palace. Tiepolo died in Madrid in 1769.

In spite of its art and commerce Venice in the eighteenth
century was first and last a playground. Its numerous nobility,
with less than ever to do, owing to the loss of the Republic's
power and overseas possessions, were given up to pleasure.
Gambling and the theatre were their great pursuits. Venice,
always much given to festivals, processions, ceremonies, became a city of ' shows.' The nobles, though they would not
admit the ' people ' to any share in power, endeavoured at
least, by giving them free shows, to keep them quiet. The
licentiousness, insolence, and extravagance of the nobility were
universally known; but the laborious *bourgeoisie*, the professional and commercial folk, doctors, lawyers, and tradesmen,
retained their frugal habits and their respectability. Montesquieu wrote that the Venetian *bourgeoisie* was the best in
Europe.

The Venetian theatre was also probably the best in Europe.
The Italians, ever since the days of Plautus and Terence, had
shown an aptitude for comedy. Admirable little comic plays
were given by means of dolls and puppets. A really fine comedy
was developed; and in the eighteenth century Goldoni, a

Venetian, aspired, not without success, to do for contemporary
Italian life what Molière had done for French. Carlo Goldoni
was born in 1707 in the city of Venice, and was trained to be a
lawyer. He spent his time, however, in reading the Greek and
Latin poets rather than law, and assiduously practised the
writing of plays. He first tried tragedies, but after 1736 turned
to comedy with *Momolo the Courtier*. An incessant stream of
light, graceful plays followed every year, once as many as sixteen in a single year. The best, perhaps, is *La Bottega di
Caffè*, which depicts the characteristic life of the coffee-house,
as vivid an institution in Venice as in Paris and London, where
people talked, read, discussed the journals, sipped coffee, ate
sausage, and lounged away innumerable hours before they
sallied forth to their homes or to the play. In 1760 he removed
to Paris, where he lived to a frivolous, cheerful old age, dying
" unnoticed amid the chaos and darkness of '93." [1]

The beauty of the city, its temperate, healthy climate, its
pleasant inns and hotels, its cheerful, versatile people, its concerts, plays, and *fêtes*, attracted all who could afford to come
when they sought rest, amusement, recreation. Emperors and
kings came in the eighteenth century—Joseph II and Leopold
II of Austria, Gustavus III of Sweden; German princes and
dukes; a Russian Grand Duke; English royal princes and
grand noblemen; men of letters, clergymen, scholars. The
Carnival, which opened every year on December 26, was a
European event. The Government gave permission for the
wearing of masks; the barriers of class were removed, as by a
magician's wand. All classes met and talked, ate and danced
together; and no one knew whether the mask concealed the
features of a great lady, a " *bourgeois* " girl, or even, it was said,
some nun who left the convent for the Carnival, to return like
Cinderella at a stated hour. There the Englishman William
Beckford was moved to imagine his strange Arabian tale *Vathek*,
published in 1787. Voltaire, when in his novel of *Candide* he
sends his heroes round the world, inevitably brings them to
Venice at the time of the Carnival in the year 1757. One

[1] Vernon Lee, *Studies in Eighteenth-century Italy*, p. 412.

evening Martin and Candide at the *table d'hôte* of their hotel
fall into conversation with six strangers, who, to the astonishment of the rest, are called " Majesty " by the domestics.

When the domestics have gone silence falls upon the table.
The strangers are a little sad. At last Candide, who thinks that
the strangers are merely carrying out some joke or farce of the
Carnival, breaks the silence with: " Sirs, this is a curious pleas-
antry. Why are you all kings? For me, I confess that neither I
nor Martin are." Thereupon one of the strangers gravely answers
in Italian:

" I am not joking. I am called Achmet III; for several years
I was Grand Sultan; I dethroned my brother; my nephew
dethroned me; they cut off my viziers' heads; I am finishing my
life in the old seraglio; my nephew the Grand Sultan Mahmoud
sometimes allows me to travel for my health; I have come to
spend the Carnival at Venice."

A young man who was near Achmet spoke after him and said:
" My name is Ivan; I was Emperor of all the Russias; I was
dethroned when in the cradle; my father and mother were
imprisoned; I was brought up in prison; sometimes I am given
permission to travel, accompanied by those who keep guard over
me; and I have come to spend the Carnival at Venice."

The third said: " I am Charles Edward, King of England; my
father ceded to me his right to the throne; I fought to uphold it;
they tore the hearts out of eight hundred of my followers; they
beat them about the face; I was put in prison; I went to Rome
to visit the king my father, who was dethroned as well as myself
and my grandfather; and I have come to spend the Carnival at
Venice."

The fourth then took up the tale and said: " I am the King
of the Poles; the fortunes of war deprived me of my hereditary
estates; my father suffered a similar fate; I resigned myself to
Providence, like the Sultan Achmet, the Emperor Ivan, and the
King Charles Edward, to whom may God give long life; and I
have come to spend the Carnival at Venice."

The fifth said: " I am also King of the Poles; I lost my Kingdom twice; but Providence has given me another estate in which
I have done more good than all the Kings of the Sarmatians
together have been able to do on the banks of the Vistula; I also

resign myself to Providence; and I have come to spend the Carnival at Venice."

It remained for the sixth monarch to speak: " Gentlemen," said he, " I am not such a great nobleman as you, though I have been a King like the rest of you; I am Theodore; I was elected King in Corsica; I was addressed as ' your Majesty '; and now I am scarcely addressed as ' sir '; I caused money to be coined; and now I do not possess a farthing; I had two secretaries of State, and now I hardly have a servant; I have seen myself on a throne, and now for a long time I have been in prison in London sleeping on straw; I am very much afraid of being treated the same here, though I have come like your Majesties to spend the Carnival at Venice."

The five other kings listened to this discourse with a noble compassion. Each of them gave twenty sequins to King Theodore to buy coats and shirts; Candide made him a present of a diamond worth two thousand sequins. " Who can this simple private gentleman be," said the five Kings, " who is well enough off to give away a hundred times as much as any of us, and who does so? "

Just as they left the table there arrived at the same inn four other serene Highnesses who had also lost their estates through the fortunes of war and had come to spend the Carnival at Venice; but Candide took no notice of these newcomers.[1]

In Bonaparte's campaign of 1796 in North Italy against the Austrians (who possessed Lombardy) the territory and neutrality of Venice were violated by the belligerents. Bonaparte used this as an excuse for suppressing the feeble state, *le Lion valétudinaire de Saint Marc*, as he called it. On May 12, 1797, Ludovico Manin, the last Doge, resigned his office. The Franco-Austrian Treaty of Campo Formio, October 17, 1797, annexed Venetia to Austria, in exchange for Austrian cessions to France on the left bank of the Rhine.

---

[1] Voltaire, *Candide*, Chapter XXVI. The monarchs or ' Pretenders ' brought together in this scene are (1) Achmet III of Turkey, (2) Ivan VI, (3) Charles Edward Stuart, " Charles III of England," (4) Augustus III of Poland, Elector of Saxony, (5) Stanislaus Leszczynski, King of Poland, Duke of Lorraine, (6) Theodore Neuhoff, who had a brief reign in Corsica in 1736.

Literature in Italy after the death of Tasso in 1595 fell into poor ways. Its great man was Giambattista Marino (1569–1625), who is considered perhaps the most artificial, precocious, and affected poet who ever rose to high repute. " With Marino, the last son of the literary Renaissance, art was precipitated into the abyss of decadence." [1] His influence dominated Italian letters through the seventeenth century, and is said even to have been responsible for the ' preciosity ' that afflicted all Europe, and which Molière pilloried in *Les Précieuses Ridicules*. The men of letters who met in the Palazzo Corsini, the home of Queen Christina of Sweden in her last years in Rome, cultivated nature and simplicity, in reaction against the turgid followers of Marino. In 1690, the year after Christina's death, her literary group founded the Arcadian Academy. The new Academy captured Roman society. Cardinals and princes gave it their patronage. The movement spread all over Italy. [2] The great Metastasio was, in a sense, an outcome of the movement, for he was adopted and brought up by an Arcadian. His genius and power of originality carried him far beyond the Arcadians. From the time when he wrote the *libretto* of *Didone abbandonata*, an opera produced at Naples in 1722, his position in the world of Italian letters was unchallenged. He may not himself have felt deeply, but there is no doubt that he had the gift of pure song. Like many of the Italian poets, he removed to Vienna, the greatest market for librettists of operas. He lived there, working rather lazily, a good-natured, selfish old valetudinarian, until his death in 1782. Besides Metastasio's, real poetry was also written by the Milanese priest Giuseppe Parini, a member of the Trasformati, an academy founded at Milan in 1743. His great poem, *Il Giorno*, a day in the life of a young man of fashion, began to appear in 1763. The liberal Austrian Governor of Lombardy, Count Firmian, recognized the poetic and also the political value of *Il Giorno*, and gave Parini a

[1] Vittoria Rossi, quoted in L. Collison-Morley, *Modern Italian Literature* (1911), p. 5.
[2] See below, pp. 261–262.

Government office. The satirical descriptions of the poem would, it was hoped, arouse the Milanese aristocracy, elegant pleasure-loving triflers, to a sense of duty.

Parini is believed to have been influenced by contemporary English poetry, particularly Pope's *Rape of the Lock*. French influence was also strong in Italy; Molière was the model for Goldoni, whose admirable comedies of *bourgeois* life were written and acted at Venice mainly between 1748 and 1760. Italian tragedy reached a lofty peak in Alfieri, a Piedmontese nobleman, and officer in the Asti Regiment of the Sardinian Army. He found time to travel in most of the countries of Europe, from Spain to Russia, including England. He conceived a great respect for the English gentry and ladies and for English government and liberty. A man of healthy tastes, he liked riding horses and reading Plutarch. All this gave him the ambition to write in the grand style. His first tragedy, *Cleopatra*, was produced at Turin in 1775. The horse-riding officer became an earnest, indefatigable student, working hard at Tacitus, Homer, Dante, Petrarch, Ariosto, to improve his style. He made friends with the professors of the University of Pisa, in the Grand Duchy of Tuscany. Florence became his home, and there in 1776 he met Princess Louise of Stolberg, Countess of Albany, wife of Prince Charles Edward Stuart, the Young Pretender to the throne of Great Britain. The Princess was abandoned by her husband, whose character had not stood the test of adversity. Alfieri and the princess fell in love; and for the rest of their lives, wherever she went, Paris, Strasbourg, Florence, he was there. Yet he never relaxed his studies and his composition, writing *Virginia*, *Timoleon, Maria Stuarda, Bruto Secondo, Filippo, Merope*, and many others. Alfieri was a patriot and a republican. Practically all his tragedies have the same theme, the struggle against tyranny. He died at Florence in 1803, a few months after finishing his *Autobiography*, and was buried in a noble tomb, with a monument by Canova, a tribute to his memory from the Countess of Albany.

In philosophy Italy had a notable representative in the first

half of the eighteenth century, Giambattista Vico (1668–1744),
Professor of Rhetoric in the University of Naples. Vico was
the son of a Neapolitan bookseller. Like Kant and many other
scholars of the age, he had to be content for a long time to earn
his living and a certain amount of leisure as a private tutor in a
family. In 1697 he obtained his professorship, which gave him a
regular if very small income (100 scudi or £20 a year). In 1735
the Spanish Infant Don Carlos (later Charles III of Spain),
who had just become King of Naples in the War of the Polish
Succession, made him his historiographer royal. This position
carried a pension with it. Vico had already brought out his
Scienza Nuova in 1725. It is a magnificent work, a definite
stage in the process of broadening and freeing man's intellect
which another great Neapolitan philosopher, Benedetto Croce,
has so passionately championed in a later age. Vico's book deals
substantially with law and history, and owed much to his
studies of Grotius' profound and learned work *On the Laws
of War and Peace* (1625). He arrived at the conclusion " that
systems of law are always relative to the general state of society
in which they appear," and that " laws are not made, but
grow." He was a sincere Christian, a member of the Roman
Catholic Church; but his philosophical views were absolutely
incompatible with the rigid system of the Roman Catholic
Church at that time, which believed that truth had been
revealed to it once and for all, unchangeable. Vico held " that
truth and justice come from God, but that human reason
gradually comprehends them." His *New Science*, his view of
society as something always growing, changing, led him to
formulate a law of progress and decay, through which, he
believed, all societies, all nations, like the human organism,
inevitably pass.[1] These views of Vico profoundly influenced
subsequent thought, that of Montesquieu in particular, both
in his *Considérations sur les Causes de la grandeur des Romains
et de leur décadence* (1734) and *De l'Esprit des lois* (1748).
Montesquieu wrote the *Grandeur et décadence* after three years

[1] Vico's philosophy is explained, with a sketch of his life, in Robert
Flint, *Vico* (1901).

of travel in Austria, Poland, Italy, Switzerland, Holland, and England. There can be no doubt that in the " great village," which was the society of the cultured men of Europe, he must often have heard Vico's *Scienza Nuova* being discussed.

With the name of Vico in philosophy there should be coupled that of Muratori. Ludovico Muratori was the official librarian and archivist of the Duke of Modena. The collection of medieval chronicles of Italy, *Rerum Italicarum Scriptores*, which he planned and edited, was published in twenty-nine folio volumes between 1723 and 1751 through the enterprising bookseller Argelati of Modena. It is scarcely too much to say that Muratori and the French Benedictine monk Jean Mabillon are the founders of the modern study of history, for (except contemporary history, like Clarendon and Burnet) there was really none worth speaking about before their time.[1]

Italy has always thrown a glamour over every aspect of life in the eyes of Northern people. Italian literature, though not as eminent as French, in the eighteenth century, continued to wield the Italian spell. Whether the scene is that of Arcadians making verses and discoursing on letters in the elegant country villa of a nobleman, or Muratori patiently and skilfully working at his documents, alone, fireless, through the winter months, in the chill library at Modena, there is always a touch of distinction. Nor was it all *dilettante* work. Giuseppe Baretti (1719–89), a well-known figure in Johnson's circle in London, was a strong and fearless critic, a wholesome, sane judge of literary standard. " His account of Italy," said Johnson, " is a very entertaining book. And, Sir, I know no man who carries his head higher in conversation than Baretti. There are strong powers in his mind. He has not, indeed, many hooks, but with what hooks he has, he grapples very forcibly." Baretti, during his London period, fell into trouble by stabbing a Haymarket bully in self-defence. He

---

[1] Clarendon wrote the classical *History of the Rebellion*, not published till 1704 ; Burnet the *History of My Own Times* (1723) ; Mabillon *De Re Diplomatica*, which founded the scientific study of ancient charters and documents (1681). Mabillon died in 1707.

was arraigned at the Old Bailey, but was acquitted. " Never did such a constellation of genius enlighten the awful sessions house," wrote Boswell. Burke, Garrick, Topham Beauclerk, Dr Johnson, Sir Joshua Reynolds, and Goldsmith were among the witnesses who testified to Baretti's good character.[1]

Italy in the eighteenth century was a happy country. It is true that there was little progress there, as progress is understood in modern times. Trade, commerce, industry, population, were not increasing. Forms of government remained fixed, immobile: in the monarchies despotic, in the republics oligarchic. There were no politics. There also were no wars, or almost none, between 1713 and 1793. The War of the Polish Succession (1733–38), the War of the Austrian Succession (1740–48), just touched Italy; the Seven Years War (1756–63) not at all. The Italian states had few troops. Austria was the dominating Great Power. France and, except for a brief period in the time of Queen Elizabeth Farnese, Spain had renounced ambitions in Italy. Under the temporal hegemony of Austria and the spiritual hegemony of the Pope the people slumbered politically, but lived vividly enough in their social and intellectual activities. The local royal Courts and Government Houses had their operas, libraries, and universities. In a genial climate, the soil yielded a reasonable subsistence under the industrious hands of the peasantry. A hereditary craftsmanship produced characteristic Italian wares; the little seaports maintained a hardy race of fisher-folk and an active commerce in Mediterranean produce. The dance, the comedy, the opera, found a congenial home in the cities, and elementary forms of these arts continued to flourish among the simple villagers. Intellectually there was plenty of stimulus in Italy, but a complete absence of moral and political *malaise*. Goethe had some reason for apprehension, when the time came for him to leave the fortunate country after a long sojourn, that he would never experience unalloyed happiness again.

"*Italiam ! Italiam !*" cried Montesquieu as he wrote the last

[1] James Boswell, *Life of Johnson, sub anno* 1769.

lines of *De l'Esprit des lois*, thinking, doubtless, of the leisure which he was now to enjoy, but also of his sunny days in Venice and Rome. He felt like Æneas and Achates and their company after the long journeys.

> *Cum procul obscuros colles humilemque videmus*
> *Italiam. Italiam! primus conclamat Achates:*
> *Italiam læto socii clamore salutant.*[1]

---

[1] " From afar we see dim hills and the low-lying coast of Italy. 'Italy,' first exclaims Achates ; 'Italy,' the crews salute with joyous cries." (*Æneid*, III, 522–524.)

CHAPTER XI

THE OPERA

MUSIC is essentially a modern and European art, for neither the ancient world nor peoples with another than European culture produced any that was great. The men of the Elizabethan age and seventeenth century were highly musical; their common means of amusement in company was to sing and play to each other, as is charmingly described in the last scene of *John Inglesant*. By the opening of the eighteenth century the class of professional musician was extending beyond the organists and choristers, who had hitherto been almost the only professionals; and people were going to the theatre not only to hear the spoken drama, but to hear opera, that remarkable branch of the dramatic art where acting and scenery are subordinate to music, and an enchanted world is created, over and above the mirrors of nature.

Opera on the grand scale began comparatively late, with Peri's *Eurydice*, produced at Florence in 1600. Monteverde of Cremona, who in his later years lived and worked at Venice, composed and produced *Ariana* at the Court of the Duke of Mantua in 1607 and *Orfeo* in 1608. This new branch of the dramatic art, however, did not make great headway in the seventeenth century, although Scarlatti, the Neapolitan, and Purcell, the Englishman, did some notable work. The native place of the opera was Italy, and the *libretto* of nearly every opera was Italian. Nevertheless the highest development was attained elsewhere, in Vienna, Paris, Dresden, Hamburg, London. Smollett in 1764 found the opera at Florence only "tolerable," and the audience "not very attentive to the music." [1]

[1] Tobias Smollett, *Travels through France and Italy*, Letter XXVII (January 28, 1765).

Yet the Italians have the credit for the early development of the opera, and particularly for its development of melody; but the German composers carried onward the work of the Italians to still greater success.

The advance of opera came with the advance of Courts. Sovereigns and princes and the high aristocracy like expensive amusement, and have the means of paying for it. In the eighteenth century every prince wanted to have a ' Versailles.' Louis XIV, the model of grand monarchs, encouraged the legitimate drama, the magnificent classical pieces of Corneille and Racine; but the eighteenth-century monarchs, though willing and pleased to view a classical play from time to time, frequently wanted something lighter. The opera gave them what they looked for, amusement, interesting dramatic representation, and music with plenty of those airs that their souls delighted in.

Besides the monarchs, the rich, cultured *bourgeoisie* were taking a great interest in opera. The old merchant families of Hamburg, in their great town-houses and country-houses, had splendid libraries and music-rooms, and patronized talent. It was at Hamburg that Handel produced his *Almira* on January 8, 1705. Although music has never been an easy profession, nor one which conferred much wealth, the great musicians of the eighteenth century may be said, on the whole, to have fared passably well. Certainly two of the masters of the age, Handel and Gluck, did so.

George Frederick Handel was born at Halle, in Prussian Saxony (Prussian since 1648), on February 23, 1685, the same year as Johann Sebastian Bach was born. The father was a barber-surgeon, who tried to keep his son away from the career of music; but even as a small boy Handel showed a determination to do nothing else, and adhered steadily to this. A half-brother was *valet de chambre*, or footman, at the little Court of the Duke of Saxe-Weissenfels. The boy Handel, on a visit to his brother, made friends with the Court musicians, and was allowed to play on the organ. The good Duke, hearing Handel play, and taking a kindly interest, advised the father to let the boy follow a musical career. On returning to Halle the elder Handel placed his son as a pupil with the Cathedral organist, who gave him a thorough training in playing and composition; at the same time the father attended to Handel's general education.

After his father died Handel remained with his mother at Halle, and dutifully entered the University there and studied law for a short time, until he was appointed organist at the Cathedral (1702). After a year in this employment he went off to seek his musical fortune at Hamburg, where, under the patronage of the rich and cultured *bourgeoisie*, opera was now regularly established. He was well received there by the premier musician, Matheson, who allowed him to conduct for the opera. Handel was very hot-tempered and sensitive. He fought a duel with swords with his benefactor, and narrowly escaped death. Nevertheless, the elder and younger musician soon became friends again; and in the next year, when he was only twenty years old, Handel had the joy of seeing two of his operas, *Almira* and *Nero*, performed in quick succession at Hamburg. Handel was a prudent economist. He saved money at Hamburg, and then, putting aside sufficient to maintain his mother at Halle while he was away, he left Hamburg for Italy, the gay and sunny country where music chiefly flourished. The generous Italian musicians, Corelli, who was composing violin music, and Alessandro Scarlatti, who was composing opera (both at Naples), received the talented young German in friendly manner. At Rome, Naples, Florence, and Venice he found opportunities to practise his art and to produce operas which he composed there—*Rodrigo* and *Agrippina*.

Handel passed three years in Italy, leaving it in 1709 to become Kapellmeister to the Elector of Hanover, afterwards George I of Great Britain. He was allowed liberal leave of absence from the Court of Hanover, and spent most of his time in England. His opera, *Rinaldo*, was produced at the Haymarket in 1711. The London public took kindly to opera, though Joseph Addison, in the *Spectator*, directed the shafts of his gentle irony against it. Indeed, he went further than this, and in the year in which *Rinaldo* was produced roundly complained of "the forced thoughts, cold conceits, and unnatural expressions of an Italian opera." A week or two later he wrote:

> There is no question but our great-grandchildren will be curious to know the reason why their forefathers used to sit together like an audience of foreigners in their own country, and to hear whole plays acted before them in a tongue which they did not understand. . . . We do not know what it is we like; only, in general, we are transported with anything which is not English.

He allowed, however, that the *recitativo* (which was rather a new thing) was an improvement.

> There is nothing that has more startled our English audience than the Italian *recitativo* at its first entrance upon the stage. People were wonderfully surprised to hear generals singing the word of command, and ladies delivering messages in music. Our countrymen could not forbear laughing when they heard a lover chanting out a *billet-doux*, and even the superscription of a letter set to a tune.

Nevertheless, he was of opinion that the change was for the better.

> But however this Italian method of acting in *recitativo* might appear at first hearing, I cannot but think it much more just than that which prevailed in our English opera before the innovation; the transition from an air to recitative music being more natural than the passing from a song to plain and ordinary speaking, which was the common method in Purcell's operas.[1]

The hospitable English gentry opened their great houses to Handel. He received a pension of £400 a year from George I, and made further considerable sums by teaching and by composing opera and concert music. Gradually, however, he devoted himself more and more to the composition of religious music, and produced the great series of oratorios for which his name will live for ever. He occasionally composed Italian

[1] *Spectator*, March 15 and 21, April 3, 1711.

opera for the Haymarket Theatre. *Radamisto*, produced there in 1720, had great success. His last opera, *Deidamia*, appeared in 1741. In religious music he has no peer except his contemporary Johann Sebastian Bach, whom he never met. The oratorios *Saul* and *Israel in Egypt* were performed first in 1738, in London. The *Messiah* was first produced in 1742, at Dublin. Thereafter most of his work came out at Covent Garden Theatre; *Judas Maccabæus* was produced there in 1747. The crowds which thronged to hear the oratorios are a disproof of the allegation of religious lethargy so often levelled against the English of the eighteenth century, for Handel did not *impose* religious music upon England. He placed his genius at the service of the public; there was a greater demand for oratorio than for opera in England of the seventeen-forties.

Not all Handel's ventures were successful, and his quarrels with other musicians damaged his practice. He was twice bankrupt, but recovered his position, and ultimately paid all his debts, and was well enough off to be able to present an organ to the Foundling Hospital of London. He became almost blind towards the end of his life, but continued working to the last. He died in 1759, and is buried in Westminster Abbey. The other great master of religious music, Bach, who at the end of his life was choir-master of the Thomas Schule at Leipzig, had died in 1750. It seemed that with the death of these masters grandeur passed out of musical composition. " The gigantic days of Handel and Bach were exchanged for a time of peruke and powder, when the highest ideal was neatness, smoothness, and elegance. Depth, force, and originality were gone, and taste was the most important word in all things." [1] This criticism is not justified, for a composer of great power as well as of elegant taste was growing to maturity.

The mantle of classical opera which Handel had worn fell to Christopher Willibald Gluck. This tranquil genius was born in 1714, the son of a gamekeeper on the estates of the great German Bohemian family of Lobkowitz. He obtained a

[1] Maczewski in Grove's *Dictionary of Music* (1900), vol, i, p. 113. *Cf.* W. H. Hadow, *Oxford History of Music* (1904), vol. v, p. 6.

good education in a Jesuit school, and later studied music at Prague. He had no great patron at this time, and had to maintain himself by playing the violin at country fairs and dances. When he went to Vienna, however, he was brought to the notice of the nobility there by Prince Lobkowitz, and was taken on a tour to Italy by Prince Melzi. Gluck spent some years in Italy, composing tuneful operas, which found ready acceptance with the public of the Italian cities. When he went to London, however, in 1745, he had no success; so he turned back to the Continent, and found a home in Vienna. Here was the musical centre of Europe. The great landed families, the Austrian, Bohemian, and Hungarian aristocracies, maintained their own orchestras, and were ever ready to support the production of good music. Gluck wrote operas for the Court of the Empress Maria Theresa, and taught music to the Archduchess Marie Antoinette. His opera *Orfeo*, produced in 1762, " startled the entire Viennese world," [1] and marks the real beginning of operatic reform. He ignored the fixed rules which governed the number of characters, the length of airs and such things, and he composed opera entirely different from any which had hitherto appeared. Marie Antoinette, after her marriage to the Dauphin, invited Gluck to Paris. He went there in 1774, the year in which Marie Antoinette and her husband succeeded to the throne of France; and he lived there until 1787. Before he went to Paris Gluck had produced *Alceste* at Vienna. His Paris period opened with *Iphigénie en Aulide*; after this came *Iphigénie en Tauride*, *Écho et Narcisse*, *Les Danaïdes*. By careful study of the libretto of the drama provided for his music Gluck set himself to assist the poetry " by intensifying the expression of sentiments and the interest of situations "; he was thus dramatist as well as musician. The words were not just a convenient vehicle for his music; he could only compose to good literature; the words, the poetry, inspired him. No other writer of opera was so much master of dramatic technique and so genuinely poetic as Gluck until

[1] W. H. Hadow, *op. cit.*, vol. v, p. 91. *Cf.* Vernon Lee, *Studies of the Eighteenth Century in Italy* (1907), p. xxvi.

Mozart arrived. Gluck's last years were spent with dignity and serenity at Vienna, in the pleasant society of that queen of eighteenth-century capitals.

Down to the middle of the eighteenth century opera, though produced in great quantity, had been somewhat stagnant. There were few works of genius; the *Olimpiade* of the young Pergolese, produced at Rome in 1735, with a fine *libretto* by Metastasio, is exceptional. Even Handel's operas were a little mechanical; he was prepared to fit his music almost to any words. The rules of composition were inclined to be somewhat rigid. Every opera was expected to contain only six characters, three men and three women, and these must make three pairs of lovers. Thus the poets or poetasters who wrote the *libretto*, as well as the musicians who composed the score, were absurdly confined in their style and in their inventiveness. Gluck broke away from all this and raised opera to a high art, to something much more than just smooth and elegant and pleasant composition for people to see and hear. " Grandeur, dignity, purity, were his qualities." [1] His influence on Mozart was pronounced and beneficent. Dr Burney met the composer at Vienna and saw his works. " In some of his scenes," he wrote, " M. Gluck, transported beyond the bounds of ordinary genius, gives such energy and colouring to passion as to become at once poet, painter, and musician. He seems to be the Michel Angelo of music, and is as happy in painting difficult attitudes and situations of the mind as that painter was of the body." [2] Thus Gluck shares some of the glory of bringing eighteenth-century opera to its grand culmination.

Another composer who shared this distinction was Franz Joseph Haydn. This musician is known all over the world for having composed the magnificent Austrian national anthem in 1797, when gigantic battles were being fought in South Germany and North Italy between the Austrian and French armies. A great composer, he was also a great teacher. Born

---

[1] Sacheverell Sitwell, *Mozart* (1932), p. 30.
[2] Charles Burney, *The Present State of Music in Germany, the Netherlands, and the United Provinces* (1773), vol. ii, p. 289.

in Austria in 1732, one of the twelve sons of a village wheel-wright, Haydn was trained as a chorister and given a good general education. From Hamburg (near his native village), where Haydn was chorister, he obtained a place in the choir of the Court church, St Stephen's, at Vienna. He gave lessons on the clavichord and in singing, and was patronized by the cultured family of Martinez. In the middle of the century Metastasio, the Italian lyric poet and writer of *libretti* for opera, who lived in Vienna and was then the most famous man of letters in Europe, became his friend. Haydn composed operas to Metastasio's *libretti*. In 1759 he was made conductor to the private band of Count Morzin; in 1760 sub-director of Prince Paul Esterházy's *Kapelle*, or orchestra; in 1766 he became *Oberkapellmeister*, or head director. Thereafter much of his time was spent at one great seat or another of the Esterházy, chiefly at Eisenstadt, in Hungary; he had to work with the Prince's orchestra and to compose for it. Successful, admired, established in the highest circles of the Austrian musical world, incessantly engaged in composition, concerts, practices for his exacting, artistic masters, Haydn had time to befriend and encourage young musicians, among whom were two of the very greatest, Mozart and Beethoven.

Wolfgang Amadeus Mozart was born at Salzburg on January 27, 1756. His father, Leopold Mozart, was one of the Court musicians or chapel musicians of the Prince Arch-bishop of Salzburg, who kept a hundred performers, vocal and instrumental, in his service. The father wrote a treatise on the violin, " which formed the basis of violin-playing in Germany during the whole of the latter part of the eighteenth century." [1] He carefully trained the young Mozart, exercising him especially, and almost from the earliest years, in the art of musical composition. At the age of six the boy wrote a concerto for the clavier. Although paid a very small salary by the Archbishop, Leopold Mozart lived in a pleasant, *bourgeois* house (on the first floor), brought up his family carefully, and took them on tours through Germany. The young Mozart

[1] Sacheverell Sitwell, *op. cit.*, p. 9.

" astonished all Europe by his infant knowledge." [1] The tours paid for themselves, for the family gave concerts as it went along. The first tour—father, son, and daughter—to Munich was made in January 1762, the second, to Vienna, in September–October of the same year. The cheerful Viennese received the infant prodigy with kindness and indeed with enthusiasm; " we conversed with the first Ministers and ladies," wrote the father in a letter to the landlord of his Salzburg house. The Empress Maria Theresa took the boy Mozart on to her lap, and gave him and his sister each a rich robe, made for a young archduke and archduchess. The solemn, good-natured Emperor Francis sat beside the clavier and watched the little boy's fingers as they wandered over the keyboard. Kaunitz, Count Harrach, Count Hardegg, had the Mozarts to perform, and sent carriages to bring them to the great houses. The third tour was made to Munich in 1763. The boy played before the Elector of Bavaria in the Palace of Nymphenburg, and before the Duke of Zweibrücken in the Court's summer residence at Schwetzingen. The family—father, mother, son, and daughter —proceeded to Heidelberg, Frankfort (where Goethe heard the boy play at a concert), Bonn, and Aix-la-Chapelle, where they played before Princess Amalia, sister of the King of Prussia. From Aix they went on to Paris, where the Bavarian ambassador lodged them in his hotel. They played before the Court at Versailles; the boy did not like Madame de Pompadour. " Who is this who won't kiss me? " he said aloud. " My empress kissed me." Grimm, the secretary to the Duke of Orléans, the correspondent of Catherine II and other famous people, was extremely active on their behalf, and sold 320 tickets for their first concert.

After Paris came London. The Mozarts were there from April 1764 to September 1765. They stayed first in Frith Street, Soho, and later in Chelsea. The King and Queen took a keen interest in the boy. George III tried him on the piano with pieces of Bach and Handel. Once when the Mozarts were walking in St James's Park the royal carriage, which was

[1] Charles Burney, *op. cit.*, vol. ii, p. 323.

passing them, stopped; the King put his head and hands out, laughing and beckoning to the boy and his sister. The Mozart family remained over a year in England. When the London visit came to an end the Dutch ambassador followed the post-chaise of the Mozarts, and, catching them up, said that he was commanded by Princess von Weilburg, sister of the Prince of Orange, to invite them urgently to The Hague. The invitation was accepted. Finally the family returned home by Malines (on the invitation of the Archbishop, an old friend of the elder Mozart), Paris, where they were sought out and visited by the Hereditary Prince of Brunswick (the famous general of Frederick the Great, mortally wounded forty years later at Auerstädt), Dijon, Lyons, Winterthur, Schaffhausen, Donau-eschingen, and last, towards the end of the year 1766, Salzburg. The Archbishop took back Leopold Mozart, after his somewhat extended leave of absence, into the chapel orchestra. This tour is an example of others which followed, and shows how even in those years of bad roads and lumbering post-chaises travelling was a common thing in Western and Central Europe, even for people of moderate means, provided they were enterprising and talented. The Courts and aristocracies and the cultured *bourgeoisie* of the larger towns provided enthusiastic audiences or patrons. All this travelling and excitement was rather hard on the small boy, who would sometimes climb down in the middle of a concert, from his seat at the harpsichord, to stroke a cat; or he would be found by some rich patron hopping about the room with a stick between his legs for a horse.

A few months' quiet work at Salzburg soon renewed the Mozarts' zest for travelling; so, with another leave of absence from the Archbishop, they went to Vienna in September 1767. The Emperor Joseph II proposed that the young Mozart should compose an opera, and seems even to have outlined the plan of one. The boy, who was now twelve years old, quickly (as his way was throughout life) composed an opera, a large work of 558 manuscript pages, *La finta Semplice* (*The Pretended Simpleton*), which was played in private in the houses of Prince Kaunitz, the Duke of Braganza, and other amateurs. " The whole hell of music," however, as Mozart's father called the jealous Viennese artists, set themselves, successfully, to prevent a public performance. Returning to Salzburg, the Mozarts settled down, for a time, to what they felt to be the dull round of duty in the Archbishop's choir; the boy wrote church music and studied the Italian language, for Italy was the lure of all composers of church music and opera. In December 1769 the father and his son set forth to Italy for a two-year tour.

It is a beautiful route from Salzburg (known as the " Strada d'Italia ") through the mountains to the Venetian plain. The Mozarts stopped at Verona, and the boy wrote letters home, in a mixture of childish German and Italian, to his sister. " The German clown now ceases, and the Italian begins," he modestly said. Every Italian city had a philharmonic society or academy, which welcomed Mozart and let him give concerts to them: at Mantua; at Milan, where the famous Governor-General of Lombardy, Count Firmian, was a great friend; at Bologna, where they stayed in the country-house of the Austrian field-marshal Pallavicini and made the acquaintance of Padre Martini; at Rome, where they saw Pope Clement XIV and were kindly received by Cardinal Pallavicini, who complimented young Mozart on his Italian, and said, "*Ick kann auk ein benig deutsch sprekken* "; at Naples, where they played before King Ferdinand I and were kindly received by the English Ambassador, Sir William Hamilton, and his wife (Nelson's Lady Hamilton), an accomplished player on the clavier. On the return journey they stopped for a long time at Milan for the production of an opera which Mozart had just written, called *Mithridates*. It was performed twenty times there. The Mozarts arrived back at Salzburg in March 1771. The boy's mind and spirit had bloomed amid the vivid artistic conditions of Italy, and his health had benefited from its climate and simple, plentiful food. He had found in Italy the genius of opera; and in the Sistine Chapel and elsewhere he had heard church music in its noblest expression.

Scarcely were the Mozarts returned to Salzburg than they

were invited to return to Milan for the marriage of the Archduke
Ferdinand, third son of Maria Theresa and the Emperor
Francis, to Maria Beatrice, heiress of the Duchy of Modena.
Mozart, now aged fifteen, composed for the marriage a dramatic
serenade, *Ascanio in Alba*. On hearing this piece at Milan
Hasse (whose charming character Dr Burney has described),[1]
himself considered to be the peer and rival of Handel, said
generously, " This boy will throw us all into the shade."
From the brilliant Court of Milan the Mozarts returned to
their old life at Salzburg.

At this time a new, unsympathetic archbishop, Hieronymus
Colloredo, succeeded to the saintly Sigismund. Archbishop
Hieronymus is described as " coarse, brutal, overbearing,
wholly indifferent to art and letters." [2] Young Mozart was his
concert-master, at a salary equivalent to twenty-one shillings
a year. The youth produced endless music for him, church
music, concert music, canticles, serenatas with *libretti* by
Metastasio—all to no effect, for the Archbishop showed no
inclination to promote the wonderful genius in his service. A
brilliant visit to Milan in 1772 consoled Mozart somewhat for
this neglect. He composed the opera *Lucio Silla* for the
carnival at Milan, with *libretto* by Metastasio, and was warmly
welcomed by Count Firmian. Then back to Salzburg, and
another trip to Vienna, 1773 ; so finished Mozart's boyhood.
He was the most famous youthful prodigy of all ages, and his
later performances amply fulfilled and more than fulfilled this
early promise ; yet as a man he never met the worldly fame and
success which as a boy had been showered upon him.

Mozart was now eighteen years old. With the careful and
sympathetic tuition and guidance of his father, he was making
an independent career. In 1774 he went (still with his father)
to Munich, to compose an *opera buffa* (comic opera, with
recitative) for the carnival. *La finta Giardiniera* was produced
there amid great enthusiasm on January 14, 1775. There
followed three years of unrequited labour at Salzburg. In 1777

[1] Charles Burney, *op. cit.*, vol. ii, p. 274.
[2] W. H. Hadow, *The Oxford History of Music*, vol. v, p. 14.

he embarked on another tour; this time his father stayed behind, but he took his mother with him. He wanted a permanent post at Munich, where there was magnificent church music, but though he was well known there, and the Bishop of Chiemsee befriended him, he could not obtain a place from the Elector. From Munich mother and son went on to Augsburg, a famous place for organ-making. There he played and wrote. Next to Donauwörth, Nordlingen, Hochenaltheim (the residence of the Prince of Wallerstein), Mannheim, the chief residence of Charles Theodore, the Elector Palatine. Charles Theodore was a sort of Augustus the Strong, one of the most dissolute princes of the age, but also interested in the arts. He heard the great young musician play, and said, " Mozart stays here for the winter," but actually did nothing for him. His old friend the Princess of Orange entertained him at her palace, Kirchheim-Poland, for a few days, along with Herr Weber, a citizen of Munich, and his daughter Aloysia, with whom Mozart had fallen in love. After this brief interval of romance Mozart and his mother went to Paris. They lodged in the " Rue du Gros Chênet vis-à-vis celle du Croissant," at the Hôtel des Quatre Fils Aimont. There Mozart's mother fell ill and died, July 3, 1778. Mozart moved into the house of the kind Baron Grimm. He gave lessons in music, had concerts, and just managed to maintain himself well enough, but saw no prospect of permanent success in Paris; so he returned for consolation to Munich, only to find that his sweetheart Aloysia Weber had grown cold. He easily fell in love, however, with Aloysia's sister Constance, and she ultimately became his wife. Aloysia was later a well-known singer on the Munich, Vienna, Hamburg, and Amsterdam stages; the friendly and chivalrous Mozart composed pieces specially to suit her.

At the age of twenty-three Mozart in 1779 was Court and Cathedral organist to the Archbishop of Salzburg, with a salary of 500 florins a year. His fame was now all over Germany. In 1780 Charles Theodore of the Palatinate, who had also succeeded to the Electoral throne of Bavaria (1775), invited him to go to Munich, to compose an opera for the next year's carnival. Mozart accepted, went to Munich, and composed rapidly, as was his usual way, the piece which the Elector had commanded. The *libretto* was written by one of the Salzburg priests, the Abbate Varesco. *Idomeneo* came out in all the splendour of the Munich theatre, with the best voices in Europe, and the magnificent combined orchestra of Munich and Mannheim (under the conductor Stamitz, " unhesitatingly accepted "[1] as the finest of the time) on January 29, 1781. Although not entirely original in conception, for it was much influenced by the classical models of Gluck's operas, it is considered by its brilliant airs and recitative to have constituted a revolution in the history of opera. In March 1781 the Archbishop of Salzburg, who was a great Austrian nobleman, went with all his Court to Vienna, and commanded Mozart to go there too. Mozart obeyed, and found that though the Viennese nobility were glad to hear his music the Archbishop, while giving him a good room in the house to live in, left him to dine with the footmen and valets. After about six weeks Mozart decided to give up service with the Archbishop and to become an independent musician, teaching, playing (violin or pianoforte), and composing in Vienna (May 1781). The break came after the Archbishop, in a fit of jealousy at Mozart's popularity with the Viennese aristocracy, had ordered him to cancel all his musical engagements and to return to Salzburg. Mozart went to protest, and was greeted with a torrent of abuse; the temper of the much-tried musician gave way, and in a white heat of indignation he resigned his post on the spot. " In that memorable interview the *ancien régime* of music signed its death-warrant." [2]

In the wonderful social and artistic life of the great Habsburg capital Mozart ' found ' himself. The Court and the great noble families—the Esterházy, Palffy, Harrach, Kaunitz, Waldstein, Thun, and the rest—took the liveliest interest in music, so that Mozart's series of subscription concerts went off with the greatest success. The majestic Gluck retired to

---

[1] W. H. Hadow, *op. cit.*, vol. v, p. 8.
[2] *Ibid*, vol. v, p. 15.

Vienna in preference to living even in the great social capital of Paris. Joseph Haydn, Mozart's senior, was still in active career. They became friends and profound admirers of each other. " To Mozart, the greatest composer of the day was Haydn—and to Haydn it was Mozart." [1] All the best Italian composers and librettists came to Vienna. The talented native society was further supported by distinguished visitors from France, Russia, England. A few hours' journey away was Prague, something more than a provincial capital, where an especially enthusiastic aristocracy (Thun, Chotek, Waldstein, Lobkowitz) and *bourgeoisie* were ready to welcome with almost frenzied delight the productions of the great composer. For ten happy years Mozart worked—and worked extremely hard— at his concerts, his teaching, and his composing, at Vienna or between Vienna and Prague. The Emperor Joseph, always rather inscrutable, was the centre of the great scene. Polite, attentive, almost flattering, yet a trifle cold; living unostentatiously, dining off the simplest dishes, thoroughly enjoying a bowl of chocolate, bread and cream, which he demanded at the grand Viennese evening parties, he was still every whit an emperor, and had as definite ideas about music as about everything else, and expected to be listened to. He often offered suggestions for musical composition to Mozart, which indeed Mozart seems to have found very helpful. Joseph would sit near Mozart at a concert, and at the appropriate moment would say, in his curious mixture of French and German, " *Allons, d'rauflos!* " (" Come, let go! "), as if he were giving commands to a battery of artillery. This meant that Mozart had to start playing. Sometimes his criticism was a little embarrassing. " Too many notes, my dear Mozart," he once remarked, *à propos* of the opera *Die Entführung aus dem Serail*. " There are just as many, may it please your Majesty, as there should be," replied the unabashed musician.

Mozart's first big work in his Viennese period was *Die Entführung aus dem Serail* (1782) (known to English operagoers as *The Seraglio*), which he composed, with the approval

[1] Sacheverell Sitwell, *Mozart*, p. 35.

and possibly at the suggestion of Joseph II, to show that German, as well as Italian, could make good *libretto* for opera. The text was adapted from the drama of Bretzner. Austria and Hungary had for 300 years been the bulwark of the Empire against Turkey; Turkish life, the subject of the opera, was a real thing to the Viennese public. In the same year, 1782, Mozart married Constance Weber, and settled down to a happy domestic life of nine years, incessantly occupied with concerts and composition, working hard to make a living which was never regular, a mixture of prosperity and adversity. " Just at the right time he met the adventurer Lorenzo da Ponte, a converted Jew, a priest, a character who might have been the twin-brother of Casanova, and, it may be added, a most able librettist." [1] *Le Nozze di Figaro (The Marriage of Figaro)*, the *libretto* an adaptation by da Ponte of Beaumarchais' comedy on the suggestion of Joseph II, came out at Vienna in 1786; " it set the model for all comic opera of the future." [2] *Don Giovanni*, also with a very spirited *libretto* by da Ponte, was produced at Prague in 1787. Mozart had been invited by Count Thun to come to Prague and write the opera there. He accepted the invitation, came to Prague, and was soon followed by da Ponte. They were thus able to compose the opera, music and *libretto*, together.[3] Mozart was delighted with his reception by the Bohemian public. The production at Prague of *Don Giovanni*, vivid, spirited, humorous, with an undertone of deep gravity, lovely and haunting in its melodies, dramatic in its characters and scenes, was the most resounding musical success in the eighteenth century. Curiously it had a very poor reception at Vienna, where it was produced in 1788, though it became established in popularity by the end of the century.

In the same year, but before *Don Giovanni* came out, Mozart's kind and wise father died, rather solitary, at Salzburg. Worldly success had now definitely come to Mozart. He had scarcely returned from Prague to Vienna when Gluck died. The

[1] Sacheverell Sitwell, *op. cit.*, p. 42.   [2] *Ibid.*, p. 42.
[3] H. V. F. Somerset, *Notes on Mozart's Opera Don Giovanni*, p. 2 ; see also L. da Ponte, *Memorie* (Biblioteca di Classici, serie iv, vol. 78), pp. 175–189.

THE FOYER OF THE OPERA, PARIS

Emperor Joseph now, as it were, recognized Mozart's acknowledged supremacy in the world of opera and concert music by appointing him Composer to the Court, with an annual pension. The great musician's character, however, was declining. He lapsed into dissolute habits, though he continued his fruitful musical activity. Two operas, *La Clemenza di Tito* (*The Clemency of Titus*) and *Die Zauberflöte* (*The Magic Flute*), were produced, the first at Prague, the second at Vienna, in 1791. " With *Figaro, Don Giovanni*, and *Die Zauberflöte*, the opera of the eighteenth century attains its climax." [1] Mozart died, aged thirty-five years, on December 1, 1791, leaving the manuscript of the *Requiem* completed at his bedside. In the previous year his friend Joseph II had died, broken-hearted. The troubles of Europe, the French Revolution, rebellion in Belgium, unrest in Hungary, war in north and south, had cast their baleful influence upon Vienna. Mozart was buried, unnoticed by the public, in St Marxer Linie Cemetery, the actual site of the grave unmarked, and never subsequently ascertained. He possessed a genius for melody such as the world had never seen. " Voi che sapete " from *Figaro* and " Batti, batti " and " Là ci darem la mano " from *Don Giovanni* stay for ever in the memory of those who hear. His insight into human character, though limited in range, gives to his operas the human and sympathetic touch, which beauty of melody alone cannot command. Rich, brilliant, and vivid orchestration crowned the success of his dramatic achievement. He had known not only the primrose paths of life, but also the furnace fires; and he could express equally well these aspects of existence " in the learned and spontaneous pages of his superb, yet delicate, music." [2]

After Mozart's light went out the geographical centre of opera shifted from Vienna to Paris. France had been in revolution, but attained to internal peace and prosperity under Napoleon. Austria, on the contrary, suffered from unsuccessful war, was many times invaded, and had her capital twice

[1] W. H. Hadow, *op. cit.*, vol. v, p. 113.
[2] H. V. F. Somerset, *op. cit.*, p. 7.

occupied by Napoleon's army. It was during the second
occupation, after the battle of Wagram in 1809, that Haydn
died. Art, which has no frontiers, was recognized by the
polished and chivalrous French officers who paid the last
respects to the great Austrian maker of music by attending his
funeral.

Gluck had previously shown that Paris was a favourable
city for the development of musical talent. He was followed
by another master, Cherubini, a Florentine, who, after producing operas in Italy and England, made his home in Paris
from the year 1786. Gradually he abandoned the light Italian
style and produced works of a lofty and somewhat severe
grandeur. *Lodoiska* (1791), a brilliant, masterful work, now
seldom, if ever, performed, *Médée* (1797), and *Les deux Journées*
(1801) brought him to the height of European fame. Cherubini was not sufficiently obsequious to Napoleon to please that
master of destiny, though he consented to conduct concerts
for the Emperor in Vienna when the French occupied the
Austrian capital in 1805. Under the restored Bourbons he
became conductor at the Chapel Royal and teacher at the Con-
servatoire. Cherubini lived until 1842, having produced not
merely opera of his own, but having helped to bring forward
others to follow him, like Auber and Rossini, to maintain the
musical greatness of Paris.

The brilliant home of opera was no longer to be primarily
Vienna, but Paris. If it may be said that the creative period
of the Viennese opera attained its grand climax in *Figaro, Don
Giovanni,* and *Die Zauberflöte,* its ending came magnificently
with *Fidelio.* Ludwig van Beethoven, the most passionate and,
with Bach and Handel, the most profound of the eighteenth-
century composers, was born at Bonn in 1770. His father was
a singer in the Elector-Archbishop's choir and band. He was
educated for the profession of music, and joined the Archbishop's corps of musicians as piano accompanist in 1783, becoming second organist in 1784. He was befriended by the
cultured and kind Count Waldstein (the same who gave shelter
and work to Casanova at the end of that scapegrace's life).

The *Waldstein Sonata*, composed by Beethoven in 1805, is one of his finest works.

In 1791 Haydn, on his way back from London, broke his journey at Bonn, and was shown the score of a cantata composed by the young second organist of the Elector's chapel. Haydn was struck with the work, sent for Beethoven, and offered to take him as a pupil in composition. Beethoven consented, obtained permission to resign from his position at Bonn, and in 1792 took up his residence at Vienna, where Haydn, in his visits to the capital, carried out his promise to teach him, though in rather a desultory fashion. His compositions at Vienna were chiefly chamber music for concerts. He had the desire and ambition to compose opera, but he was a simple, stern moralist, a Puritan, to whom the frivolity and immorality of the average *libretto* were distasteful and, indeed, repulsive. At last somebody brought from Dresden the text of Paër's *Eleonora, or Conjugal Love* (*Eleonora, ossia l'amore conjugale*), which, if not a great drama, taught the good domestic virtues. It was translated into German; and all through the year 1805 Beethoven worked at a score to make an opera out of *Eleonora*; later the name was changed into *Fidelio*. It was produced in Vienna in 1806. Beethoven worked over it again and again. The final version was produced in 1814. For richness of melody and brilliance of orchestration it stands out as a grand achievement, a fitting close to that great Viennese school of which Haydn, Gluck, Mozart, and Beethoven are immortal figures, beckoning to the later, perplexed centuries to turn for relief and guidance to that mellow and melodious age.

CHAPTER XII

SCOUNDRELS

CARLYLE'S opinion that the eighteenth century was an age of shams and cheats, morally bankrupt, and therefore heading inevitably for the deluge of revolution, can be definitely challenged. Europe in that age had a very complete civilization; and in many respects a very fine one. Carlyle himself loved reading and writing about the eighteenth more than any other century. A hater of shams and cheats, he would scarcely have found rest and pleasure for his soul, as he obviously did, in returning again and again to an age of such things.

There are some bad men in the society of every age. Lazy and dissolute characters, aided by sharp wits, live at the expense of hardworking and respectable people, who are the great majority. The eighteenth-century scoundrel, not encountered more frequently, so far as can be ascertained, than the type in any century, was perhaps more picturesque. He aped his betters in polite society, and caught some of the glamour of a romantic age. The cosmopolitanism of the eighteenth century, the coming and going of strangers of all countries in spas, casinos, and coffee-houses, gave opportunities to the polite swindler, who, however, was by no means peculiar to that age. The Spanish novelists, the " Picaresque " school of the sixteenth and of the seventeenth centuries, had set the fashion of writing about rogues. For a long time the European public was served with literary fare about Dick Turpins and Moll Flanderses, about sham priests and broken-down card-sharping students. Next, the gossip of watering-places gave prominence to the achievements of a superior kind of rogue. The taste for memoir-writing completed their fame.

Scoundrelism takes various forms; the polite, educated

scoundrel is usually a man with some inclination towards virtue, which, however, he does not follow. He knows that his course of life is vicious, and, though he hopes to escape punishment, he does not think it to be unjust when, being found out, he is put in prison. The really and wholly bad man is uncommon—the man who, seeing perfectly clearly the choice between good and evil, coolly, deliberately, and after mature consideration chooses evil. Of this rare type Frederick the Great seems to be the example in the eighteenth century. A man of high intellect and of perfect self-control, fully alive to the distinction between right and wrong, conscious of the dictates of the moral law, he calmly chose to be wicked: a frankly bad man. He never even tried to persuade himself that the invasion of Silesia was just. He states quite simply in his *Histoire de mon temps* that he wanted the province and he wanted to make a name for himself. That by so doing he should destroy respect for the law of nations, inaugurate an era of European war, cause the death of many thousands, ruin the happiness of countless families, was nothing to him. He would probably keep·disaster away from himself, and save his kingdom, but if not he would shoot himself. Without religion, without scruple, without hope, looking forward ultimately to annihilation, he would annihilate himself at once if society seemed like getting the better of him. He would do as he pleased, live and die unfettered and unrestrained—*penser, vivre et mourir en roi*. That he slept on a camp-bed, rose at six in the morning, and worked hard at the business of ruling was not due to a sense of duty or to any sort of moral inclination. He had a happily tempered physique; he liked air, exercise, work, simple food. He liked efficiency. Like Bonaparte, he had a tidy mind, and the rare ability to impose tidiness on the complex feudal society round him. He had no urgings towards cruelty. He was too cynical to be intolerant. Like Bonaparte, he had no inclination to make money; if so inclined, he would have made it, with complete indifference to the means. He happened to have no passions; but if he wanted a thing he took it; if he wished to do a thing he did it. He and Bonaparte

are the complete egoists of the century, absolutely devoid of
any other-regarding quality or inclination. Frederick's self-
indulgences, always on a moderate scale, were actually infamous. Voltaire, who, though spiteful, was not a liar, hints
quite plainly at them, and no disproof seems ever to have been
attempted.

Cagliostro and Casanova were of a different type from the
great Frederick, in respect not merely of ability, but of morality.
They were sorry rogues, dissolute, self-indulgent, greedy;
merely scoundrels, desirous of living softly without having to
work hard, avoiding routine and restraint, preferring to receive
something and to give nothing, followers of evil courses, as
being more seductive, but not deliberate choosers of them—
bad enough men, but not frankly and deliberately wicked. It
is conceivable that Cagliostro or Casanova could have experienced a conversion and been turned to good ways, but Frederick
never.

Any good thing is liable to be abused. The social cosmopolitanism of the eighteenth century gave opportunities to the
cosmopolitan adventurer, just as the international finance of
the twentieth century provides opportunities for the international swindler; this kind of man appears always to be found
out, but not always soon enough to save his victims. Cagliostro had a long ' run ' before he was found out and caught.

Giuseppe Balsamo, known to history as Count Cagliostro,
was born at Palermo, in the Kingdom of Naples, in 1743. His
father soon died. The widow had to bring up a greedy, fat,
ungovernable boy. An uncle paid for his schooling, and then
sent him, at the age of thirteen, to the Convent of the Ben-
fratelli at Caltagirone, outside Palermo, to be trained as a
novice. There he was put to assist the convent apothecary,
and obtained some familiarity with the drugs in use at that
time, and with their high-sounding names. He did not, however, remain long under the discipline of the monks; he was
greedy, lazy, given to pilfering. So he was returned to his
squalid home in Palermo. Naturally he soon fell in with the
worst sort of companions among the lower orders of the city;

he was just suited to them. He had a profession, too, painting, but he found it easier to make money in other ways—carrying letters for intriguers, forging signatures, perhaps even compassing an assassination; fat and greasy, he looked simply heavy and stupid, but he was really shrewd and sly. Cheating at cards and forging bequests might pass unnoticed for a long time; robbing and poniarding, however, even on the darkest nights, is a dangerous game. Giuseppe felt the eyes of the police upon him, vanished from Palermo, and began the tour of Europe. This was, apparently, in 1769, the year in which Bonaparte, Castlereagh, and Metternich were born.

From Palermo Giuseppe found means to cross the Strait of Messina, attaching himself to a quack who called himself a Greek, Althotas, who seems to have specialized in making hemp look like silk. They drifted through Calabria, and were lost to sight in the great sink of Naples. Next he turned up in Rome, which had an easy-going *régime* under the Pope, so long as blasphemy and politics were avoided. Giuseppe lodged in an inn near the Corso, and sold his pen-and-ink drawings, which he called etchings and engravings. He made the acquaintance of a good-looking Roman girl, called Lorenza, daughter of a craftsman, a girdle-maker, and married her. For a time he and his wife lived in the father's house, for Giuseppe always managed to sponge upon somebody. The girdle-maker could not keep his daughter and son-in-law for ever; they had to go out into the great world, and start living on their wits. Lorenza and he kept together all their life—at least, all their active career. They must have been attached to each other by some sort of sentiment, though at best they seem only to have been comrades in roguery.

Taking the name of Count Cagliostro, and donning the uniform of a Prussian colonel, Giuseppe fared forth from Rome with his handsome and complaisant wife. Inevitably they worked upward to Venice, where anybody could make some money among the crowds of visitors spending freely, carelessly, blindly, at the Carnival. He was now established in his profession of parasite and minor scourge of society, ably assisted by Lorenza, who called herself Countess Seraphina, and had no scruples about inveigling wealthy youths into her company while Cagliostro cheated them of their gold. Most places only yielded a harvest once or at long intervals; for Cagliostro could not afford to become too well known. So from Venice the precious pair went over to Lombardy, and by way of Genoa to Marseilles and the south of France. Next they descended upon the Iberian peninsula and Madrid, a good place for eating, drinking, and gambling, but a little too strictly supervised by the efficient Charles III. From Madrid Cagliostro and Lorenza went on to Cadiz, and into Portugal. Lisbon had a cosmopolitan society of nobles, wine merchants, rich foreigners with weak lungs, passing voyagers to India and America. After Lisbon apparently France was traversed again, on the way to Brussels, a great capital under Austrian rule, with a governor-general, a garrison, a Court of Imperial Belgian nobles, a concourse of strangers going to Spa or Aix-la-Chapelle for the waters. From Brussels the way is open into Germany, where there were many little dynastic Courts ready to be duped with recipes of cures for this and that trouble, cures even for old age and death, for Cagliostro had a brew of the elixir of eternal youth.

In 1772 and 1776 the Cagliostros seem to have visited England, making some money, though the husband once could not escape his duns, and had to undergo a term in the King's Bench Gaol. He established good relations with the new sect called Swedenborgians, obtained an invitation into some Freemason's Lodge, and himself founded, or refounded as he said, " Egyptian Freemasonry," with cabalistic signs, high officers, rites, jargon. Money poured in, and the harvest was reaped; then back to the Continent again. In 1780 they were in St Petersburg. Nobody knew who Cagliostro was, and all sorts of nationality were imputed to him. He spoke several languages, all badly. There, on the extreme confines—or beyond—of ' Europe,' in the Court of Catherine the Great at St Petersburg, the Cagliostros had their first serious check. In Tsarist Russia, in the half-Byzantine Court, so prone (down to its latest days) to be misled by superstition, fraud, treachery, vice, Cagliostro was unveiled. A Scottish physician saw through his pretensions, his patter, and his professional style, laughed at his elixir of life and at his food of the gods. Cagliostro and his wife fled. Courland, East Prussia, Poland, Saxony—the luxurious Dresden, the cultured, wealthy Leipzig—were all visited in turn, until Strasbourg, which had a very wealthy, good-natured, and gullible archbishop, was reached. There the Cagliostros met another of their kind, the adventuress called Countess de la Motte-Valois, a genuine though very fallen descendant of the old royal line, illegitimate branch. Cagliostro was clever enough not to appear as a principal; but there seems no reason to doubt that he went deeply with La Motte into the conspiracy of the Diamond Necklace.

This affair was one of the scandals which have preceded the fall of grand dynasties. High society had become unwholesome. An Austrian physician, Friedrich Anton Mesmer, was creating a vogue in Paris for ' occultism,' hypnotism,' mesmerism.' People were gullible. The Prince-Cardinal Louis de Rohan, Archbishop of Strasbourg, was rich, vain, easy with his money. Countess de la Motte, who was simply an unprincipled adventuress, obtained access to him and intimated that the Queen Marie Antoinette would favourably receive him. The Prince-Cardinal went to Versailles. La Motte arranged a meeting on the night, probably, of July 28, 1784, in the garden of the Château, between him and ' the Queen,' impersonated by a young woman in white gown and hood, called Marie-Nicole Leguay d'Oliva. The hooded figure dropped a rose into the hands of the kneeling Cardinal, and then vanished into the night.

The next step in the conspiracy was for the Countess de la Motte to induce the Cardinal to stand surety to a jeweller for a diamond necklace (costing about £80,000) which the Queen wished to purchase, but for which, at the moment, she had not sufficient cash. A forged agreement, purporting to be signed by the Queen, containing an undertaking to purchase the necklace, was then given to him by La Motte. The Paris jeweller then delivered the necklace to the Cardinal, who

handed it over to La Motte, to be given to the Queen. La
Motte and her husband disappeared with the diamonds.

Cagliostro's part in this impudent plot was apparently, by
crystal-gazing and other prophetic means which he possessed,
to assure the Cardinal that great things were in store for him,
and to lure him on to the garden and the necklace. Whether
Cagliostro was himself the dupe of Madame de la Motte is
uncertain; in the inevitable trial it was not proved that he was
one of the conspirators. Discovery came when the jeweller,
finding that no payment for the necklace arrived on the agreed
date, sent in a demand to the royal Court. The police at once
arrested Rohan, Madame de la Motte (the husband escaped),
Mademoiselle d'Oliva, and Cagliostro. They were incarcer-
ated in the Bastille, and the whole affair was sifted before
the *parlement* of Paris. The real culprit, Madame de la Motte,
was severely punished; she was branded and imprisoned for
life, but later escaped. The Cardinal was acquitted but was
exiled to his estates. Mademoiselle d'Oliva and Cagliostro
were released. The judgment was delivered on May 31, 1786.

Cagliostro was a free man, but now too well known and
under a cloud. He set out to resume the old life with his
staunch but now rather faded Lorenza, Countess Seraphina,
as he called her. He tried England; took lodgings in Knights-
bridge, and found a few fools—among them Lord George
Gordon, of Popish Riots fame—to buy his pills and elixirs;
but not for long. Next he tried Bâle, Aix-les-Bains, Turin,
Trent in the dominions of Joseph II, finally Rome; and there
the Holy Inquisition snapped him up for practising Egyptian
magic or freemasonry, in December 1789. For over four years
he lay in prison, and died on August 26, 1795, aged fifty-two.
Donna Lorenza, or Countess Seraphina, was placed in some
convent, where the patient and kind nuns let her live out her
life.

It is very difficult to realize how Cagliostro found means to
live. For he had expensive tastes, and indulged them. He
travelled in the post-carriage, like a great lord, with full com-
plement of couriers and lackeys in grand uniforms supplied

by Paris tailors. He lodged in fine apartments. The ' physiognomist ' Lavater said that Cagliostro had a face such as was
only to be seen once in a century. He was a furious gambler
for heavy stakes, and frequently lost. He professed to take
no fees for his medical and prophetic services, and to accept
no presents; if a too-grateful client pressed a gift upon him
he gave a better one in return. He had certainly no funds of
his own, and he must, surreptitiously, have received enormous
sums, probably from foolish women whose youth he was to
renew with elixirs, and from crapulous old *roués* who also had
faith in his magic potions and Egyptian incantations. Where
one may lose two may gain; and Countess Seraphina may
have accepted gifts which the husband refused. Anyhow, they
lived, and lived well, while his old mother and his widowed
sister were found by the inquisitive Goethe (in his Italian
journey in 1787) living in a single room at the top of a wretched
stair in Palermo.

Casanova is a different kind of scoundrel from Cagliostro,
though the two crossed each other's path at least once; and
Casanova for a time practised some of the Cagliostro quackery.
He was not, however, completely worthless, for he had talent,
and was capable of sustained work, otherwise he could never
have written those twelve volumes (or six, in the more compact
edition) of memoirs. The Prince de Ligne, in his own *Mémoires*,
includes Casanova, along with Frederick the Great, Louis XV,
Potemkin, Beaumarchais, Crébillon, d'Alembert, and Hasse,
among the interesting people that he had known. Casanova's
trades were various—secretary, soldier, violinist. He earned
a living by one or other form of service; and even in the last
years of his life found a patron who gave him wages, board,
and lodging in return for his services as librarian. He was
known in every capital of Europe, and was disliked in them
all; for though he was witty and amusing he was greedy, cun-
ning, and vicious. He was very little use to anybody, but good
health, quick wits, and adaptability enabled him to pass from
city to city finding something to do in each, until sheer disgust
or some particularly bad scandal drove him out. His long life,

his keen power of observation, his innumerable sojourns, and his retentive memory make his *Mémoires* a picture of eighteenth-century Europe as seen by a disreputable man. He completed these *Mémoires* in 1797, when he was seventy-two years old, choosing the French tongue because it was more widely spread than his native Italian.

Casanova died in 1798. For years the *Mémoires* were unknown to the public. In 1820, however, a certain Frederick Guntzel, a clerk, offered to the Brockhaus publishing firm at Leipzig a manuscript in French called *The Story of My Life until 1797*. The author, Casanova, had been quite forgotten. " Like a wall, the French Revolution and the career of Napoleon lay between 1820 and the last year of the eighteenth century." [1] Examined, the manuscript was found to contain 600 folio sheets, thirty lines to a page, but the narrative only extended to 1774. Brockhaus accepted the manuscript for publication, and brought it out, at first in a German translation, in 1828.

If the great public failing of the eighteenth century was war, the great private failing was immorality towards women. Cultured high society in every country was profligate; no notable improvement is discernible before the middle of the nineteenth century. Casanova was particularly indecent; the slime trails all through his *Mémoires*, at first revolting, and soon inconceivably tedious. Yet, but for this perpetual harping upon sex, the *Mémoires* would be an exciting and varied story; and, indeed, they are an historical document of value, accurate, as far as they can be tested, and charged with the vivid life of the age.

The interest is not in Casanova's *Mémoires* as *erotica*, which sensible people find dull and nauseating. The *Mémoires* may be regarded partly as a remarkable pageant of a remarkable age; partly as a detective story—following Casanova through Italy, France, Austria, Bohemia, Holland, Spain, England, Italy. Scholars have devoted themselves to tracing his movements further by searching parish registers, police files, packets of old gazettes. Tested in small detail or obscure matters, like

[1] S. G. Endore, *Casanova: his Known and Unknown Life*, Introduction.

the distances between inns or country-houses or convents, or the names of people casually mentioned, Casanova is found to be, as a rule, accurate. His anecdotes of his own exploits may tend to exaggeration, to a 'drawing of the long bow,' though even this has not been proved. His descriptions of people and of historical events or institutions are the result of personal observation by a man whose mind was naturally scientific and accurate. His bust, which was discovered in the Château de Waldstein, has the face not of a leering satyr, but of a man of frank, open, and earnest expression. The features are firm and clean-cut. It is the face not of a Southerner, but rather like that of a vigorous Northern man, a German or Englishman, a type, however, not uncommon among the inhabitants of the North Italian hills.

Giovanni Jacopo Casanova de Seingalt was born in Venice on April 2, 1725, the son of a comedian dancer who had married the daughter of a respectable Venetian *bourgeois*. He had two brothers, who became noted painters, exercising their profession at Dresden. The father died when Jacopo was young; the mother, who had taken to the stage, had to travel about Europe; the children were brought up by their maternal grandmother. The young Casanova, after the age of nine, was boarded out at Padua (the educational centre of the Republic), and sent to school and college there. At the age of sixteen, if his account is correct, he graduated Doctor of Law. The Patriarch of Venice, Monseigneur Correr, admitted him to the four minor orders. Casanova shaved his head; but this was as far as he went towards the vocation of a clergyman. He became companion-secretary to a gluttonous Venetian senator. When the senator died Casanova, who had become notorious, even among the uncensorious public of Venice, for his licentiousness, was placed by his family in a seminary at Murano, to proceed with studies for the profession of priest. Fortunately for that profession, though he was tempted to take what seemed an easy way of gaining safety and a living, he declined to enter it. This was one of the few good resolutions of his life, for he would have been the worst possible priest. His mother, who knew the Bishop of Martirano, in South Italy, procured from him promise of employment in Rome. So Casanova, after trying and just failing to murder a man against whom he had a grudge, went off to Rome in 1743. He had only fifty sequins for the journey, and he lost all by gambling, but a good-natured, drunken, begging friar became his companion, and begged for both of them. At Rome he obtained the position of secretary to Cardinal Acquaviva. As usual, he made himself pleasant, and for a time was almost popular for his wit, his cynicism, and his boldness; but after a while the Cardinal advised him to leave. " I shall pretend I am sending you on a mission," said the Cardinal indulgently. Casanova put off the *abbé's* habit which he had been wearing, donned that of a soldier, and obtained a commission in a Venetian regiment. On May 5, 1744, according to his own account, he sailed for Corfu, where his regiment was in garrison. At Corfu he gambled away his money, and was glad of the opportunity to take six months' leave and go to Constantinople. There, he says, he met and regularly dined with the celebrated Pasha Bonneval, who had been a distinguished officer in the French Army, a general in the Austrian Army under Prince Eugène, and was now a Turkish general and a Mohammedan, old, devoted to books and to wine. The *Mémoires* describe Constantinople and its life in a lively, convincing way; but it is very doubtful if Casanova ever went there. The whole story is probably a daring lie, made up from a study of travel books in the library of Dux. After more quarrelling and gambling at Corfu, and a spell in a small island, Casopo, as a sort of Robinson Crusoe (only it was an inhabited island), Casanova returned to Venice and sold his commission. Doubtless the regiment was glad to be quit of him. He earned a miserable living by playing the fiddle, without any talent at all, in an orchestra. A chance meeting with a rich and invalid senator gave Casanova the opportunity to exercise his wits against the stupid physicians; his good sense was useful to the senator, and his fortune seemed made. A rival called Demetrio, a Greek, contrived a trap by which Casanova fell into a canal and was nearly drowned. Casanova stole a corpse from a cemetery, cut off an arm, put the arm in Demetrio's bed, and gave the Greek such a shock that he became mad. For this, and for rifling the tomb, Casanova thought it best to leave Venice. He came back, however, and during the Carnival at Venice was lucky enough to win 3000 ducats. With this money he went off in 1750 to Paris, and at a supper-party given by the celebrated actress Silvia met Crébillon the elder, the veteran dramatist of the age of Louis XIV, who was experiencing something of a popular revival. Crébillon had Casanova at his house three times a week to teach him the best French. Casanova remained in Paris for two years. With his ready adaptability, he took to spiritualism, and persuaded several silly fashionable women to regard him as an oracle. From Paris he seems to have made a trip to London, though this is not mentioned in the *Mémoires*. He certainly went to Dresden, Prague, and Vienna in 1753. The strict control of Vienna's morals under the administration of the Empress Maria Theresa irked him, and he soon returned to Venice. There he kept a casino, where he practised gambling and crystal-gazing. He says that the Abbé de Bernis, Ambassador of France to Venice, frequented his casino in disguise, and that together they used to stroll about Venice at night and amuse themselves with light suppers in a nunnery and such intrigues. Bernis left Venice in 1757 for Paris to become Foreign Minister of France and maker of the Habsburg-Bourbon alliance. In his own *Mémoires* he never mentions Casanova.

As was his way, Casanova made Venice again too hot for him. The cause of his trouble, he says, was that he read a composition of his own, an atheistical poem, in a *café*. This time he was not able to escape. One morning an officer entered his room and told him to go to the Tribunal of the Inquisition, a department of the Government in the Ducal Palace. Casanova was brought to the room of the Secretary of the Tribunal, who looked at him fixedly for a moment, then said simply, "*È quello. Mettetelo in deposito*" ("It is he. Put him in safe keeping"). He was taken away to the Piombi ('the Leads'), the garrets under the roof which served as prison-cells. He was there for months, and then, after prolonged planning and many disappointments, and much burrowing with improvised tools, cryptic messages to other prisoners, and all the devices of the stage villain, made a wonderful escape over the roofs. How lovely it was to see the stars again and to breathe the cool night air! The incident supplied Alexandre Dumas with one of his ideas for *Monte Cristo*.

Paris in 1756 was the next scene of his activities. Bernis received him in a friendly way. He was in Paris when Damiens tried to assassinate Louis XV. He persuaded the brothers Paris-Duvernay, the great bankers, to admit him into partnership in a State lottery enterprise. The rich, celebrated, and ancient Marquise d'Urfé admitted him to her magnificent house on the Quai des Théatins, with its splendid collections of books and objects of *virtu*. Casanova became a ' Rosicrucian,'[1] and helped the marquise in her investigations in alchemy and magic. She thought that he had the means of renewing her youth and turning her into a boy ; Casanova was able to work upon her delusions for a considerable time. He had some artistry, and started a factory for producing silks with beautiful printed designs ; he made some money—or, at any rate, obtained a good deal of capital from his wealthy friends. A charge of forgery was brought against him, and he says that he spent a term in prison, in Fort l'Évêque. Tireless researchers have discovered that he was not in prison, but that he fled for safety from Paris, in 1759 ; he arrived in Holland with a smart Spanish manservant. He won a good deal of money by gambling at Amsterdam, but some people blackmailed him and made him give up most of it. The chief of police induced him to move on, and Casanova set forth into Germany ; but he took with him letters of credit for 100,000 Dutch florins ; perhaps the gift or loan of a rich banker of Holland who believed in his

---

[1] The 'Hermetic' Fraternity of the Rosy Cross started in Germany probably in the fifteenth century, and existed as a secret association or number of associations for practising magic down to about 1790 or 1800. Hermes, or Mercury, was the fabled inventor of alchemy.

skill or magic. His money enabled him to figure as a fine gentleman at Cologne and Bonn; the Elector of Cologne tolerated him for a time. Then he went on to Stuttgart, where the Duke of Würtemberg kept an infamous Court, and where Casanova found and recognized the gay and extravagant riff-raff of the second-rate theatres of Europe. One night he lost a lot of money gambling when completely drunk. He was going to be made a bankrupt and perhaps forcibly enrolled in the Duke's army (and in that case might one day have found himself hired to fight for Great Britain in America); but he saved himself by flight—to Zürich. He liked the country and the open air, and went for long walks by the lakes. The open doors of the church of Einsiedeln, one of the most famous monasteries in Europe, drew him inside. Casanova entered, found a sympathetic priest, confessed his sins for three hours, and decided to be a monk. He stayed in the monastery that night, and then on the advice of the good abbot left for a few days to think over and confirm his resolve. He never returned. A little later, 1761, he was in the Free Imperial City of Augsburg as representative of the King of Portugal. Most of the year, however, he was in Switzerland, at Zürich, where again he nearly became a monk; at Lausanne, where he made many friends; at Bern, where he discussed literature with the famous scientist and man of letters Albrecht von Haller; and at Geneva, where he went several times to Voltaire's home, Les Délices. Voltaire conversed with him, and was rather ironical and almost rude; so Casanova moved on to Aix-les-Bains. He won a lot of money from an Englishman who lost with a laugh and a wave of the hand. With luck now in his favour, Casanova proceeded to Grenoble, Avignon, Marseilles, Toulon, Nice, Leghorn, Genoa, and up the Arno to Florence; after sojourning there some time he went to Rome, where his brother Giovanni (later Director of the Dresden Academy) was doing well as an artist in the company of Raphael Mengs and Winckelmann. At Rome Casanova kept a coach and a footman, was blessed by the Pope, Clement XIII, and received from His Holiness the Cross of the Order of the Golden Spur. His next place of halt was Naples, next Florence and Modena; the police made him leave the last two cities. So he went back to Paris, where his spiritualism and magic earned easy money from Madame d'Urfé. He put her through strange rites to be made young, and at the end she seemed to believe that the miracle had taken place. " I owe all my happiness to you," said the deluded sixty-year-old lady. He obtained plenty of money, and went off to England, with introductions to the Duke of Bedford, and rented a nice house in Pall Mall. After some months of gay suppers and theatre-parties he cashed a false draft at a bank and had to flee, by way of Dover and Dunkirk, to Germany. At Berlin he obtained an interview with King Frederick, and seemed to convince the great monarch that he, Casanova, was a skilful hydraulic engineer. Waiting for royal employment, he was shocked and pained by an offer from the King to give him a post as schoolmaster. So he dashed off to St Petersburg by way of Königsberg and Mittau. He had several interviews with the great Empress Catherine, and remained on, expecting employment, until he saw his departure significantly announced in the official gazette. He departed for Warsaw, was kindly received by Prince Adam Czartoryski and King Stanislaus, and spent long hours studying Polish history and politics in the great library of the Bishop of Kiev. The notes which he then made he used later in writing a *History of the Troubles of Poland.* An intrigue and a duel resulted in his having to leave Warsaw; King Stanislaus gave him a thousand ducats, glad to see the last of him.

Next Casanova went to Dresden, where his brother, the painter, was now successfully established; to Vienna, where Maria Theresa's strict administration soon made him move on, to Augsburg; then he set forth, by way of Paris, to Spain, where he decided to engage in the development of mines. He had letters of introduction to Count d'Aranda, chief Minister of Charles III. The Minister coldly told him to be on his good behaviour. Raphael Mengs was at Madrid now, as Court Painter. He did not welcome Casanova, who was soon shut up in prison, either for possessing forbidden weapons or for com-

plicity in a murder. He was released, but could not induce the
Spanish authorities to use him in their projects of mining development in the Sierra Morena. He travelled about Spain, and
was interested in the Roman ruins. At Saragossa he had a term
in prison, and began to write his *History of the Venetian Government*. From Saragossa he went to Barcelona, to the south of
France and into Italy, and wandered about Italy and Dalmatia.
He procured a pardon from the Venetian Inquisition, and
settled down in Venice, his old home. It was now the year 1774,
and he was forty-nine years old, and there the *Mémoires* end.

For over thirty years he had been a parasite, licentious,
extravagant, reckless. Now he was middle-aged and had to
earn his living. He became a spy under the Venetian Inquisition, and remained in the service for nine years. The business
of a spy was to assist the Inquisitors in preserving the morals
of Venice and extirpating scoundrelism. Casanova was, it
seems, an active and conscientious spy, and obtained some
promotion in the service, but in 1780 he was retired. He
remained at Venice, earning a living by literary work, trans-
lating Homer, contributing short poems to journals, working
for the stage, and writing a novel, which was published in 1782
under the title of *Venetian Anecdotes*. He lived poorly, but
his two brothers, the successful painters, the one at Dresden
and the other at Vienna, may have helped him. For a year
he obtained the post of secretary to the Venetian Ambassador
at Vienna, and at a dinner-party met Joseph Charles Emmanuel,
Count of Waldstein-Würtemberg, nephew of the Prince de
Ligne, and a descendant of the Wallenstein of the Thirty Years
War. Waldstein, rich, extravagant, impetuous, invited Casanova
to his castle, Dux, in Bohemia. He did not at once accept,
but stayed on in Vienna, and is mentioned in the *Mémoires*
of da Ponte (the librettist of Mozart's operas) as living there,
no one knew how, but having access to the Court and Joseph II,
advising the Emperor occasionally (or perhaps only once)
on theatrical matters. At last, in 1785, travelling by the rising
spas of Carlsbad and Teplitz, he arrived at Dux, which became
his headquarters for the rest of his life—thirteen years. The

generous and tolerant Count Waldstein paid him a salary of a thousand florins (£100) a year, with board and lodging in the castle, and gave him charge of the library. There, in lazy, tranquil days (he was not very tranquil himself, for his temper was always bad), with the echoes of fashionable Europe coming to him from Carlsbad and Teplitz, Casanova wrote his *Mémoires*.[1]

In 1798 the long, pleasant task, the tranquil occupation of some thirteen years' residence in the great nobleman's castle in Bohemia, was finished. The old voluptuary, in his seventy-third year, taking a final survey of his interesting career, writes his *apologia*. Like many people in their cool age, he sees his character as he would have liked it to be, rather than as it really was; or, rather, he sees his character as it was when at its best, in the intervals of hot-blooded activity and error.

On the brink of the grave, he makes his confession of faith: he is no atheist, like Frederick the Great; no determined agnostic, like David Hume; no devout Catholic, like Joseph de Maistre. He professes himself to be a reasonable Christian, or (to use his curious description) a " Christian fortified by the philosophy which has never spoiled anything." Like all people who are subject to moods of exaltation and dejection, he had found prayer the most steadying influence. " Despair kills; prayer causes it to disappear. When a man has prayed he feels confident and he acts." Though man is free, passion makes him a slave. He who has strength to restrain his steps until calm returns is the true sage; " but such beings are rare." The *Mémoires* may help thoughtful readers to attain this wisdom; the writer's aberrations will teach them either to take the opposite path or at least " to keep their saddle over the ditch."

Confessing that he has been the slave of his senses (for he was too cynical to have passions), he ascribes this to his temperament—full of ' humour ' in infancy, sanguineous in youth, bilious in middle age, melancholic at the end. Temperament, however, he contends, is not character. " Faults of temperament," avers this unrepentant sinner, " are incorrigible, because

---

[1] The truth and falsehood in the *Mémoires* have been skilfully elucidated by S. G. Endore, *op. cit.* See also Da Ponte, *op. cit.*, pp. 229–236.

temperament is independent of our forces. It is not so with character, which is spirit and heart [*esprit et cœur*]." Character, he holds, is mainly independent of temperament, is largely the result of education, and therefore can be corrected and reformed. Here we have the essence of the laxity of eighteenth-century morality; the men of this enlightened age sinned against the light.

Temperate in his old age, eating one meal of simple food each day, he remembers with pleasure the dishes which he enjoyed in his vigorous age, though never taken to excess: the macaroni *pâté* of a good Neapolitan cook; the *olla podrida* of the Spaniards; the Newfoundland codfish, cured and glutinous; game at the right moment, rather 'high'; and cheeses, which are perfect just when the tiny creatures produced there begin to show themselves. And then the women he had loved—he seems to feel their scent still.

Altogether, it is a better old age than he deserved. Anyhow, he faced the unknown tranquilly, writing his *Mémoires* as a pleasant occupation, without desire for profit or credit, because he would be dead before they appeared. The only thing which disturbed him was the idea, the certainty, that he would be criticized, hissed probably, after the publication of these memoirs. Their posthumous publication was not arranged to save him from this irritation; for he would never make a " compact with death," which he detested; happy or miserable, " life is the only good that man possesses." This slave of his own pleasures was not insensible to the fact that people when they should read these memoirs would say unpleasant things about him. Evidently some remains of conscience pricked him, if conscience is our realization of what a good man would say in surveying our motives and actions. It looks as if punishment for an immoral, though not a wholly discreditable, life came to him at last, perhaps, indeed, had been with him all the time; and this explains why he wrote his *Mémoires*, confessed all, and concealed nothing.

CHAPTER XIII

THE *SALON*

SALONS have existed in all the countries of Western civilization. The French *salon* is, however, particularly notable, for definite reasons. Its precise origin is known; there was a deliberate intention of continuing its tradition and succession; and it was peculiarly suitable to the spirit of educated French people, to their wit, scepticism, intellectual curiosity, love of conversation.

A *salon* is simply the drawing-room of a private house, and the company which habitually meets there. The essence of the thing is that the same men and women should find themselves together at fairly regular periods for social and cultured intercourse. They form a little ' court,' where all are equal, where there is a dominant though not insistent note of politics, art, letters, or other intellectual interest, and where the prevailing tone is given by the personality of the gifted hostess.

The first recognized *salon* was in the *hôtel* of the Marquise de Rambouillet at Paris for about fifty years in the seventeenth century, from 1610 to 1660. Fortunately it arose and established itself before Louis XIV insisted upon concentrating all the aristocracy at Versailles. More spontaneous than the Court, the *salon* maintained its prestige undimmed throughout the eighteenth century, and survived the Revolution. It was, of course, the personality of the hostess which kept a *salon* together, and, to a large extent, gave it its character. Some of the hostesses were remarkable women.

As places where men and women gathered together who had genius or talent and social inclination and refinement, the *salon* attained real importance. The object was pleasure—the pleasure that people of taste and intelligence have in each other's society. It was not an academy; nevertheless, as in the academies, so in the *salons*, men of talent, whatever their rank, were in a certain sense socially equal; also, a standard—a very high standard—of politeness and good manners was observed and became habitual.

A succession of *salons* can be recognized in France in the eighteenth century, mostly, of course, in Paris. The *salon* of the Duchesse de Maine was in the Château des Sceaux, where Voltaire in 1747 wrote *Zadig* in one day and had it performed the same evening. For over fifty years (1700–53) eminent men of letters visited at Sceaux. It was a *salon* of grand ' shows '— plays, torchlit *fêtes* in the park, pageants. The most characteristic *salons*, however, were places of conversation, such as that of the Marquise de Lambert, from 1710 to 1733, where Fontenelle, the Abbé de Saint-Pierre, d'Argenson, the President Hénault, and others met to dine and then pass the evening in talking. " If anyone wished to write," says Sainte-Beuve, " a regular history of the *salons* of the eighteenth century, it would be necessary to begin with Madame de Lambert's." [1] This was held in her house, the Hôtel de Nevers, Paris. Madame de Lambert was followed by Madame de Tencin, whose *salon* from 1726 to 1749 was frequented by the Abbé de Saint-Pierre, Montesquieu, Marivaux, the philosophic *débauché* Helvétius, and, when they were in Paris, Bolingbroke and Chesterfield. Madame Geoffrin's *salon* (1749–77) was the social centre of the Encyclopædists, who frequently came to her Wednesday dinner—the Monday dinner was for artists. Madame du Deffand's *salon* in the Rue de Beaune from 1730 to 1780 was frequented by very high society, but the Marquis d'Alembert introduced the Encyclopædists there too. Mademoiselle de Lespinasse, from 1762 to 1776, in the Rue Saint-Honoré, received d'Alembert, Turgot, Condorcet, Condillac, the Abbé Mably. Besides society people and men of letters, resident ambassadors—nearly always cultured, witty men—formed a constant part of the circles of the *salons*.

[1] *Causeries de Lundi*, vol. iv, p. 223.

The *salons* of the eighteenth century open with the Regency (1715–23), when there prevailed a greater freedom of manners and ideas. The *salon* of Madame de Lambert is grave and moral; but that of the Hôtel de Sully, attended by Chaulieu, Fontenelle, and Voltaire, is already bolder, and then come the great *salons* of the century, where literature, science, philosophy, politics, and religion are to be the object of the freest conversations and discussions. The most celebrated " Queens of the *Salons* " of the epoch were Madame de Tencin, Madame du Deffand, Mademoiselle de Lespinasse, Madame Geoffrin, Madame d'Épinay, Mademoiselle Quinault, etc. To these reunions it is necessary to add many others, held at the Maréchal de Luxembourg's, at the house of Holbach, or of Madame Helvétius, not to mention the famous suppers of the financier La Popelinière. The last *salon* of the century was that of Madame Necker, where shone the daughter of the house, Germaine Necker, the future Baroness de Staël.[1]

The *salons* and the *Encyclopædia* were the two great fields, the refuges and supports, for *philosophes*. It must not be thought, however, that the *salons* were all or always serious. Some, and even the best, were attended at times simply for amusement; quite justifiably, for rational amusement is a necessary element of life. The distinguishing mark of the *salon* was that feminine society was the outstanding feature in it. Therefore it differed completely from the clubs (chiefly in coffee-houses)—exclusively of men—which were so prominent in English urban life of the eighteenth century. The *salons* were not given to drinking alcohol, and the manners observed were always refined. It is true that Dr Johnson said after his visit to Paris: " The French are an indelicate people; they will spit upon any place. At Madame du Bocage's, a literary lady of rank, the footman took the sugar in his fingers, and threw it into my coffee. I was going to put it aside; but hearing it was made on purpose for me, I e'en tasted Tom's fingers. The same lady would needs make tea *à l'Angloise*. The spout of the tea-pot did not pour freely; she bade the footman blow into it." In spite of this anecdote (the truth of which is confirmed from another

[1] *Nouveau Larousse, s.v. "* Salon."

source)[1] the fact remains that French society was, in the broad view, the most refined in Europe in the eighteenth century, and its example did much to raise the standard elsewhere. Joseph Addison wrote, in the early part of the century, " I do not doubt but England is at present as polite a nation as any in the world."[2] But most people would give the palm for manners to the French.

In the Louvre there is a picture by Ollivier, *Le Thé à l'Anglaise chez la Princesse de Conti*, 1766. It depicts a lofty panelled drawing-room, with windows reaching from ceiling to floor, a painted portrait at the head of two of the panels, some beautiful, simple baroque ornamentation; little furniture, but ample, carpeted floor space; two small dogs. The ladies and gentlemen are seated at two tables, the ladies in full-bodied flowing silk dresses, the men in blue or red brocaded coats down to the knees, white silk stockings, buckled shoes. A few of the men are standing in conversation. One is playing the guitar to the accompaniment of another, who is sitting at the clavier-piano; another is following the music on the score, his 'cello resting unused on the floor beside him. The younger ladies are handing round plates of cakes. The princess is pouring out tea at one table. At another table are cold meats, and a domestic is offering a guest a glass of wine from a flagon ; there is no smoking.[3]

Some *salons* are said to have been merely frivolous, given up to gossip. Others, like Madame Geoffrin's, in the Rue Saint-Honoré, were either artistic or literary: Mondays artistic, Wednesdays literary. On Mondays Boucher, Vernet, La Tour, Bouchardon, might be found there; on Wednesdays Fontenelle, Marivaux, d'Alembert, Voltaire, Montesquieu, Marmontel. If politics or religion were broached Madame Geoffrin would calmly interrupt with, "*Voilà qui est bien*," and divert the conversation to her chosen channel. Madame Geoffrin

---

[1] See Boswell's *Johnson*, edition of Croker (1816), *sub anno* 1775, and note 1, p. 467.
[2] *Spectator*, March 10, 1711.
[3] The picture is reproduced in Bédier et Hazard, *Histoire de la littérature française, illustrée*, vol. ii, p. 92.

was an excellent rich *bourgeoise* who at the age of fourteen had made a happy marriage with a man of forty-eight. She held her *salon* from the year 1749 almost to her death, in 1791. Madame du Deffand's *salon* near the Sainte-Chapelle was philosophic; indeed, her insatiable curiosity extended to all subjects, so that in her circle thought and speech were free. She was a keen critic, who knew talent when she met it. Among the frequenters of her house was the brilliant and ironic Horace Walpole, upon whom she lavished the last friendship of her long life, a friendship of which it has been said, " its enduring quality, its half-fierce, half-wistful intensity, invest it with a queer pathos and raise it above the level of a mere infatuation." She died in 1780. The philosophic tradition in the *salon* was maintained by Mademoiselle de Lespinasse near the Convent of St Joseph, and by Madame Helvétius in the Rue Sainte-Anne; Diderot, Raynal, Turgot, Condorcet, Grimm, were regular visitors. Madame de Lespinasse's *salon* has been called " the laboratory of the *Encyclopædia* "; that of Madame Helvétius *les États Généraux de l'esprit humain*.[1]

Dinner was served in some houses as early as one o'clock or half-past one (this was Mademoiselle de Lespinasse's hour) or as late as four-thirty (the hour adopted by Madame Necker). The *salon* proper, however, was not the dinner-party, but rather the afternoon or evening reception. Mademoiselle de Lespinasse's reception in the Rue Saint-Honoré was in the evening, from five to nine o'clock. It might be said that all distinguished persons, residents in Paris or visitors to it (like David Hume or Lord Shelburne), would be found there. Marmontel, the critic, the author of *Contes Moraux*, writes in his *Mémoires*:[2]

> I do not reckon among my particular societies the assembly which took place in the evening at Mademoiselle de Lespinasse's: because, with the exception of some friends of d'Alembert, such as the Chevalier de Chastellux, the Abbé Morellet, Saint-Lambert, and myself, this circle was formed of people who were not connected with each other. She had chosen them here and there in

---

[1] Bédier et Hazard, *op. cit.*, vol. ii, p. 93.
[2] *Mémoires de Marmontel* (1891), vol. ii, pp. 229 ff.

MADAME LA MARQUISE DU DEFFAND

218

society, but so well assorted that, when they were there, they
were found to be in harmony, like the cords of a musical instrument played by a clever hand. Pursuing this comparison, I
would say that she played on this instrument with an art which
amounted to genius; she seemed to know what sound the cord
which she was going to touch would give. I mean that our minds
and characters were so well known to her that, to start them into
play, she had only to say a single word. Nowhere was the conversation more lively, or more brilliant, or better conducted than
at her house. The moderate and always equable temperature at
which she managed to keep it, either by checking it or by stimulating it alternately, was a rare achievement. Her unquenchable
enthusiasm communicated itself to our minds, but without excess; her imagination was the motive force, but her reason held
it in check. Moreover, it must be observed that the minds which
she kindled at her pleasure were neither weak nor light; men like
Condillac and Turgot were among the number; d'Alembert was
like a simple and docile child when with her. Her talent for
throwing out an idea and provoking discussion among men of
this class; her talent for discussing it with as much precision and
even eloquence as they; her talent for introducing new ideas
and varying the discourse always with the ease and skill of a fairy
who with a simple wave of her wand changes at pleasure the
scene of her enchantments; such talent, I repeat, was not that
of an ordinary woman. The follies of fashion and vanity were
not the subjects by which she made herself interesting to a circle
of highly intellectual people day after day during four hours of
conversation without sign of fatigue and without a break. It is
true that one of her charms was her enthusiastic disposition,
which impassioned her language, and which added to her opinions
the warmth, the interest, and the eloquence of feeling. Sometimes,
nay, very often, at her parties reason yielded to mirth; a mild
philosophy allowed itself then to become light banter: d'Alembert
set the example, and who knew better than he " how to mingle
the grave with the gay and jest with earnest "?

When M. Necker had grown rich with his bank, and was
becoming influential with the Government, he moved his
Paris home from the Marais, Rue Michel le Comte, to the
more fashionable and more airy Rue de Cléry, to a vast *hôtel*,

which once belonged to Claude Leblanc, Secretary of State for the Department of War. Madame Necker chose Fridays for her *salon*, so as not to compete with the Wednesdays of Madame Geoffrin, the Thursdays of Madame Helvétius, the Tuesdays and Sundays of Baron Holbach.

Madame Necker's Fridays were particularly attended by men of letters and philosophers; for somewhat more *mondain* people she had a Tuesday *salon*, with a rather more intimate character. Sometimes her evenings began with dinner, at four o'clock, sometimes with supper, for selected guests; the reception began after the meal. Madame Necker gave every guest a warm welcome; her manner was almost too warm, in contrast to M. Necker's, which was proud and somewhat cold. In summer the *salon* was continued at the Château de Saint-Ouen, on the banks of the Seine, just outside Paris. Madame Necker would send her carriage to fetch her guests from town. "The evening passed away in agreeable conversation under the great trees on the terrace; and the guests who did not wish to stay overnight were driven back to Paris."[1]

Count Haussonville, in his book on *Le Salon de Madame Necker*, based on materials drawn from the archives of Coppet,[2] gives a fragment of the conversation from the first Friday dinner-party. The guests were Bernard, a minor poet; Suard, a man of learning, member of the Academy; Thomas, an "honest man of letters, without any genius"; the celebrated Abbé Morellet; and Marmontel. Afterwards Madame Necker jotted down her impressions of the conversation, which, as in nearly all such renderings, was much more lively when it occurred than it appears to be in the written notes:[3]

M. BERNARD. You look wonderfully well, madame; your complexion is fresher than these flowers.

MADAME NECKER. Poets are full of gallantries—flatterers.

M. BERNARD. Call them rather impressionable, sensitive.

[1] Claude Haussonville, *Le Salon de Mme Necker* (1900), vol. i, pp. 125-126.

[2] The Swiss village where the Neckers found a refuge during the Revolution; Necker purchased an estate there in 1784.

[3] Claude Haussonville, *op. cit.*, vol. i, p. 127. I am indebted to Messrs Calmann-Lévy, publishers, Paris, for permission to quote from this work.

MADAME NECKER. One can combine these two qualities; but I am very much afraid they get lost in one another; in truth, the Abbé makes me despair; for an hour he has been fuming against women, and these gentlemen urge him on and applaud him.

THE ABBÉ MORELLET. Yes, madame, I uphold that women have not a shadow of good sense, and I should have convinced you if you had deigned to listen to me, but it is impossible to reason with you, and you prove our thesis wonderfully. What do you say to that, M. Necker?

M. NECKER [*abstractedly*]. Many thanks, sir, I won't have any more.

MADAME NECKER. Madame Riccoboni, for example, excels in her own style.

M. SUARD. But *has* she a style, in the first place?

MADAME NECKER. To write with warmth, with grace, and to interest her readers is to have style.

M. SUARD. To write! I don't know what writing is; she arranges her sentences pretty well without imagination and without ideas.

MADAME NECKER. Oh, sir! You exaggerate.

M. SUARD. I don't know what you mean by exaggeration; to exaggerate is a word which has no meaning; no one exaggerates; one expresses one's thought, and that is all.

MADAME NECKER. I never agree with M. Suard, not even about the weather; for if I say it is raining he does not know what rain is.

M. SUARD. Ah, dear lady, you are making merry! But, now I think of it, M. Thomas seems to be remaining neutral; that is not well.

M. THOMAS. I confess, sir, that women may lack that divine fire which animates us, that noble enthusiasm which prolongs our nightly studies and makes them penetrate into the most distant past; but if they do not rise with us to the skies, they embellish the earth; a good woman is the most beautiful sight for a sensitive soul.

M. MARMONTEL. Good! Capital, my dear Thomas; if you really wish to carry those with you to the skies and leave the others to grovel with us on the earth.

M. BERNARD. Fie, sir! You speak like a heathen—you forget that you are in the sanctuary.

Marmontel, Grimm, Diderot, and Naigeon (a devoted friend of Diderot) were regular frequenters of the *salon*. Another fragment from the Coppet archives shows how Madame Necker tactfully and decisively directed the conversation: [1]

NAIGEON. Fancies! Errors! Prejudices!

MADAME NECKER [*without listening to M. Naigeon*]. M. Diderot, let us renew a conversation which interests me and makes my existence more supportable. Did you not tell me that it was possible to explain thought by the succession of sensations?

NAIGEON. Yes, certainly, with the greatest clearness. Ah, without doubt!

DIDEROT. All nature is nothing but a series of progressive sensations; the stone feels, but very feebly; the plant feels more than the stone, the oyster more than the plant, and so on till I reach man. Weak sensations leave no trace of themselves behind. The light impress of my finger on a hard body could not be preserved, but stronger sensations do actually produce a remembrance—remembrance which is nothing other than thought, or, if you prefer it, a durable impression. Matter alone, therefore, suffices for the explanation of all these phenomena, and if matter is susceptible to sensation it is also susceptible to thought.

MADAME NECKER. Granted that ideas come to us through the senses. What shall we conclude from that? [*She vigorously refutes Diderot's argument by opposing to it the unity of the being who receives the tribute of our senses and the variety of our sensations.*] I consider myself to be a unity, and the centre of these ideas, such as it is, is certainly indivisible.

DIDEROT. It is a sense which gathers together all the other senses.

MADAME NECKER. What is the nature of the sense which contains abstract things, which is tormented by metaphysical considerations, for which nothingness is something, since it distinguishes it from existence; this sense which reacts on itself, which is formed from new thoughts, and which, in spite of the millions of objects which it represents, which it comprises, and on which it exercises itself, remains always one and indivisible? What are the operations of matter which resemble these mira-

[1] Claude Haussonville, *op. cit.*, vol. i, p. 166.

culous acts of the soul? Ah, M. Diderot, let us confess our ignorance! The more our ideas about these matters multiply, the more am I persuaded that God has treated these metaphysicians as He did the architects of Babel, who wanted to mount to the sky in spite of their littleness. He granted them the gift of languages only that He might confound them with the multiplicity of words and prevent them from understanding each other.

Madame Necker's brilliant daughter, Germaine, growing up in the stimulating, romantic, and intellectual environment of Coppet, Saint-Ouen, and of the *hôtel* of the Contrôle Général in the Rue Neuve des Petits Champs and of the Rue Bergère (whither the family removed after Necker left the Contrôle Général in 1781), gradually came to take a more and more leading part in the mother's *salon*, until she herself became its centre. In 1786 Germaine married the Baron de Staël-Holstein, Ambassador of Sweden at Paris; but although she and her husband lived in their own *hôtel*, the Swedish Embassy in the Rue du Bac, Madame de Staël continued to be the chief figure in the Necker *salon*, which with her retained more than all its former brilliance down to 1790, when after Necker's second Ministry the family left Paris for Coppet.

Madame de Staël, after her mother's death, continued, as it were, her mother's *salon* at Coppet, the charming country-house on the Lake of Geneva. Sainte-Beuve describes the society there:

The life at Coppet was "*château* life." There were often as many as thirty people there, strangers and friends; the most frequent visitors were Benjamin Constant, M. August Wilhelm von Schlegel, M. de Sabran, M. de Sismondi, M. de Bonstetten, the Barons de Voght, de Balk, etc. Every year brought back there once or oftener M. Matthieu de Montmorency, M. Prosper de Barante, Prince August of Prussia, the celebrated beauty designated at the moment by Madame de Genlis under the name of Athénais; a crowd of fashionable people, of acquaintances of Germany or of Geneva.

The philosophical and literary conversations, always witty or lofty, began about eleven o'clock in the morning at the breakfast-table. They were resumed at dinner, and during the interval between dinner and supper, which took place at eleven o'clock in the evening; and again afterwards, often beyond midnight. Benjamin Constant and Madame de Staël above all took the lead. We, younger people, had scarcely ever seen Benjamin Constant otherwise than bored, departing from his too-inveterate raillery with enthusiasm which was a little forced, a conversationalist who was always prodigiously lively, but whose spirit, in turn, had inherited all the other most powerful faculties and passions. It was at Coppet that he displayed with fire and naturalness what Madame de Staël without equivocation proclaimed *the most eminent living intelligence*. He was certainly the greatest of the distinguished men. His mind and Madame de Staël's at any rate always were in harmony; therefore they were sure of understanding one another. Nothing, according to witnesses, was so dazzling and remarkable as their conversation when they engaged in this chosen circle, these two holding the magic racquets of the discussion, and sending back to each other, for hours at a time, without ever missing, the ball of a thousand related thoughts. But one need not believe that people were at all sentimental or solemn there; often they were just gay; Corinne had some frivolous days, when she resembled the Signora Fantastici. They often played at Coppet tragedies, dramas, or the Chivalry-pieces of Voltaire, *Zaïre*, *Tancrède*, so much preferred by Madame de Staël, or pieces composed for the purpose by her or by her friends. These last were sometimes printed at Paris, in order that the parts might then more easily be learned. The interest which was taken in these dispatches to Paris was lively; and if in the meantime important corrections were thought of, a messenger was quickly sent off, and, in certain circumstances, a second one to catch up or alter the correction which was already on its way. European poetry was present at Coppet in the person of several famous representatives.[1]

The *salon*, properly speaking, never came into existence in Germany. The characteristic social medium of wit and intellect was the *table d'hôte* in a tavern or coffee-house or, more generally, in the house of some good woman of the *bourgeoisie* who kept the table. Such *tables d'hôte* existed in every university

[1] Sainte-Beuve, *Portraits de Femmes* (1845), pp. 145–147.

town. The same young men, students, unmarried lawyers, and business men, would take their midday or evening meal regularly at the same house, and naturally often formed stimulating and lasting friendships. Goethe has described his *table d'hôte* at Leipzig in the " Bombshell " (*Feuerkugel*) Tavern, between the Old and the New Market, when he attended the university there in 1765–68. There, curiously enough (for Leipzig was the literary centre of Germany at that time), his friends were mainly medical men and botanists, who agreeably stimulated his lifelong scientific interests.

Literature, however, was not ignored. " I spent the dinner-hours with my friends cheerfully and profitably," writes Goethe. "During this intercourse I perceived through conversation, through examples, and through my own reflections, that the first step in delivering ourselves from the wishy-washy, long-winded, empty epoch could be taken only by definiteness, precision, and brevity." He proceeds to analyse the literary qualities of Lessing, Ramler, Wieland, Klopstock; evidently such discussions formed the subject of the *table d'hôte* conversation.

At his *table d'hôte* in Strasbourg, when Goethe went to the university there in 1770–71, the senior member of his circle was another medical man, Dr Salzmann, over fifty years old, whose strong character, high philosophy, and piety greatly impressed everybody. " He had attended the dinner-table for many years, and maintained its good order and respectability." There also Goethe met and learned to love Jung Stilling, charcoal-burner, tailor, schoolmaster, private tutor, and now medical student at the university. Jung Stilling was a man of " simple and mystical piety." Goethe later published Stilling's *Autobiography* at his own expense and for the benefit of his friend. A temporary visitor at the Strasbourg *table d'hôte* was Johann Gottfried Herder, Kant's most famous student, and, after Lessing, Germany's greatest literary critic.

All this *table d'hôte* society, however, did not make a *salon*; nor did the parties of students and other scholars who met and still meet in the houses of kindly and hospitable professors on certain evenings every month. The essence of the *salon* is its consistent aim at the exercise of wit and intellect, and its continuous tradition. At Weimar, in the great time of Goethe and Duke Carl August, from 1775 to 1828, Goethe's circle in the *Gartenhaus* (the beautiful residence presented to him by Carl August) was almost a *salon*, except that there was no lady of the drawing-room. Frau von Stein, whom Goethe loved at Weimar until he broke away on his Italian journey, had an intellectual circle.

Berlin had no *salon* until the eighteenth century had ended. Then Bettina von Arnim, once Goethe's friend and correspondent, wife of the poet-novelist Achim von Arnim, had a home for men of letters and enlightenment; and Rachel, wife of Varnhagen von Ense, for years entertained the literary society of the " Liberation " period and tradition.

It would be foolish to claim for the French gentry a monopoly of the art of conversation or of polite and agreeable reception. In various town and country houses, and at various times, *coteries* or circles have been formed round some celebrated and talented hostess. The French *salon*, however, and particularly in the eighteenth century, was the most perfect thing of its kind, because it expressed two French characteristics—tradition and a standard. The *salon* was traditional; it went on from generation to generation, with recognized leaders, with an almost continuous existence. It maintained a standard; the persons who attended were intellectual, and were people of taste. They were interested in the things of the mind and spirit; they knew what wit and talent were. They conversed with liveliness, but not with frivolity; and bores were not tolerated. Within its magic circle it was democratic. It was seldom political; taste, letters, philosophy, were its predominant interests. Intellectual conversation in congenial company, a quiet repast among friends, " the sincere love of letters and the innocent charm of the Muses," are among the simpler and more lasting joys of life. The *salon*, as an almost permanent institution, dispensing these good things with a traditional distinction, is one of the characteristic features of a sociable age which knew the *douceur de vivre*.

CHAPTER XIV

SCHOOLS

UNIVERSITY education in the eighteenth century was not very different from university education before or since. Dealing, as it does, with young men who attend the university voluntarily, and not, as at school, by compulsion, and being concerned with the higher studies, it necessarily leaves them much time to themselves. University instruction is a loose and elastic system, much the same in every age; what differs from time to time, and from place to place, is the spirit in which the teachers and students do their work.

The case of school education is quite otherwise. Unlike universities, schools have carefully to organize every moment. Pupils of tender age require constant supervision; their time has to be filled up, otherwise they will learn very little. The method of conducting schools, of occupying the pupils' time, and leading them onward through various studies, and of training their minds, has varied greatly from age to age.

In the seventeenth century the great international order, the Society of Jesus, assumed responsibility for most of the education in the Roman Catholic countries of Europe. The Society did not itself maintain all the schools which it managed. In many cases benefactors, princes, nobles, or wealthy burghers, would found a school, and make it over to the Jesuits to conduct it. The Society would accept responsibility for a school only if given complete control of it, the right to appoint all the masters, to admit pupils, to determine the curriculum and discipline. Many of the schools thus undertaken by the Society of Jesus had boarders and day pupils. A charge was made for the maintenance of the boarders, but the teaching was gratuitous; therefore the day pupils paid nothing. As the Society was both a religious and an international order, Latin was commonly taught, and even formed the general means of communication in teaching the sciences and history. The teachers were very carefully chosen out of the best students of the Order, and they provided their pupils with a very thorough education, with, however, a tendency distinctly towards submission to authority, repression of the individual will, rather than towards initiative, self-confidence, curiosity. For this reason, in the eighteenth century, the Age of Reason and Enlightenment, the reputation of the Jesuit schools declined; and the Protestant schools, which welcomed the growing tendency towards philosophic speculation and scientific investigation, drew ahead and supplanted the Jesuits as the great educators of Europe. With the suppression of the Jesuit Order in 1773 its teaching activities came to an end, until the Order was re-established in the early nineteenth century. The Jesuits' schools were good and inexpensive. Their saying is well known: " Give me the child, and I care not who has the man." They had developed a system of instruction out of the medieval curriculum, and they taught grammar, rhetoric, mathematics, and cognate ' disciplines' with great success. Most of the great men of Roman Catholic countries were educated at Jesuit schools, including Pascal, the most outstanding antagonist of the Order, and Voltaire, the sceptic of sceptics. After the fall of the Order its schools were for the most part taken over by the central or local government authorities.

In Protestant countries ' secondary' school education (as distinct from ' elementary') was provided in town high schools (called *Gymnasien* in Germany), maintained either by the civic authorities or by charitable funds. Some churches maintained schools out of their funded property; the well-known Thomas Schule at Leipzig was a church school. Schulpforte, a boarding-school of the type of an English ' public' school, was at the charges of the Treasury of Electoral Saxony. There was a similar boarding-school at Halle, part of the magnificent Francke foundation.[1]

The Halle Pädagogium, established by Francke in 1698, was a boarding-school, much favoured by the sons of the Prussian and other North German aristocracies. It used the German tongue more than did the old seventeenth-century schools, and it taught modern languages and the sciences.[2] In the reign of Frederick II, whose accession in 1740 inaugurated the age of enlightenment, the study of Greek classics was introduced or greatly increased in all the Prussian secondary schools, or *Gymnasien*. This was partly due to Baron von Zeidlitz, Frederick's Minister of Public Instruction, and to the " Neo-Humanism " of Winckelmann, the interpreter of Greek sculpture to Germany in the eighteenth century, and to Goethe. Nevertheless, the Greek and Latin classics did not dominate German education. A school for ' modern subjects,' as we should say—what the Germans call a *Realschule*—was established at Berlin in 1747; its full title was *œkonomisch-mathematische Realschule*. This school, in the Kochstrasse, still flourishes, along with others in every district and city. Every German city had one or more good high schools. The ambition of the well-to-do parents to have their sons taught French (the fashionable language in the eighteenth century) led to the employment of many French tutors, and also to the establishing of a good number of private boarding-schools. Goethe's father helped to set up his valet-secretary, called Pfeil, probably an Alsatian, who spoke French well, as the master of a private boarding-school or ' academy ' in Frankfort; but Goethe himself was sent to the *Gymnasium* in the old cloisters once occupied by the Barefoot Friars.[3]

Elementary education was conducted by tutors in well-to-do families; poorer people were taught in the charitable schools of the cities. In villages the schoolmaster was often a retired

[1] See below, p. 278.
[2] Prince Bülow, German Chancellor from 1901 to 1909, was a schoolboy at the Halle Pädagogium; see *Denkwürdigkeiten*, Chapter VI.
[3] *Dichtung und Wahrheit*, Book IV.

soldier, a non-commissioned officer who had kept the regimental accounts, and had perhaps been employed occasionally in teaching recruits, for Frederick the Great, at any rate, seems to have had some regimental schoolmasters in his army. It is surprising how many poor boys obtained a respectable education in the eighteenth century. Except, however, in rich families which could afford tutors, there seems to have been no provision for the education of girls. Protestant parents sometimes taught their children, sons and daughters, to read the Bible, so that Luther may be considered the great educator of Protestant Germany and of German Switzerland.

The *lycées* and the *Gymnasien* have always had a fairly heavy curriculum. In order to equip the pupils for life, and to bring them abreast of modern knowledge, the high schools have imposed upon them a reasonably heavy load of learning. The results in the eighteenth century were like the results now, not particularly striking, though not by any means wholly disappointing. They were, however, not sufficiently brilliant to satisfy the idealists who believed in the perfectibility of the human race. Rousseau, never a systematic thinker, but a man whose ideas were always interesting, considered that children's minds were really being confused by having too much put upon them and too early. The result, according to his view, was that they just gave up trying to understand. Rousseau's cure for this, as explained in his novel *Émile* (1762), was that children should not be put to school until they were twelve or thirteen. " Plants are fashioned by culture, and men by education," he wrote. " This education comes from nature, from men, or from things. The internal development of our faculties and our organs is the education from nature; the use which we are taught to make of this development is the education from men; and the acquisition of our own experience of objects is the education from things." Rousseau did not try to pursue these three methods in his system, but considered that they are combined in " domestic education or that of nature." This must be education of a general kind, fitting the youth for any place in society; for Europe in the eighteenth century was not like ancient Egypt, where the son automatically stepped into the office or craft of his father. " Among us, where the ranks alone remain, and the individuals in them ceaselessly change, nobody knows, in raising his son for his own position, whether he is not working against the youth's interest. . . . In the natural order of things, men being all equal, their common vocation is the condition of man; and whoever is well educated for that will not badly fulfil any other to which he is called." Neither in Rousseau's time nor later did Europe adopt his plan of keeping the child from school until he is twelve or thirteen. It is felt, as Madame de Staël wrote in criticism, that if school education were deferred until that age some six or seven precious years would have been lost; and that, on arriving at the late school age, the children would have grown up without the inclination and capacity to study and to attend. Madame de Staël, having spent all of her time before the French Revolution in her mother's *salon* at Paris, where every subject of liberal conversation was discussed, or in Switzerland, where new methods of education were being judiciously applied, advocated the system of Pestalozzi as the most helpful line of educational advance.[1]

The German Rousseau was Johann Bernard Basedow. This man was a product of enlightenment and nature. Big, clumsy, ill-dressed, exuberant; continually smoking, and filling the air around him with particularly foul tobacco-smoke; boisterous, excitable, quarrelsome—he was not welcome everywhere, and not anywhere for long; and as a schoolmaster he was no striking success. Yet his influence on German education, and, indeed, on education throughout all Central Europe, was decided and beneficial.

Basedow was born in 1723 at Hamburg, the son of a peruke-maker. In 1753 he became a teacher at Sorö, in Seeland, at the Ritter-Akademie there, one of the schools of polite instruction for young nobles which arose in Germany in the last half of the seventeenth century. Later he was teacher in a

---

[1] Madame de Staël's views on education are in Chapter XIX of *De l'Allemagne*.

Gymnasium at Altona, near Hamburg, and was expelled in 1761 because of his heterodox opinions (the doctrine of the Trinity was his ' pet aversion ').[1] In 1762, after reading *Émile*, he determined to work for the reform of education according to nature. His book *Elementarwerk* was published in magnificent style, having been generously subscribed by nobles and reigning princes. It is a " utilitarian and encyclopædic " work, with numerous and fine illustrations, and is a selection from all branches of learning for the use of young scholars. In 1777, with the help of his enlightened and highly born patrons, he established his school, the Philanthropinum, at Dessau. School life was to be natural and happy. Learning was to be playing, or as amusing and interesting as playing; for instance, French and Latin were used by the pupils when playing games, and later teaching of the sciences was carried out in these tongues. Learning was to be not merely pleasant, and natural; it was also to be strictly useful. Unfortunately Basedow was quarrelsome; he has even been called incompetent.[2] He had to leave Dessau, and died in 1790. The Philanthropinum came to an end in 1793. It is doubtful whether the school had ever been conducted on right lines; probably it lacked thoroughness and discipline. Metternich, an able but rather superficial man, says in his *Mémoires* that he was brought up in Basedow's " easy and amusing " system. His tutor, Friedrich Simon, had been a teacher in the Dessau Philanthropinum.

Basedow was one of the men who early recognized Goethe's genius. In 1774 the two ardent men, one young, the other middle-aged (Goethe was twenty-five, Basedow fifty-one), spent a summer holiday on the Rhine and the Lahn, chiefly at Ems and Coblenz. Goethe at this time of his life was full of high spirits, something of a madcap, brilliant, witty, reckless. Basedow was turbulent, shouting forth his educational theories, his religious heresies, his beliefs in nature and mankind. He travelled with a secretary, to whom he dictated his educational essays at unexpected moments, for his practice was never to go

[1] P. Hume Brown, *The Life of Goethe* (1920), vol. i, p. 168.
[2] F. Paulson, *German Education* (1908), p. 135.

to bed, and, it appears, seldom if ever to take off his clothes. Along with Basedow and Goethe for part of the time on this holiday was the saintly ' physiognomist ' of Zürich, Johann Kaspar Lavater. Goethe's classical humanism, Basedow's naturalism, Lavater's scientific (or half-scientific) theories of the connexion between physiognomy and character, made of that summer holiday a stimulating, if somewhat disturbing, element in the cultural homes of the rich Rhineland *bourgeoisie*.

Pestalozzi's school or schools (he had several, one after the other, and never succeeded in establishing any one permanently) attracted much attention all over that small eighteenth-century ' Europe ' where all literary people knew each other, discussed the latest thing, and exchanged views. His ' system,' after all, was simple enough ; he was doing what all the teachers of the *lycées* and *Gymnasien* were equally trying to do ; but Pestalozzi had started fresh, thinking out his method for himself, outside the traditional system and routine of the existing high schools. His method was to instruct the pupils very gradually, by carefully adapted stages, so that the pupils should arrive without fatigue and without perplexity at advanced results. Sympathetic, patient, thoughtful, in many respects childlike himself, Pestalozzi merely applied a better child psychology to his teaching than did the traditional schools. He was a private schoolmaster, in charge of his own school, and therefore had the advantage of not being involved in an already developed and established system. Madame de Staël wrote :

What tires children is to make them leap the intermediaries, to make them advance without knowing what they believe they have already learned. This fills their head with a sort of confusion which makes all examination repellent, and inspires them with an invincible dislike for work. There are none of these inconveniences with Pestalozzi. The children have pleasure in their studies ; not that it is play to them, for that only puts *ennui* into pleasure and frivolity into study ; but because from early years they experience the pleasure of educated men—the pleasure of knowing, understanding, and of going to the end of the tasks which they are set. The method of Pestalozzi, like all that is truly good, is not an entirely new discovery, but an enlightened and persevering application of truths already known. Patience, observation, the philosophic study of the processes of the human mind, have made him realize what is elementary in thoughts and what follows naturally in their development. He has pushed further than anyone else the theory and practice of graduation in teaching. His method has been applied with success to grammar, geography, and music.

Such was the primary virtue of the Pestalozzi system; other noticeable characteristics were that it was practised—in theory, at any rate—in his school without the use of punishments or rewards (as a matter of fact, he did use corporal punishment, but always shook hands afterwards); and that charges were low, so that the common people could afford to have their sons educated. Pestalozzi's complete loyalty to his ideal, his obvious genuineness and simplicity of spirit, attracted and kept round him a corps of teachers who laboured with disinterested devotion for the good of their pupils. Fichte, the patriotic German philosopher, said that he looked for the regeneration of the German nation from the institute of Pestalozzi. When, after the disaster and downfall of the old Prussian state at Jena, Stein and his far-seeing colleagues were working at their great reforms the Prussian Government sent seventeen persons to Yverdon to study Pestalozzi's method.

Johann Heinrich Pestalozzi was born at Zürich on January 12, 1745, of an old Protestant family. He lost his father early, and was brought up partly by women and partly by an uncle who was a Protestant pastor at Höngg, in charming country, three miles from Zürich. Throughout his life Pestalozzi was deeply religious; he was a true Christian.

Zürich in the eighteenth century had an academy or university. In the middle of the century Wolff, Professor of Philosophy there, had aroused enthusiasm for a 'return to nature,' for simplicity of manners, and for a 'renewing' of German literature—for Zürich was a German-speaking town. Pestalozzi, a student in the Academy, felt the call of this early 'romantic movement,' and was further inspired by Johann Jakob Bodmer, Professor of History and Politics, who upheld the ideals of freedom, justice, liberty, limitation of wants, the simple joys of the domestic hearth. Thus was the ' decadence ' of the age to be checked. Lavater, who was a pastor at Zürich, was a friend of Pestalozzi.

In 1768 Pestalozzi set up in business as a market-gardener at Neuhof, on the plain of Birr, built a house, married, and had a family. After seven years he was making no success of the business. It was then that Pestalozzi converted his house and land into a school for poor children, about thirty, between the ages of four and nineteen. The children worked in the field as well as in the classroom, and so were to earn the means for the upkeep of the school. They were to be brought up ' according to nature,' in liberty regulated by the teacher's wisdom; they were to be taught to feel in their heart the reality of God; their instruction was to be physical and moral, as well as intellectual; and training in agriculture and some kinds of industrial craftsmanship was to be supplied. As the poor pupils earned their ' keep,' the school was not a charity. Pestalozzi was against the benevolent institutions which " gave a poor man a loaf which he had not earned." Such was the Neuhof experiment. It was successful in the sense that the children increased in weight and in mental capacity and took on a cheerful manner; but their labours as market-gardeners could not pay for the school. After five years (1780) Pestalozzi had to give it up. He was evidently a poor man of business and not much of a farmer. His wife fell ill, but a devoted servant took charge of the whole household and carried on the market-gardening too.

For eighteen years there was no more attempt at teaching. The market-garden just supported the family. The untidy Pestalozzi (he was always badly dressed) was reflecting and occasionally putting pen to paper. Gradually he wrote out a novel, a typical product of eighteenth-century romanticism, long, sentimental, philosophical, with charming pictures of the countryside. It was published in four volumes, the last appearing in 1787, and was called *Lienhard und Gertrud—* the story of the regeneration of a feeble husband by his wife, and of a backward village by the humane proprietor. Later

Pestalozzi let Gertrude, after reforming her husband, educate her children, in his novel *Wie Gertrud ihre Kinder lehrt* (1801). His work was attracting attention. The German philosopher Fichte carried on a correspondence with him.

Eighteen years was a long time for the pedagogue to go without teaching. He was recognized, however, as an educator; and when in 1798 French soldiers killed 400 of the inhabitants of Stans the Government of the Helvetic Republic gave to Pestalozzi the charge of a relief school for orphans there. There were boys and girls of all ages at the Stans school. Pestalozzi threw all his energy into the work, and alone taught the whole school, about eighty children, all the intellectual subjects; he also regularly instructed them in manual work. After about a year the French military authorities took over the school for an army hospital. So Pestalozzi's second school came to a sudden end, but it was the foundation of European primary education of the nineteenth century.

Pestalozzi's work was not nearly finished with the breaking up of the Stans school. He was soon (1801) established in a big school, well equipped through State and private subscriptions. This was the Institut de Berthoud, with three schools, or sections: a primary school, for poor boys; a secondary school, for paying pupils; a normal school, for training teachers. The boys boarded at the Institut; the poor boarders earned their charges by waiting on the rest. Later, day-pupils were also admitted. When the Château of Berthoud, in which the Institut was lodged, was required by the Canton of Bern for other purposes, Pestalozzi, on the invitation of the town of Yverdon, Canton Neuchâtel, moved his school to the Château there. His last period began; the school at Yverdon (where he added a girls' school to his *institut*) won European fame, and was studied as a model by Governments and educationists who in the stirring time of the " War of Liberation " were looking forward to a new Europe, based on culture, humanity, faith in mankind. By the year 1824, however, Pestalozzi's school was losing pupils; in 1825 it was closed. The great master retired to Brugg, in the Canton of Aargau, and died in 1827.

CHAPTER XV

UNIVERSITIES

THE rationalism and self-confidence of the men of the eighteenth century led them somewhat to despise, or at least to neglect, classical antiquity. They felt that they had nothing to learn from the ancients in regard to science and philosophy, and therefore they ceased to regard the universities, which were still largely devoted to classical studies, as places of the first importance.

The universities and the schools had to suffer from the same contempt as Aristotle, to whom they still adhered; they were considered as institutions which had remained behind the times, and where nothing was taught but disputation and idle talk— certainly not any true science! With similar feelings the courtier looked upon the humanistic schools; and upon Latin poetry and eloquence, as taught there: obsolete arts which had ceased to be of any earthly use in real life.[1]

This contempt for the ancient university studies was not the rule in England, where Oxford and Cambridge exercised a social ascendancy among the well-to-do classes, and where a vigorous Parliamentary life put a premium upon oratory and, to some extent, on polite learning. On the Continent, however, Parliaments were dead or in decay, and the universities had never enjoyed any social prestige.

Perhaps it is not quite true to say that German universities enjoyed *no* social prestige, for from time to time one or another has been, so to speak, in fashion, though not predominantly —Bonn in the early twentieth century, Göttingen in the late eighteenth. Göttingen was founded—nominally by King George II of Great Britain, Elector of Hanover—in 1737. It

[1] F. Paulson, *German Education* (1908), pp. 102–103.

adopted the tradition of academic freedom which had made Halle so fruitful, and it became particularly distinguished in history and law. The German aristocracy sent to Göttingen their sons who were meant to be statesmen or diplomatists, and they learned history, law, and political science. This aristocratic tradition lasted down to the first half of the nineteenth century; Bismarck was a student at Göttingen. The connexion of Hanover with England brought a good number of young Englishmen to Göttingen, and further promoted its liberal tradition. Canning's poem in the *Anti-Jacobin* on the " University of Göttingen " illustrates its popularity.

The professors of Göttingen, fully alive to their own dignity and to the importance of their mission, enjoying a considerable income and high-sounding titles, and also distinguished not a little by their connexion with a foreign Court, materially assisted in that great change by which the unworldly and pedantic scholar and teacher of the seventeenth century was transformed into the well-bred man of the world, counting himself among the upper classes, and almost considering himself above teaching.[1]

The eighteenth century was certainly not a great age for universities; it kept them in their place. It was not necessary in that aristocratic age for everybody who aspired to be somebody to go to a university. Some people went there; many distinguished men did not. " Vigorous personalities, like Leibniz and also Lessing, kept away from them " (although both were students at Leipzig).[2] The most cultured people of the eighteenth century, the French and Italian gentry, went comparatively little to their universities, which were chiefly professional schools for lawyers and physicians. Turgot, the Abbé Morellet, and Loménie de Brienne were students at the Sorbonne; but neither Voltaire, Montesquieu, Helvétius, the Abbé Raynal, Diderot, nor the scientists Maupertuis and Buffon, were students or professors at a French university. The wit and intellect of France were in her *salons*, country-houses, and academies. " The Sorbonne still sits there in its old mansion," writes Carlyle, concerning

[1] F. Paulson, *op. cit.*, p. 121.   [2] *Ibid.*, p. 116.

the reign of Louis XV, " but mumbles only jargon of dotage, and no longer leads the consciences of men : not the Sorbonne; it is the *Encyclopédies, Philosophie,* and who knows what nameless innumerable multitude of ready Writers, profane Singers, Romancers, Players, Disputators, and Pamphleteers, that now form the spiritual Guidance of the world." [1]

Rousseau, in Chapter I of *Émile,* obviously alluding to France, speaks of " those laughable establishments called Colleges." Rousseau and Carlyle were not quite fair in their estimates. Gibbon, while a youth at Lausanne, corresponded with " a professor in the University of Paris " who had never heard of him, called M. Crevier. Gibbon was then seventeen years of age, living in the home of a Calvinist pastor, M. Pavillard. He thought that he discovered the proper reading of a corrupt passage of Livy, and he wrote off to M. Crevier, the editor of a big edition of Livy. " His answer was speedy and polite. He praised my ingenuity and adopted my conjecture." [2] The only French university with an international reputation was Strasbourg. A frontier city, it offered equal facilities for the study of French and German. The Strasbourg medical school had a high reputation, and greatly attracted the young Goethe when he was a student of jurisprudence there in 1770. He attended the lectures of Lobstein on anatomy and of Spielmann on chemistry. There were medical students at the house at which Goethe boarded, and they all talked medicine continually. " It is well known," wrote Goethe in his autobiography, " that medical students are the only ones who zealously converse about their science and profession out of the hours of study." He found the social life of the university very stimulating. Referring to his Strasbourg experiences, he wrote : " University life, even if in the course of it we may not have to boast of our own proper industry, nevertheless affords endless advantages in every kind of cultivation, because we are always surrounded by men who either possess or are seeking science, so that, even if unconsciously, we are constantly

[1] Thomas Carlyle, *French Revolution,* Book I, Chapter II.
[2] Edward Gibbon, *Autobiography* (ed. 1907), p. 79.

drawing some nourishment from such an atmosphere."[1]
Studies stopped, however, when the young and beautiful
Austrian Archduchess Marie Antoinette, daughter of Maria
Theresa, passed through Strasbourg on her way to be married
to the Dauphin, afterwards Louis XVI. The university had a
whole succession of holidays for the occasion. Goethe had a
good view of the Archduchess, and noted her " beautiful lofty
mien, as cheerful as it was imposing," as she drove through
the streets with her women, in a glass carriage.

Goethe said that the medical faculty at the University outshone all others. Yet Strasbourg had a great faculty in international law and diplomacy at that time, represented by
Christophe Guillaume de Koch, whose lectures were a regular
school for young diplomatists. Koch was born in 1737 at
Buchswiller, the town of a district belonging to Hesse-Darmstadt, but *enclavé* in Alsace. He was educated in the excellent
Gymnasium of Buchswiller, and passed on from there to the
University of Strasbourg. For years he devoted himself to
law, and to ' diplomatic '—that is, the art of deciphering and
dating ancient manuscripts. He made a name for high scholarship in this study, and published some important works. In
time, however, the claims of international law and diplomacy
(the conduct of international relations) overcame his other
interests. Students came out of France and Germany to attend
his classes, and to learn the technique of statesmanship. A
Protestant, of simple life, serene disposition, with a passion
for public service, Koch was an ideal educator of young men
who were going to enter political life. From about 1780, when
he became Professor of Public Law at Strasbourg, down to
the French Revolution Koch's ' school of diplomatists ' was
famous throughout Western and Central Europe. Metternich,
Talleyrand, Benjamin Constant, Montgelas (the Bavarian statesman), were among his pupils. He represented Alsace in some
of the legislative assemblies of the French Revolutionary
Governments, but settled down again with feelings of relief
in his professorship at Strasbourg in 1795. He died in 1813,

[1] *Dichtung und Wahrheit*, Book IX.

beloved by his colleagues, who raised a monument to his memory. His great works, *Histoire des Traités de paix* and *Abrégé de l'Histoire des traités de paix*, are indispensable to all students of the diplomacy and international relations since the Peace of Westphalia.

Metternich, the future ambassador and Austrian Chancellor, and his brother were at the University of Strasbourg in 1788–90, from the age of fifteen and a half to seventeen.[1] The University was popular not merely because of its eminent professors, but also because French and German, being commonly spoken, could be learned with equal facility there. Metternich in his *Mémoires*, curiously, does not mention Koch, nor, indeed, any of his professors by name. He writes: "When I arrived in this city the young Napoleon Bonaparte had just left it. He had finished his special studies there as officer in the artillery regiment which was in garrison at Strasbourg. I had the same professors of mathematics and fencing as he had. . . . But during my sojourn at Strasbourg I never heard his name mentioned." One of the reasons, in addition to the reputation of Koch, for Metternich coming to Strasbourg was that he and his brother had each the income of a prebend in the Cathedral of Mainz, and that, in order to qualify as prebendaries, they had to study for two years at a university recognized by the Mainz Chapter. Strasbourg was one of the universities thus recognized.

The Germans used their universities more than the French used theirs, and had the habit of going there. Leibniz and Lessing and Goethe were students at Leipzig; Christian von Wolff, the philosopher, was a student at Jena, Kant at Königsberg. To the Germans then, as now, the university was just a normal means of carrying forward the education received at the high school; it conferred no social distinction and was sought much more by the small *bourgeoisie* than by the gentry. In Scotland the universities were largely attended, and were well-managed institutions for providing liberal and scientific instruction. Oxford and Cambridge, the

[1] Metternich, *Mémoires* (1886), vol. i, p. 6.

only universities in England, tended to be regarded as places where gentlemen, other than sailors and soldiers, should pass the years of from nineteen to twenty-two; they had the merit, however, according to Madame de Staël, of providing the young men who were to be orators and statesmen with a particularly useful equipment. " The English universities have singularly contributed to spread among the English that knowledge of ancient languages and literature which gives the orators and the statesmen in England such liberal and brilliant instruction." [1]

Owing to the number of German states, many of them having their own universities, there was a great variety of tradition and manner of life in the various schools. Goethe said that in his time (about 1768) Halle and Jena were noted for the roughness of their students, for their physical strength, skill in fighting, and insolence towards the citizens. At Leipzig, on the other hand, all was politeness; " a student could scarcely be anything else than polite as soon as he wished to stand on any footing at all with the rich, well-bred, and punctilious inhabitants." The politeness of Leipzig was believed to be due to the large number of cultured Huguenot families which had settled there after the Revocation of the Edict of Nantes; their descendants are still among the leading families of Leipzig. In Goethe's time many of the professors came from these families, and were men of high culture and of independent means. [2]

The German universities, though education there, as in England, was mainly classical and linguistic, had not a similar result in producing statesmen for the Cabinet and Legislature. The reason for this was obvious: properly speaking, there were no Cabinets or Legislatures. Governments, being paternal and despotic, provided no opportunities for the development and exercise of statesmanlike qualities on the part of the citizens. In no country in Europe were the means of higher education, and opportunities for instruction and for perfecting the faculties, so common as in Germany; yet, in spite of this, said Madame de Staël, " it was obvious that the Germans

---

[1] Madame de Staël, *De l'Allemagne*, Chapter XVIII.
[2] *Dichtung und Wahrheit*, Book IX.

lacked energy, were heavy, and narrow in outlook." The fault
for this, she concluded, lay with the Governments, which
" are the real instructors of peoples." The Governments
provided no politics, no career, no interest. The students,
who had lived a busy intellectual life, free, independent,
rejoicing in their corporate privileges and strength, at Halle,
Göttingen, Jena, and the rest, on leaving the university fell
back into the monotonous and homely habits which dominated
Germany; and by degrees they lost all the elasticity and resolu-
tion with which their student life had inspired them. " All
that remained was a very extended knowledge." Salzmann,
the president of the students' ' mess ' at which Goethe dined
when a student at Strasbourg, said that the fault of the German
universities lay in their aiming at education in too large and
learned a sense. Strasbourg, being a French university, was
more practical.[1]

All this was a great waste of ability, a great misfortune for
the public, for in no country was university education so good.
" Education in the German universities," wrote a French
observer (anonymous, quoted by Madame de Staël), " begins
where that of several nations of Europe finishes." The professors were recognized as men not merely of ' astonishing '
erudition, but of extreme scrupulousness. In Germany everything was done with conscientiousness; university instruction
had the same degree of accuracy and thoroughness as everything else. From the point of view of universities, the only (and
that a questionable) advantage of the absence of political life
in Germany was that it directed the minds of thinkers into
realms of pure thought. The mind, at any rate, could be free
and active; and thus a very high level of metaphysical speculation was attained—but only by the few. " An immense
distance separates minds of the first and second order." [2]

In Germany the most famous university of the eighteenth
century was Leipzig, although Halle, so long at least as
Wolff taught there, had a reputation, and was the best in the

---

[1] *Dichtung und Wahrheit*, Book IX.
[2] Madame de Staël, *op. cit.*, Chapter XVIII.

Kingdom of Prussia. It was in a far-eastern corner of Germany, at Königsberg, however, that the lamp of philosophy burned brightest, and with a steady, clear flame, during the last half of the century.

Königsberg, the chief city of East Prussia, had probably about 50,000 inhabitants. The province or state was separated then (as it is again now) from the rest of Prussia by Polish territory, generally called to-day the Polish Corridor. The Albertina, the University of Königsberg, was more local than most other German universities; it was attended by East Prussians, Poles, and Lithuanians. Its culture was thoroughly classical and German; and its connexions extended through the Baltic provinces of Russia. Kant's first great literary work, *The Critique of Pure Reason*, was brought out in 1781 by a publisher of Riga, who put it on the market at the Leipzig fair in that year.

Immanuel Kant, the most famous teacher of the University of Königsberg, was born in that city in 1724, the son of a strapmaker, a pious Lutheran, as most of the Königsbergers were. Kant was educated at the town *Gymnasium*, or grammar school, the Collegium Fredericianum, and entered the University at the age of sixteen and a half, in 1740. He finished his student days in 1746, and obtained work as private tutor to a family— the usual method by which poor men in the eighteenth century started upon a learned career. For years he was a private teacher, *privat dozent*, or lecturer without salary (but charging fees), at the University. He competed for a prize offered by the Berlin Academy in 1763 for a philosophical essay, but was defeated by Moses Mendelssohn. His lecturing went on steadily throughout the Seven Years War, when East Prussia was occupied (1758–63) by Russian troops. It was not until 1770, when he was forty-six years old, that he obtained a professorship.

Kant never travelled. All his life, except when he was tutor in a family, was spent in Königsberg. His fame was European, though never popular; and occasionally particularly keen students (Herder is the most famous) would be drawn from lands outside East Prussia to attend his lectures at Königsberg. The philosopher never felt himself to be provincial or out of touch with the great world because he had his chair only in a small university in a provincial city on the Baltic. He read the newspapers with interest, and indeed avidity, and kept abreast of current politics. He was particularly roused by the American Revolution and by the French Revolution, approving of both. The tragic result upon Europe, however, of the French Revolution induced him at the age of seventy to engage on a serious essay for the prevention of war and the perpetuation of the blessing of peace. *Zum ewigen Frieden* (*Towards Enduring Peace*) was published in 1795.

A German professor of the eighteenth century took his duties seriously. He was a State official, and though the Prussian and other German Governments left the professors remarkably free, an inefficient or idle teacher would not have survived long. Kant's conscientiousness made him have no need of official supervision. He was a careful and assiduous teacher, lecturing every day for two or three hours for six days in the week, beginning always at 7 A.M. He carried no manuscript into his lecture-room, but simply the textbook which was the basis of the lecture course (for instance, the *Logik* of Georg Friedrich Meier, of Halle); this he followed page by page, using minute marginal notes written by his own hand. His first lecture was a complete failure, as his nerve gave way, and he found himself with nothing to say; nevertheless, he became one of the most competent lecturers of his age. He prepared his lectures with great care from 5 A.M. to 7 every morning; and without cultivating popularity was always cheerful, serene, and approachable with the students. His salary was never more than 600 thalers or £100 a year; but he lived in modest dignity in his own house, kept a manservant, entertained two or three friends to dinner every day (at one o'clock sharp), and was always neatly dressed. His clothes were not too plain, either. He liked a dash of blue or yellow about them. He was fond of conversation; the daily dinner-party to which he invited his various friends lasted from one to four o'clock, though it consisted only of three plain courses with a little wine. At four o'clock he went out for a gentle walk, returning to read the papers and to take up his writing until bedtime, at nine-forty-five.

The German university and the German professors were very much the same then as now. Students were free to make or mar themselves, but the professors were genuine, assiduous teachers, ready to help any students who took the trouble to attend lectures and showed themselves eager for instruction. The young Gibbon, aged seventeen, at Lausanne, corresponded about passages in the Latin classics with Professor Matthew Gessner of Göttingen, Breitinger of Zürich, and Crevier of Paris, all three personally unknown to him. Gessner and Breitinger were especially encouraging to him, and wrote frequently and elaborately; they were evidently pleased at being consulted. Gessner's letters were unduly prolix; in one of them he filled half a sheet enumerating his titles and offices. When not teaching, the professors were engaged in private study, which produced a steady stream of mature works, published in the *Acta Eruditorum* or in the books of the Leipzig and other publishing houses. Kant's long and fruitful life ended in 1804. There were many careers and characters not unlike his in the German professoriate, though naturally there was no comparable genius. It is a remarkable fact that in an age when German political power and national sentiment were at their lowest, and when there were almost no professors of any distinction in any other country (except Scotland), the German university teachers had never been so splendid; their fame was European. Schiller, the greatest living dramatist and poet after Goethe, was a hard-working, efficient Professor of History at Jena.

Carlyle, who was the great interpreter of Germany to England in the first half of the nineteenth century, declared in an essay, published in 1828, that the merits of Christian Gottlob Heyne, Professor of Classics at Göttingen, were " more justly appreciated in England than those of almost any other German, whether scholar, poet, or philosopher." If Carlyle was correct, it is a remarkable fact, for Heyne is totally unknown in England now. His reputation in England cannot simply have been due to the connexion of the British Crown with Hanover, although this did result in English students going to Göttingen. King George II had a good deal of common sense, but was not interested in intellectual things; the real founder was not George II of England, but the Hanoverian Premier Minister Munchausen. The Government was responsible for the stipends of the professors and the other expenses of the University.

Christian Gottlob Heyne, born in 1729, was the son of a poor weaver of Chemnitz. He was sent to the local school with the assistance of a Protestant pastor. Later he earned some money by private tuition. Finally he attained his goal by entering the University of Leipzig as a student. In the middle of the eighteenth century the great Professor of Classics at Leipzig was Johann August Ernesti. Heyne was Ernesti's most promising pupil. After completing his studies at Leipzig Heyne held another private tutorship, and then obtained a small post in the library of Count Brühl, the powerful, dissipated, but artistic and literary Premier Minister of Saxony. In the capture of Dresden by Frederick the Great in 1756 at the opening of the Seven Years War the Brühl library suffered partial destruction and Heyne was driven out on to the streets. He obtained another private tutorship (in the Schönberg family), married, and finally, in 1763, on Ernesti's recommendation, was made Professor of Classics in the University of Göttingen. He had already become known by an edition of Tibullus, produced when he was clerk in the Brühl library at Dresden. At Göttingen Heyne was the thoroughly happy man, who seemed to have taken to heart Martin's counsel in Voltaire's *Candide*, that to work without reflection is the sole way to make life supportable. He worked happily and tranquilly at the University for fifty-three years. He had a comfortable salary, beginning with 800 thalers (about £120) and rising to 1200. He held three classes a day, a number which few modern professors maintain. His *Seminar* or advanced class (nine chosen pupils) trained scholars for all the schools of Germany; it is said that this *Seminar* produced 135 professors. Notwith-

standing his long teaching hours, he continued to produce
without interruption a large series of works of classical scholarship: editions of Virgil, Pliny, Pindar, Homer, numerous
translations, some ten thick volumes of essays and studies, and
finally, the fugitive efforts of his lighter moments, 7500 reviews
in the *Gelehrte Anzeigen*. It ought to be mentioned that the
Gelehrte Anzeigen was the learned journal of Göttingen, and
that Heyne, naturally, was the editor of it. So great was the
respect in which he was held that when Napoleon's armies
overran Hanover Heyne was able to arrange that Göttingen
should be treated as neutral territory, undisturbed by war;
in this it was more fortunate than the Prussian University of
Halle, which was closed by the French, all its professors (among
whom was the great theologian Schleiermacher) being left
without occupation or means of support.[1]

Christian von Wolff, the philosopher, was professor in Halle
University from 1706 to 1731; afterwards at Marburg, in Electoral Hesse; and again at Halle from 1740 to his death in
1754. Frederick August Wolff, one of the greatest of Platonic
and Homeric scholars, was professor at Halle from 1783 to
1807. He was a pupil (not a very attentive one) of Heyne at
Göttingen, where, though he did not care much for the
lectures, he read hard and fruitfully in the splendid library of
the University. His first classical work, a dissertation on the
Homeric poems, was dedicated to Heyne. For some years he
was teacher in the Ilfeld Gymnasium, where he prepared an
edition, with German notes, of Plato's *Symposium*. This work
won for him a chair at the University of Halle. Gradually Wolff
formed there a great school of philological students. Teaching
was his first interest. In his twenty-three years of service he
delivered fifty different courses of lectures, besides conducting
Seminarien and going over the exercises of the students privately
with them. Nevertheless, he found time and energy to edit
great editions of the *Odyssey*, the *Iliad*, and other classical

[1] For Heyne see Carlyle, *Essays* (ed. 1899), vol. i, pp. 319 ff. For Halle
see Henrik Steffens (a Halle professor in 1806), *Was Ich Erlebte*, pp. 1–35,
in Rehtwisch, *Aus Vergilbten Pergamenten*, vol. vii.

works. When the University of Halle was broken up by the French in 1807 Wolff went to live in Berlin. King Frederick William III of Prussia paid him a pension. In 1809, when the Prussian Government founded the University of Berlin, Wolff was of the greatest assistance. He conducted a *Seminar* in the new university and edited a classical journal. Thus he helped to maintain continuity between the scholarship of the century which had passed away and of the new age that was opening.

The Italian and Spanish universities were ancient and of honourable reputation, but had no vigour. Padua, popularly called the " Bo " (which meant perhaps *Baccalariorum Ordo*, Order of Bachelors), was the university of the Republic of Venice, and trained the youth of that state for law or medicine; it was also attended, according to Casanova, who was a student there in 1739, by large numbers of foreign students. The Venetian Government encouraged foreign students to come by having highly paid professors, and by allowing students a great deal of liberty, a concession much prized in an age when Government interference was apt to be petty and vexatious. The Venetian *sbirri*, or police, did not inspect the students' baggage; and students freely carried arms, although nominally these were prohibited by law. The students enjoyed self-government. They conducted their relations with the civil authorities through one of themselves, a senior student called the Syndic, who was always a foreigner and was responsible for their good conduct. He had a difficult task, for the students, as described by Casanova, were undisciplined and licentious; he calls them *une jeunesse effrénée*. Life at the " Bo " was merry; and however scholarly were the lectures of the professors whom the Venetian Government paid so well, the examinations seem not to have been too exacting, for Casanova, at the age of sixteen, graduated Doctor of Law after one year's study. All the students appear to have studied either law or medicine. Casanova, who had quick wits, wanted to study medicine because, he said, it was easier to practise charlatanry as a physician than as a barrister; but his guardians insisted upon his taking law. He satisfied the examiners on two theses;

one in civil law, *Concerning Wills* (*De Testamentis*), another in canon law, *Whether the Hebrews can construct New Synagogues* (*Utrum Hebræi possint construere novas synagogas*). Shortly before Casanova left the " Bo " there was a riot arising out of a dispute between a *sbirro* and a student in a *café*. The student tried to shoot the *sbirro*, who, however, was the quicker and shot first, and wounded the student. This provoked a riot; the students collected in masses, and set out to kill all the *sbirri* they could find. In the ensuing fights two students were killed. The Government, however, negotiated with them through the Syndic, and arranged peace after hanging the *sbirro* whose altercation with the student in the coffee-house had started the trouble. Casanova, who was never behindhand in debauchery, soon outran his income and contracted debts. Naturally he wrote home to Venice to the grandmother who was in charge of him, asking for more money, but instead the grandmother came herself to Padua, took Casanova away from the " Bo," and carried him back to Venice.[1]

At Rome the old college or university called the Sapienza maintained an undistinguished existence. In the *Diatribe du Docteur Akakia*, a satire written against the scientific theories of Maupertuis, Voltaire makes the Sapienza condemn the theories by an absurd reasoning.[2]

Of the Dutch universities Leyden had a very high reputation, and, on account of its sound Protestant tradition, was particularly frequented by young Englishmen and young Scotsmen if, for religious and other reasons, they did not go to Oxford and Cambridge. Boerhave of Leyden was the greatest physician and medical teacher of the age. Utrecht University also was in high repute. As Dutch Protestantism was Calvinist, English Presbyterians were especially drawn to the universities of Holland. There was a " Presbyterian Fund " maintained in the English Presbyterian communities for providing exhibitions or bursaries for study abroad.

A Scotsman, Alexander Carlyle, who passed a session at

[1] For the University of Padua see Casanova, *Mémoires*, Chapter II.
[2] Voltaire, *Œuvres* (1785), vol. xlvi, p. 24.

Leyden in 1745, has little to say about the instruction there
except that the lectures were rather dull; but another source
of exactly the same date declares that " the Professors' chairs
were filled with men who were an ornament to the Republic
of Letters, and greatly advanced its interests by their writings
and other labours." Carlyle associated almost entirely with
British students, of whom two became famous. One was John
Wilkes, then aged eighteen, who already had ambitions to
be " a fine gentleman," and showed something of his later
" daring profligacy." The other was Charles Townshend, who
later, as Chancellor of the Exchequer in 1768, imposed certain momentous customs duties on the American Colonies.
Townshend was a man of wit and humour, and of the most
charming conversation, " which not only took the ear, but
elevated the thoughts." The students lodged usually in parties
of four or five with Leyden citizens, and were well entertained.
Dinner cost sixteen stivers (one shilling and fourpence), breakfast six, supper six. Every student could have sixty ' stoups '
of wine free of town duty, so that a good small claret cost one
shilling a bottle; tobacco forty stivers a pound. Students met
a good deal together in one another's rooms and chatted about
politics, drank claret and coffee (which was particularly good),
and had supper of egg and salad and red herring (called buk-
kan). Occasionally they visited the neighbouring University
of Utrecht, where there were other British students, including
young noblemen with their tutors. In general, students found
that Leyden and Utrecht lodgings were cheap and clean, and
the surroundings pleasant.[1]

Education at Dutch universities had a decidedly rationalizing
and liberalizing tendency. Their Calvinism was of a moderate
kind, and influenced the English Presbyterians who attended
Dutch universities, such as Lardner, Peirce, Tomkins, Samuel
Jones, in a liberal direction theologically. Samuel Jones, after
studying under Witsius at Leyden, established an academy, or
higher school, in the ancient Gloucestershire abbey-town of

[1] See *Autobiography of the Rev. Alexander Carlyle of Inveresk* (ed. Burton,
1910), pp. 174–190.

Tewkesbury, which for a time became quite a centre of free discussion. Some students when they returned from Holland to England ceased to hold with any form of organized Christian religion, and became simple deists. Since that time strict Anglicans or Presbyterians have felt doubtful about the orthodoxy of the Dutch universities.[1]

By the end of the eighteenth century the universities (as represented chiefly by German schools) had re-established themselves in the respect and opinion of Europe. Gibbon, writing in 1792, could declare: " In all the universities of Europe, excepting our own, the languages and sciences are distributed among a numerous list of effective professors; the students, according to their taste, their calling, and their diligence, apply themselves to the proper masters; and in the annual repetition of public and private lectures these masters are assiduously employed." [2]

This good result may be traced back to the foundation of the University of Halle in 1694, for here a school was formed in which the professors were neither pledged nor expected (as in the older Catholic schools) to teach conformably to certain accepted views on science or theology, but were free to pursue their researches and to teach as their unbiased knowledge should direct them. Halle, and through its successful example all the other German universities, established a right to academic freedom, *akademische Freiheit*. In the last half of the century the mighty reputation of Kant, with his unswerving pursuit of pure reason and the autonomy of mind and will, set the seal upon this prize of freedom; and the inspiring work of Fichte and the new University of Berlin (1809) in the period of the building up of modern Prussia after the disaster of Jena, and the consequent political and moral collapse, established the idea of a university as a place not merely of intellectual interest and learning, but of practical influence and vitality.

[1] I am indebted for the information in this paragraph to one of my pupils, Miss O. M. Griffiths, Ph.D.
[2] Edward Gibbon, *Autobiography* (ed. 1907), p. 38.

CHAPTER XVI

ACADEMIES

EUROPE—the small ' Europe ' from Lisbon to the Vistula
—was, and is, a cultural unit, in which all the men of
polite learning recognized themselves as forming, in the phrase
of Bayle and Goldsmith, a ' republic of letters.' Although
there were no international conferences of learned men in the
eighteenth century, the solidarity of the scholars and men of
letters was maintained by their frequent travels and their long
periods in different places. They also joined learned academies,
of which there were a great number, most of them very active.
It was not merely the pleasure of association and mutual
esteem that learned men and writers sought in these societies;
they enjoyed also a certain, though limited, degree of freedom
of expression, for academies were privileged, and some were
even powerful. The most famous of all academies, the Académie
Française, numbered only forty members and was restricted
to Frenchmen only. Founded by Cardinal Richelieu in 1634,
registered by the *parlement* of Paris in 1637, it was always a
body of considerable distinction. Its elections were keenly
canvassed, and in the eighteenth century were subject to royal
influence. Voltaire was certainly the most eminent man of
letters in France, though not the most popular, when Cardinal
Fleury, Premier Minister of France and member of the
Académie, died, in 1743, at the age of ninety. " Ingratitude
excepted, he was a tolerably good man," writes Voltaire. Anyhow, Voltaire wanted his place. King Louis XV said he should
have it; the Duchesse de Châteauroux, the King's mistress,
would have it so. The Comte de Maurepas, however, the
Secretary of State, who quarrelled with Châteauroux, and,
indeed, with all the King's mistresses, naturally went against

253

Voltaire and prevented the appointment. In 1744, however, when campaigning in the War of the Austrian Succession, Louis XV fell ill at Metz, and being, as it was thought, on the point of death was induced by his almoner, the Bishop of Soissons, son of James II of England, to dismiss Châteauroux. He did so, and recovered, and at once wanted Châteauroux back; but she had died from the spiritual mortification caused by her dismissal. So another mistress had to be found, and the choice fell upon the graceful and well-educated wife of a farmer-general of taxes called le Normand, the squire of Étiole. Voltaire, who liked country life and graceful, well-educated women, was a friend of the Étiole household; so the next time there was a vacancy in the Académie he had no difficulty in obtaining the place, through the influence of Madame le Normand. " From this I concluded," he writes, " it was better, in order to make the most trifling fortune, to speak four words to a King's mistress, than to write a hundred volumes." [1] On the whole, the Académie Française was not a very distinguished body in the eighteenth century. The eminent naturalist Buffon came up from the country every year to Paris, to perform his duties at the Jardin des Plantes and to visit his friends. He attended the Académie when at Paris. The poet Malesherbes also was a member at this time. Montesquieu was, of course, a member; for he was not merely the most distinguished writer of the day on the science of politics; he was also universally acknowledged as one of France's greatest and noblest public men. So completely was his fame established in France that he, being President of the *parlement* of Bordeaux, was simply called " the President," *tout court*, just as the Duke of Wellington later was universally spoken of simply as " the Duke."

There was another president, honorary, of the *parlement* of Paris who had a considerable name in those days. This was President Hénault. Grimm considered that Hénault must be reckoned among the most fortunate and happy men of the age. Of respectable ability and amiable disposition, inheriting a

[1] *Memoirs of Voltaire* (trans. 1826), p. 60.

large fortune from his father, who was a rich farmer-general
of taxes, Hénault naturally obtained a place as judge or member
of the *parlement* of Paris with ease. He soon, however, quitted
the Palais de Justice, and obtained by purchase a position at
Court—superintendent of the household of Queen Marie, wife
of Louis XV. The rest of his life was passed in the fashionable
and intellectual, if rather small, circle of high society in Paris,
where he lived in dignity and affluence, and gave excellent
suppers. He wrote, or composed, as Grimm prefers to say,
the *Abrégé chronologique de l'histoire de France*, a very neat
piece of work, which established the model for French school
text-books ever since. He was elected member of the Académie,
and was known universally as President Hénault, and by the
wits as the President *à l'abrégé*; but when the great Montesquieu died in 1755 Hénault attained the height of bliss and
fame, by succeeding, as it were, to the title of " the President,"
tout court. He died in 1770, at the age of eighty-six, having
for many years done nothing but talk with his friend Madame
du Deffand and other *beaux esprits*, give suppers, and supervise
one edition after another of the *Abrégé chronologique*. With
him the Académie Française lost one of its most distinguished
contemporary members. Another president, Charles de
Brosses, of the *parlement* of Dijon, the distinguished author of
the discoveries at Herculaneum, made several efforts to enter
the Académie, but was refused every time. His continued
failure to be elected is said to have been due to intrigues of
Voltaire. President de Brosses had sold an estate near Ferney
to Voltaire; some time later an acrimonious and long dispute
broke out between the buyer and seller concerning some loads
of wood, worth 281 francs, to which Voltaire thought that
he was entitled free of charge. The president had right
on his side, but Voltaire kept him out of the Académie.[1]
For 281 francs de Brosses failed to become one of the Im-
mortals.

The Académie had become rather a pointless body, which

[1] See Lytton Strachey, " The President de Brosses," in *Portraits in
Miniature* (1931), pp. 70–86.

used up its energy in the quarrel of two factions, the *dévots* and the *philosophes*. The party of the *dévots* naturally included most of the prelate Academicians, while the *philosophes* were the bold and sceptical men of letters, like Voltaire, who, however, stayed at Ferney and did not take part in the Académie quarrels. La Harpe, the learned literary critic, belonged to this party. Two prelate Academicians who prided themselves on their enlightenment belonged to the party of the *philosophes*; these were the Prince de Rohan, Coadjutor Archbishop of Strasbourg, later the hero or dupe of the episode of the Diamond Necklace, and Monseigneur Dillon, Archbishop of Narbonne, who was interested in economics, was acquainted with Adam Smith, and is considered to have been a lax Christian. On the other hand, the Duc de Richelieu, Marshal of France (the conqueror of Minorca in 1756), a complete if magnificent worldling, belonged to the party of *dévots*. The Duc de Choiseul, the eminent statesman who had the misfortune to be responsible for carrying on and concluding the Seven Years War, and was dismissed by the King in 1770, was a member of the Académie; he took no part in its proceedings or its quarrels, however, but remained in dignified retirement at his magnificent country-seat of Chanteloup. The Academicians elected to succeed to the *fauteuil* of President Hénault the Prince de Beauvau, a captain in the King's bodyguard. In the eulogy of his predecessor, which it is the rule for every newly elected Academician to make, the Prince de Beauvau took the opportunity of deviating into a defence or eulogy of the administration of Choiseul. The select public which was admitted then, as now, to sessions of the Académie showed by its applause that it warmly approved of this act of chivalry or justice towards the statesman of Chanteloup. It was like an English judge using his place on the Bench to deviate into a public defence of a dismissed British general; but the arid disputes of *dévots* and *philosophes*, and intervention in the political intrigues at the Court of Versailles, were scarcely justifications for the existence of the famous Académie Française.

Its last *séance*, and also the last session of its more learned sister, the Académie des Inscriptions et Belles-lettres, was held in 1793. These royal societies could not survive the execution of the King; they were partially refounded in 1795, but not completely set up again with their old names until 1816. The Abbé Morellet, the friend of Turgot and translator of Adam Smith's *Wealth of Nations*, the last Director of the old Académie, survived into the Consulate, Empire, and even into the Bourbon Restoration. Dying in 1819, at the age of ninety-two, this perfect example of the eighteenth-century *philosophe* could contemplate the restored Académie still retaining something of the old *douceur de vivre*.[1]

Although de Tocqueville says that already before the Revolution Paris was drawing everything in France to itself, there was still interesting social life in the provinces. There was an academy of learned men at Dijon, another at Besançon, another at Nancy and elsewhere. Provincial ' capitals ' were a charming feature of eighteenth-century life. " When Edinburgh was as far from London as Vienna is to-day it was natural—it was inevitable—that it should be the centre of a local civilization which, while it remained politically and linguistically British, developed a colour and character of its own. In France there was the same pleasant phenomenon. Bordeaux, Toulouse, Aix-en-Provence—up to the end of the eighteenth century each was, in truth, a capital, where a peculiar culture had grown up that was at once French and idiosyncratic." The tradition of local culture lingered into the succeeding age, and can just be discerned in Balzac's stories, but it died out, or largely died out, with the development of railways, telephones, and the metropolitan Press. Yet aristocratic streets of the *ancien régime* are still to be found—for instance, in Dijon—the houses " so solid and yet so vivacious, with their cobbled courts and coloured tiles," withdrawn into tranquil resignation.[2]

---

[1] For Hénault, *dévots*, and *philosophes* in the Académie see Grimm, *Mémoires* (ed. 1814), vol. i, pp. 112–116, 163–168.

[2] Lytton Strachey, *Portraits in Miniature*, pp. 70–71.

In such local capitals were provincial academies which had meetings, dissertations, discussions ; and they encouraged merit by the offer of prizes. In 1749 the strange and erratic genius Rousseau had the great opportunity of his life when the Academy of Dijon offered a prize for an essay on the effect of the progress of civilization upon morals. Rousseau sent in an essay, won the prize, and published the essay the next year. Its limpid style and original and paradoxical argument (the superiority of the savage state of nature over the civilized state) took the flippant and intelligent high society of France by storm, and made for Rousseau a European reputation. In 1753 he tried for the Academy of Dijon prize again with an essay on *The Origin of Inequality*, but this time he failed, though it is a good essay, and became the basis, with the first, successful essay, of the *Contrat social*. The Academy of Lyons made the celebrated Abbé Raynal, author of *L'Histoire des deux Indes*, a member in the year 1780. The Abbé, who, of course, was a member of the Académie Française, showed his well-known humanity and munificence in accepting the Lyons membership. He offered two prizes, to be awarded by the Academy. One prize was of 600 livres (£25-£30), for an essay on the subject, *What have been the Principles which have made the Manufactures which distinguish the City of Lyons Prosperous?* The other prize was of 1200 livres, for an essay on the subject, *The Discovery of America: has it been Beneficent or Harmful to the Human Race?* The Baron Grimm, who reported this event in his correspondence, adds : " This last question is perhaps the most vast and finest which has ever been propounded since there were academies in the world." [1]

The Berlin Academy gained in distinction and fame, largely through the patronage of Frederick the Great. The Academy was founded in 1700 on the proposals of Leibniz by Frederick I, the first Hohenzollern to have the title of king. It had liberal statutes, and its membership was not limited to Prussians, nor even to Germans. Leibniz himself was a Saxon in the service of the Elector of Hanover and of the Duke of Brunswick-

[1] F. M. Grimm, *Mémoires*, vol. i, p. 227.

CHRISTIAN VON WOLFF

Wolfenbüttel; he was responsible also for the foundation of the Academy of St Petersburg by Peter the Great of Russia in 1713. Frederick the Great of Prussia invited the French scientist Maupertuis to Berlin, and had him made President of the Academy. This increased the renown of the institution, though some people considered Maupertuis to be rather ridiculous.

Pierre Louis Moreau de Maupertuis was a Breton of Saint-Malo, born in 1698. Like Descartes, another eminent mathematician before him, Maupertuis began his active career as a soldier, an officer in the French cavalry regiment La Roche-Guyon. Except in war-time, soldiers had a great deal of leisure in the eighteenth century. Maupertuis relieved the terrible *ennui* of army life, as Descartes had done, by mathematical and philosophical research. His studies brought him to the notice of the Royal Society, which, when he visited London in 1728, elected him to be a Fellow. He was now out of the army, living a scholarly life, a member of the Paris Académie des Sciences. In 1736 he led an expedition at the expense of Louis XV to Lapland, to measure a degree of the meridian. Frederick II of Prussia, in the first year of his accession to the throne, invited Maupertuis to Berlin. The French *savant* went with the King on the first Silesian campaign, and was taken prisoner by the Austrians at Mollwitz. He was soon released. In 1743 he was elected to the Académie Française. In 1746, being resident in Berlin, he was made President of the Berlin Academy. He published a book, proposing that expeditions should proceed to the North and South Poles, and that a pit or shaft should be sunk to the centre of the earth. Both proposals were ridiculed by Voltaire (in the *Diatribe du Docteur Akakia*), then at Berlin, and by Frederick the Great. Yet the scheme of exploring the Poles has now been put into effect; and the proposal of sinking a shaft as nearly as possible to the centre of the earth has been seriously made by a modern scientist and engineer.[1] Maupertuis, who was melancholic and irritable, quarrelled over his book with

[1] Sir Alfred Parsons.

Voltaire, and with Koenig, a mathematician at The Hague; and eventually he left Berlin, travelled for his health in the South of France, and died in 1759. The King permitted him to retain the presidency of the Academy to the end; but " Frederick exercised it himself, after the decease of the restless and morose Maupertuis." [1] The King also honoured Maupertuis by having Voltaire's *Diatribe du Docteur Akakia* burned by the common hangman of Berlin.

The liberal outlook of the Berlin Academy is seen in its action in 1784, when it awarded its prize to Antoine, Comte de Rivarol's *Discours sur l'Universalité de la langue française.* The Bavarian Academy of Sciences, founded in the reign of the Elector Maximilian Joseph (1745–77), maintained the tradition of solid learning in South Germany, and in the later years of the century zealously promoted secondary-school education in Bavaria.

Ever since the Renaissance there had existed societies or academies of learned men; not young students, but established scholars. These scholars, or amateurs of scholarship, joined academies because they liked the company of their fellows; because their association conferred distinction and reputation upon each other; because the ' proceedings ' of the academy gave them an opportunity of placing the results of their researches or studies before the learned world; and, in the eighteenth century, because they could exercise their wit and intellect fairly safely in the academy without the intervention of police spies or censors. The popularity of academies among the Italian *intelligentsia* of the eighteenth century is largely to be explained by this last fact. The Italian nobility, moderately rich, usually well educated, had no politics in the little paternal or despotic states—Tuscany, Modena, the Papal States, and the rest—in which they lived. They had, however, a sphere for intellectual discussion and expression in their academies. A famous society of this kind was the Accademia della Crusca of Florence. The most widely spread in its influence and

---

[1] Mirabeau, *The Secret History of the Court of Prussia*, vol. i, pp. 120–121.

membership was the Arcadia; indeed, it was probably the
most celebrated academy of the whole eighteenth century.

During the long residence of Queen Christina of Sweden
in Rome men of letters and cultured ladies and gentlemen
had frequently met together in her hospitable villa. Queen
Christina's *salon* came to an end with her death, in 1689.
Nevertheless, the company who used to forgather did not
disperse. One spring day in the year 1692 some fourteen of
them were walking and talking of literature and reciting their
verses in the Prati di Castello, the meadows behind the Castle
of Sant' Angelo. One of the company exclaimed happily,
" It seems to-day as if Arcadia were reviving for us ! " The
idea was taken up enthusiastically, and on that day Arcadia
was founded.

The new academy was a brilliant success from the first. All
the cultured Roman nobles and ecclesiastical dignitaries wished
to join it. A constitution and statutes were drafted by Gian
Vincenzo Gravina, a brilliant young Professor of Law at the
Sapienza, himself an original member of Arcadia. The first
President, or *Custode Generale*, was a literary priest, Gian Mario
Crescimbene. Ladies could become members of the Academy.
The Arcadians met at first in the palace of Don Livio Odescalchi,
but in 1725 King John V of Portugal, who was at Rome and
greatly honoured by the attentions of Arcadia, presented to
the Academy the Bosco Parrasio, a villa on the Janiculum.
This was the seat of Arcadia until the Academy disappeared
in the storm of the French Revolution.

The active life of Arcadia, from 1692 to 1795, extended over
all Italy. At first, naturally, it drew its members from Roman
society and letters and art: Alessandro Guidi, Silvio Stam-
piglia, men of letters; Carlo Maratti, painter, Arcangelo
Corelli, violinist and composer; others of less note. Some,
probably most, of the members were just interested amateurs,
cultured *abáti*, nobles who posed as Mæcenas, ladies who liked
to sparkle in an intellectual company. A famous member about
the year 1775 was Maria Maddalena Morelli, a poetess, the
original of Madame de Staël's Corinne. The great Metastasio

was, naturally, a member, and an active one, in his Roman period. The Academy published large, handsome books, recording its proceedings and chronicling the lives of its celebrated members.

By the middle of the eighteenth century Arcadia had spread over all Italy. Its centre was always the Bosco Parrasio at Rome, but there was a local Arcadian Society in every town. This spreading of Arcadia was both a cause and effect of the delightful absence of class distinctions in eighteenth-century Italy. Society had never been very feudal there. Commerce and social life had promoted a widespread *bourgeoisie*. The Church and the learned professions brought nobles and *bourgeois* together. Now they met regularly in Arcadia. In those placid, picturesque towns nobles, priests, professors, lawyers, doctors, continued to meet, read and talk, in their chosen coffee-house. All that was best in social life outside the family circle was concentrated in Arcadia. The ' utilitarianism ' which began to prevail in intellectual circles in the latter half of the century, the zeal for social reform, the stern research into economics, and also the archæological studies fostered by Winckelmann at Rome, tended to discourage Arcadia. Nevertheless, it was still flourishing when Goethe came to Rome in 1788 and was made a member. Rome, however, was now becoming more cosmopolitan than ever. The fairly large ' colonies ' of foreigners extended and transformed the cultured life of the city; no longer did everybody know everybody else. Arcadia lost its intimacy, its solidarity. In the period of the French Revolution and French occupation it peacefully died away.[1]

According to Matthew Arnold, the existence of a metropolitan academy, like the Arcadian or the Académie Française, was the result of a national bent towards culture and correctness, and in turn promoted that bent. Literatures without such a centre were, in Arnold's view, provincial; writers indulged in caprices, uncorrected, being subject to no stan-

[1] See Vernon Lee, *Studies of the Eighteenth Century in Italy* (1906), pp. 13–102.

dard. Addison has a lovely Attic style, but he is provincial
(says Arnold) because his thoughts are commonplace. Burke
is a writer of genius, but his prose is extravagant; he is provincial, distant from the centre, or, rather, there is no centre
at all to discipline him. He lacks urbanity. He writes " Asiatic "
prose, barbarously rich; " but the true prose is Attic prose." [1]
   Urbanity is the word. The academies had the secret of it.
Esprit de corps, style, finish, mutual respect, and admiration
for the classic past are the marks of the good academicians.
And if one of the sweetest things in life, and a sovereign
remedy for all ills, is the sincere love of letters and the innocent
charm of the muses (as Sainte-Beuve says), the literary
academies of the eighteenth century are supreme.

[1] Matthew Arnold, " The Literary Influence of Academies," in *Essays in Criticism*, First Series (ed. 1921), p. 64.

CHAPTER XVII

THE CHRISTIAN LIFE

THE appraisement of the moral and religious condition of any age is naturally difficult—indeed, impossible to realize completely—because morality and religion are matters of the heart as well as of outward action. Lecky made some such appraisement, with considerable success, for the Roman Empire and the Dark Ages in his *History of European Morals from Augustus to Charlemagne.* A popular judgment, based on insufficient evidence, has epitomized the Middle Ages as the " Ages of Faith." The eighteenth century has never been considered to be an exalted period in either morals or religion; it produced a fair number of *roués*, the name which Saint-Simon says the Regent Orleans applied to his boon-companions; it has been held to be essentially ' secular,' the Age of Reason. Yet it was deeply, though not sentimentally, interested in religion, and Reimarus of Hamburg (who died in 1768) produced the first critical history of the life of Christ.

An age need not necessarily be considered as essentially worldly because it is a reasonable and a tolerant age. The intolerant men of the eighteenth century—and there were still a good number—were presumably religious. Its tolerant men were not necessarily irreligious. Archbishop Leopold von Firmian of Salzburg was doubtless deeply religious. He pressed so hardly upon 30,000 Protestant Salzburgers that they left the country in 1732, and betook themselves to the Kingdom of Prussia. Voltaire was tolerant, but, though he occasionally went to Mass, he cannot be called religious. Firmian and Voltaire, however, are at extremes to each other; and there were many good people in between.

The Roman Catholic Church was then, as it still is, the greatest of the Christian communities. The Pope had a dual position, being Holy Father of the Church and sovereign of the Temporal State. His sovereignty extended over the greater part of Central Italy (except Tuscany). From the Gulf of Venice on the north to the frontier of Naples on the south, the Pope's dominion extended over a length of 240 miles. Like most of the other states of Europe, the Papal State (or States of the Church, for there were several provinces) was ruled by an absolute monarchy. The custom was by this time fully established that every successive Pope should be an Italian. This custom can only have grown up through the fact of there being always a majority of Italians in the College of Cardinals. The cardinals elected an Italian prelate as Pope; and the Italian Pope nominated a majority of Italians to the cardinalate; and this process has continued. As, however, there was no Italian nation in the political sense of the word, the Pope, sovereign of a petty state in the peninsula, was in practice international; that is to say, no great state could have any claim on him. The Temporal Power in the eighteenth century was a guarantee of internationalism on the part of the Papacy. The Papacy had no firm control over the Roman Catholic communities in the states of Europe. The monarchs of France, Spain, and Austria would not suffer the intervention of Rome inside their states. The French Church was ' Gallican.' Something like ' Gallicanism ' prevailed in the other countries too; in Germany in the late eighteenth century it was called ' Febronianism.' In fact, it might be said that in the first half of the eighteenth century the dignity of the Roman Catholic Church was diminished and almost destroyed through slights inflicted by Catholic sovereigns; and in the latter half of the century its very existence was threatened by those sovereigns. They insisted on the Pope dissolving the Jesuit Order; ' Febronianism ' looked like producing an independent German Church; Joseph II's reforms struck at the Roman Church's power in Austria; the French Revolutionary Government rejected Papal jurisdiction altogether. In the eighteenth century, it might almost be said, there existed 'national' Catholic Churches. There were, at any rate, considerable local varieties and privileges among the clergy of various states. The Papacy, the Central Roman authority, was feeble, lacking in prestige and resources. Yet at the end of the age, in the opening of the nineteenth century, there was seen the beginnings of what proved to be a steadily increasing stream of Ultramontanism, a movement towards a completely centralized and unified Church, absolutely controlled from Rome. Gradually all local differences and immunities (with small exceptions) were suppressed. The immovable, authoritative, centralized Church was recognized, one of the most notable facts, in a mutable, uncertain world.

At the beginning and end of the century the Papacy had to meet a movement which threatened its supremacy. The early movement was Jansenism, the later Febronianism. Jansenism began in the seventeenth century. Appealing to the authority of St Augustine, Cornelius Jansen (1585–1638), Bishop of Ypres, a man of great talent and high character, justified experience as a religious guide. The claim of ' experience ' or of an ' inner light ' is not far removed from the claim to the right of private judgment, which is the essence of Protestantism. The Jansenists, however, of whom the best known was Blaise Pascal, were never Protestant. They remained, or endeavoured to remain, in the Church. In 1713 Pope Clement XI, urged forward by the aged and devout King Louis XIV, issued a Bull *Unigenitus*, condemning Jansenism root and branch, in 101 propositions. Thereafter, though the *parlement* of Paris and other local *parlements* all tinged with Jansenism did their best not to recognize the Bull, Jansenism was subjected to legal and ecclesiastical pressure, and declined in France throughout the century. It lingered on, however, in country parsonages. At the end of the century there was one priest who was a Jansenist and who became famous. This was the Abbé Grégoire, a member of the Estates-General of 1789, and the first priest to take the oath of fidelity to the Revolutionary Civil Constitution of the Clergy. In Holland

Bishop Peter Codde, Vicar-General of Utrecht from 1669 to 1710, was Jansenist, and, refusing to submit to the injunctions of the Pope, practically constituted Utrecht as an independent Jansenist Church. This body, the Jansenist Church of Utrecht, which recognizes Papal and Roman Catholic dogma and discipline according to the constitutions of the Church down to and including the Council of Trent of 1563, has maintained itself in existence, with the episcopal succession renewed at the demise of each of its bishops, to the present time.

Towards the end of the century the Papacy received a much more direct attack than that of the Jansenists (who, indeed, had never meant to attack the Papacy) from Febronianism. Bishop Johann Nikolaus von Hontheim was not an obscure priest who could be ignored. He was born in 1701, the son of a noble family, which had been for many generations in the service of the Prince-Archbishop of Trier. After receiving an excellent education at the Jesuit school at Trier and the Universities of Trier, Leyden, and Louvain he entered the priesthood. In 1748 he had risen to be suffragan and vicar-general to the Archbishop of Trier. In this office he had an enormous amount of administrative business to perform, but he found time and energy also to pursue his historical and religious investigations. As historian of Trier, Hontheim is a scholar of importance; as a writer on ecclesiastical affairs he shook the Church to its foundations. His book *De Statu ecclesiæ et legitima potestate Romani pontificis*, published in 1763, was, of course, condemned by Clement XIII and subsequent Popes; and Hontheim eventually submitted and signed a form of retraction which both sides agreed to consider as satisfactory. He died in 1790 on his estate of Montquentin.

The main propositions of Hontheim's book *Concerning the Condition of the Church and the Legitimate Power of the Pope* are, briefly, that the Pope is not infallible, but is subordinate to the whole Church; that an appeal may be made from a decision of the Pope to a General Council; and that in every country the authority of the Church should be exercised by national or provincial synods of the bishops. These propositions, supported with a wealth of learning and argument by Hont-heim (under the pseudonym of "Febronius"), would, if accepted, have resulted in a decentralized Catholic Church, with the Pope enjoying only a 'primacy' among the rest of the bishops. According to Febronius, the Popes themselves were not determined to maintain their autocracy, but the College of Cardinals held them to it.

Although condemned by the Papacy, Febronius's book, or, at any rate, his conclusions, found acceptance in the minds of many clergy and also of monarchs of that age of enlightenment; and it is believed powerfully to have contributed to the move-ment which resulted in the suppression of the Jesuits, the champions of Papal supremacy, in nearly all the states of Europe. In the early years of the nineteenth century, however, the theory of Papal supremacy, or Ultramontanism, underwent a remarkable revival, and Febronianism, except as a lingering tradition, ceased to have much influence, until Bismarck revived it, in the long run unsuccessfully, in his *Kulturkampf*.

It seems unfair to call the eighteenth century irreligious, seeing that it had Jansenism in the beginning and Febronian-ism at the end, and in the middle the Wesleyan and Moravian movements. A characteristic of Jansenism, and particularly of Febronianism, was a liberal attitude towards the other Christian bodies. Febronius believed that, without a sacrifice of Catholicity, the Roman Catholic Church could draw near to the 'dissident' communions, and should be able ultimately to include them. Papal absolutism and infallibility are, how-ever, an insuperable obstacle to union with the Protestant Churches; but as Febronianism denied Papal absolutism and infallibility, it could have, and would have (if it had estab-lished itself), found common ground with the Reformed communions.

In the eighteenth century it would not have been safe to look for the Christian life particularly in the ecclesiastical principalities, any more than in Papal Rome, although con-ditions in Rome and in the Rhineland were fairly respectable. These Rhineland spiritual states were doomed, because they were indistinguishable in culture or morality or politics from secular states, and therefore had no ground for justifying themselves against the secularizing tendencies of the age. Mainz, the premier of the three ecclesiastical electorates, had no eminent prince-archbishop since Francis von Schönborn (1695–1729), the friend and employer of Leibniz. Three successors were respectable prelates, who showed some interest in education, but the last before the Revolution, the Freiherr von Erthal (1774–1802), was reported by Cardinal Pacca as leading a merely worldly life. He was a Voltairean, and appointed the Protestant scientist and man of letters Georg Forster to be his librarian. If this had been his only fault historians would have had little to criticize in him. Archbishop Clemens Wenceslas (1768–1802) of Trier, son of Frederick Augustus II of Saxony, is described as a good-natured cleric, popular and respected, of an irreproachable character; but nothing was done to bring the administrative conditions up to date. The Cologne electoral archbishopric was a perquisite of the Bavarian royal family, the Wittelsbachs, for nearly 200 years, down to the death of Clemens August, son of Maximilian II of Bavaria, in 1761. He is said to have led a life of " wild dissipation." The next archbishop, Maximilian, Graf von Königseck, was not quite so bad an example. In 1784, with the election of the Archduke Maximilian, brother of the Emperor Joseph II, Cologne obtained a zealous and respectable prelate. He was, like Joseph II, a reformer in the ' Josephist ' style, too liberal for his Roman Catholic subjects, who were Ultramontane, and who resented Max's almost ' anti-clerical ' tendencies. The smaller ecclesiastical principalities, such as Speier, appear to have been in a worse condition than the electorates.[1]

The verdict of M. de la Gorce on the Church in France before the Revolution, that scandal cannot be alleged against it, but only lack of zeal, might be applied to the Papacy too in the eighteenth century. It can scarcely be alleged that the lack of zeal in the national Roman Catholic churches was caused by the absence of firm Papal control; for the Popes themselves

[1] See G. P. Gooch, *Germany and the French Revolution* (1920), pp. 15–16.

were no great moral forces, so that power to control the other
countries, if they had had it, would have mattered little. The
personal character of all the Popes since the time of the Counter-
Reformation was reasonably high. They were good men and
good priests, but not outstanding moral forces. The Catholic
rulers of the states of Europe ignored them, with the result
that toleration became the custom if not the law everywhere,
except in Spain. The Papacy began to receive orders from
the monarchs, and in 1773 Clement XIV had to enact by Bull
the suppression of the Order of Jesus. The attack of the
monarchs on the Jesuits was not an attack upon religion, but
upon the secular power and property of the great Order and
upon its unswerving championship of Papal supremacy in
every land.

Perhaps the most saintly character of the eighteenth century
was in the Protestant community. Jean Frédéric Oberlin was
born at Strasbourg in 1740, the son of a schoolmaster. As a
student at the University of Strasbourg he came under the
influence of Dr Lorentz, a devout evangelical Lutheran
preacher. After finishing his studies at Strasbourg he was
ordained minister. There followed upon this a period as tutor
in a private family; then he became in 1767 pastor of Waldbach, in the Ban de la Roche, also called Steinthal, the stony
valley. Naturally unfertile, the Steinthal had also been devas-
tated in the Thirty Years War (1618-48), and had never
recovered. The villagers were Protestant, some of them
refugees, for only in Alsace did the French Government recognize the legality of Protestantism. The village of Waldbach
was 1800 feet above sea-level, and stood in a rocky, almost
barren countryside. The condition of education was deplor-
ably low, but Oberlin's predecessor, the Pastor Stuber, had
started schools at Waldbach and the four other villages which
were within the parish. Oberlin energetically carried on this
educational work. He resided in Waldbach, married, and became the beloved guide of all five villages. There were three
churches in the parish; Oberlin preached in each in turn, but
drew his congregation from all the parish. The peasants would

usually bring a horse to fetch him, and would take him after
the service to dinner with one of their families.

Oberlin was the ideal conscientious and kind pastor. He
prepared his sermons with the greatest care, and committed
them to memory. In order to meet the needs of his congregation he had services in German as well as in French. He
knew all his people, and kept a ' moral register ' of such as
were drunkards, idlers, bad managers. He was particularly
attentive to the needs of children, keeping Sunday School
regularly, and carefully catechizing them and explaining the
way of good life. He induced his parishioners to build a school
in each of the five villages, providing funds partly from his
own pocket, partly from gifts of his friends in Strasbourg. At
these schools children over seven years of age were taught
reading, writing, arithmetic, and the elements of geography,
agriculture, astronomy, Scriptural and secular history. From
all five villages the children came once a week to Waldbach
for an examination, so that the progress made in each village
could be compared, and a wholesome competition be maintained between them. There was a central lending library,
each village being allowed to retain its share of the books for
three months. Oberlin also induced the schools to make collections of plants; he installed a model of an electrical machine,
and published an *Almanack* without the usual superstitious
and frivolous entries.

Although Oberlin's schools were for children over seven
years of age, he was keenly alive to the needs of the younger
children. For these, from the ages of two to six, he provided
rooms under the charge of " mild and affectionate women,"
called *conductrices*. It was the duty of the *conductrice* to teach
the infants French (with their parents they would talk the local
patois), and as they grew older to sew, knit, spin, and sing.
Use was also made of geographical picture-cards and prints
of national and sacred history. While the children were in
these ' Kindergartens ' the parents were out labouring in the
fields.

The backwardness of the people of Ban de la Roche was,

in Oberlin's view, particularly caused by lack of means of communication with the world outside. He therefore induced the villagers to give part of their time to making roads and bridges. Soon there were ready means of communication with Strasbourg, as well as between the villages and with neighbouring towns. In the process of road-making and embanking opportunity was also taken to turn aside streams (so preventing floods) and to improve or rebuild the poorer cottages and cabins of the once-desolate district. In order to direct attention to better methods of agriculture, Oberlin had two model gardens of his own, always open to the villagers. The people had given up trying to cultivate the potato, and were living on inferior grain and peas and apples. Oberlin sent abroad for new varieties of potatoes, and soon found one which suited the soil of the Ban. In time the desolate hillsides took on a garden-like appearance, delightful to the eye; and in the bad years of famine in France the stony Ban de la Roche escaped the worst effects. To the reintroduced potato Oberlin added other profitable plants—flax, with seed procured from Riga, rare grasses, clover. He established nurseries for young trees, taught the science of grafting to improve the fruit, and founded an agricultural society. The quality and quantity of milk was immensely improved by the use of new feeding stuffs for cows.

Under the energetic and benevolent pastor the population of the Ban increased so rapidly that there was surplus labour; as many as 1500 were unemployed. Oberlin met this difficulty by introducing straw-plaiting, knitting, dyeing, and finally cotton-spinning. So efficient did the new industries become that a Bâle firm established a branch factory in Waldbach for making ribbons. The brighter boys of the villages were apprenticed to crafts at Strasbourg, and came back to the Ban as expert blacksmiths, masons, joiners, glaziers, and wheelwrights.

The moral improvement of the Ban was no less remarkable than the material. Oberlin made the local gentry take an interest in the people and the churches; he inspired a number of the villagers to engage in missionary work; and he induced the spirit of mutual help among them, so that if a peasant's cow died prematurely his neighbours would help the peasant to buy another; if a new cottage had to be built young people would fetch stone and timber; if a breadwinner became ill the neighbours would go out and share his work in the field.

The fame of the valley spread abroad in France, Germany, and England. Ministers of religion came to see villagers living together in sobriety, industry, and Christian charity. Members of agricultural societies came to study methods of local improvement and experiment. Louis XVIII made Oberlin a member of the Legion of Honour. The prefect of the *département* (Bas-Rhin) frequently consulted the pastor. Long-standing legal disputes about timber rights and such matters of local feud were settled outside the courts under Oberlin's advice or arbitration. The villagers were predominantly rigidly Protestant, but Oberlin induced them to be fair to the few Roman Catholics and to tolerate the Jews. Until the last years of his life he conducted all his visitations uphill and down dale, in rain or snow, upon foot. Incessantly active as he was, he never gave up the duty of study. He had no prejudices. " I am a Frenchman and a German," he once said. His house became a sort of medical dispensary as well as parsonage. After fifty-nine years of devoted labour the venerable pastor died, on June 1, 1826, at the age of eighty-six.

Though a married man and a Protestant, Oberlin's life was in many respects like that of a Roman Catholic priest of a parish. There are different aspects of saintliness; Oberlin's is almost medieval. The universal respect in which he was held, the unchallenged admiration for his wholly Christian character, are like the ' sainthood ' by popular recognition which the Middle Ages was wont to confer. Such a position was almost gained at the opening of the eighteenth century by a man of rare beauty of character. François de Salignac de la Mothe Fénelon was forty-three years old when he was nominated Archbishop of Cambrai in 1694. His book, *Explication des Maximes des Saints sur la vie intérieure*, brought him into conflict with the great Bossuet, Bishop of Meaux; and for the last fifteen years of his life, which ended on January 7, 1715,

Fénelon was exiled from Court and confined to his diocese. Saint-Simon in his *Mémoires* has charmingly described the life of the great prelate during this period at Cambrai. Hitherto known as a courtier, and as the author of *Télémaque*, Fénelon now became known as the saintly archbishop, who tended the wounded in his palace during the War of the Spanish Succession; who lived sparely but entertained largely; who thoroughly knew the affairs of the diocese and personally attended to all of them; and whose continual services in the church and daily walks in the city made him familiar to all the citizens of Cambrai and to the multitude of travellers continually passing by there.[1]

Saints, who were the fine flowers of medieval Catholicism, are less numerous in the centuries of modern history. The eighteenth century was, perhaps, too rational or too worldly; saintliness is discernible in the Roman Catholic Church of this period only rarely. There was, however, one important order founded by one acknowledged saint. Alphonsus Liguori was born at Marianella, near Naples, in 1696, the eldest of seven children. His father, who belonged to a noble but impoverished family, was a captain in the navy of the Kingdom of Naples, which at that time was under the Spanish Crown; his mother was Spanish. The boy grew up intelligent, obstinate, earnest. At sixteen he was a Doctor of Laws; and at the age of nineteen he began practising as an advocate at the Neapolitan Bar. At the age of twenty-seven he was one of the leading barristers, being reputed not to have lost a single case.

At this time, in 1723, the successful advocate, favoured by fortune and society, had an important case which turned upon the correct reading of a certain document. Alphonsus made a mistake in regard to it, and lost the case, involving for his client about £100,000. He was so filled with remorse for the mistake that he left the court in tears, resolving never to practise again. He gave himself up to contemplation and acts of charity, until suddenly, when visiting a hospital, he discerned a light shining upon him and a voice saying, *Leave the world*

[1] Saint-Simon, *Mémoires* (1830), IX, 344 ff.

and give thyself to me (August 28, 1723). On October 23 he put on clerical dress, and a year later joined the missionary association called Neapolitan Propaganda. His ordination as priest took place on December 21, 1726. He continued to live in his father's house, and from there conducted his devoted labours among the Neapolitan poor—the *lazzaroni*, as they were called.

In 1729 Alphonsus left his father's house and went to live in the Chinese College, a missionary college of Naples. There he met a guest, Father Thomas Falcoia, and made the great friendship of his life, although Alphonsus was only thirty-three years old, and Falcoia sixty-six. Falcoia was shortly afterwards consecrated Bishop of Castellamare. With his help, and supported by visions of Sister Maria Celeste, a nun of the convent of Scala, Alphonsus founded at Scala on November 9, 1732, the " Congregation of the Most Holy Redeemer," with the special object of attending to the spiritual needs of the goatherds of that mountainous region.

The Congregation of Redemptorists, which contained houses of monks and houses of nuns, had somewhat stormy times. From 1708 to 1734 the Kingdom of Naples was under Austrian rule, and the Redemptorists were tolerated. In 1734, in the War of the Polish Succession, Naples passed to Don Carlos, son of Philip V of Spain and Queen Elizabeth Farnese. Don Carlos was a reforming monarch, one of the *rois éclairés* of the century. He had a like-minded Minister of State, the Marquis Tanucci. The policy of the new *régime* in Naples was to limit the power of religious orders, which were regarded as obstacles to the complete development of state sovereignty. There were also dissensions inside the Redemptorist Order. A further blow was the appointment of Alphonsus as Bishop of St Agatha of the Goths, a Neapolitan diocese, in 1762. He tried to avoid this appointment, but King Carlos insisted, and he could not escape the position.

After thirteen years of devoted and unremitting labour in his diocese Alphonsus was permitted in 1775 to resign his see and to return to his missionary work as a Redemptorist brother. He was now old, feeble, bent with rheumatism, invalid, believed to be dying. He took up his abode in a cell at Nocera, expecting a speedy death. Actually he had twelve more years of work. It was a singularly unhappy period, for dissension broke out again in the order; the saint, crippled, deaf, nearly blind, could not control his quarrelsome foundation. Though eighty-eight, and almost bedridden, he was assailed by temptations of the devil, and had to fight night and day against sinful suggestions, apparitions, and illusions. After three years of this struggle he won his way through to peace, dying peacefully on August 1, 1787, when just short of ninety-one years of age.

Alphonsus was canonized in 1839. His reputation for saintliness was the result of a life of intense activity, and, indeed, of intense passion, spent in the service of God, unsullied, yet apparently a failure in its aims, for his order was never widespread, and seemed in perpetual danger of disintegration. His solid fame rests upon numerous published works, especially a *Theologia Moralis*, a grand treatise on problems of conduct and motive, inspired by the Jesuit system of casuistry, and carrying this system to complete and, as Alphonsus believed, unchallengeable conclusions. In an age regarded by good Catholics as one of impiety and infidelity, the age of Voltaire, Rousseau, and Frederick the Great, the long career of this passionate Papalist, whose character was like that of St Francis and St Theresa, made an impression on contemporary society which to-day can scarcely be realized. His reputed miracles are not numerous nor particularly impressive. His published works, numerous and solid though they are, do not account for his great reputation. This reputation is the result of character, or moral intensity, which, in a long and stormy life, imposed itself upon the imagination of an age beginning to react from the dictates of pure reason. It cannot have been a wholly worldly age which recognized so frankly the merit, on the one hand, of the stormy, harassed, passionate, unhappy character of the zealot Alphonsus, and, on the other, of the tranquil, harmonious, cheerful Pastor Oberlin.

In Germany in the eighteenth century there was a notable evangelical or 'Pietist' movement, which continued to have a powerful influence throughout the century, the disturbing period of the French Revolution, and even down to the late nineteenth century. The great çentre of Pietism was the Prussian University of Halle, which was founded in 1694, and almost at once became highly distinguished in theology and philosophy. The movement was Protestant, Lutheran, austere and wholly opposed to ritual or sacerdotalism—a kind of Puritan movement within the Lutheran Church, which, it was contended, had developed beyond the original views of Luther.

The originator of the movement seems to have been Philipp Jakob Spener, who was not himself connected with the University of Halle. He was born at Rappoltsweiler, in Upper Alsace, on January 13, 1635. As a youth he felt a call to the ministry. After studying at the chief Protestant centres—Strasbourg, Bâle, Tübingen, Geneva, and Stuttgart—he was ordained to the ministry in the Lutheran Church. As pastor at Frankfort he laboured to reintroduce the simple devotion, humility, charity—piety, in a word—which the spirit of theological controversy had overlaid or driven away. From the year 1670 Spener held at his house in Frankfort frequent meetings for prayer, meditation, discussion, and exposition of the Bible. The movement spread throughout Protestant Germany, and the meetings took on a regular form, under the name of Colleges of Piety (*collegia pietatis*). In 1686 he was made Court preacher at Dresden (a curious official position for a Lutheran pastor under a Roman Catholic monarch). From Dresden his influence spread to the great University of Leipzig. In 1689 the Elector of Brandenburg invited him to be Provost of the Church of St Nicholas in Berlin. Thus when in 1694 the Prussian University of Halle was founded Spener's views and Spener's disciples naturally were accorded much influence there. Spener himself remained at his work in Berlin until his death, in 1705. He was an admirable pastor, earnest, fearless, and strong. His book *Pious Desires* (*Pia Desideria*) was the handbook of the Pietist movement. Francke was his most influential disciple.

August Hermann Francke was born at Lübeck in 1663. After a distinguished student career at the universities of

Erfurt and Kiel he became a preacher at Luneburg. He corresponded with Spener, and visited him at Dresden. In 1694 he was made Professor of Oriental Languages in the University of Halle; in 1698 he exchanged this chair for that of theology in the same university. A follower of Spener, Francke made Halle the centre of the Pietist movement. Like Spener, he was no mystic, but a practical man, whose piety expressed itself, among other ways, in founding educational and charitable institutions—an orphanage, a school for poor boys, a college for training teachers, schools for girls, higher schools for teaching Latin and also modern subjects. These institutions are still flourishing in Halle. He died there in 1727.

Francke's most influential follower was the pious Count Zinzendorf. Nicolaus Ludwig, Graf von Zinzendorf, was born at Dresden in 1700, son of a Minister of State of Frederick Augustus I, the Strong, Elector of Saxony. Brought up in the Protestant Lutheran faith, under the influence of Spener (a friend of his family), Zinzendorf was from the first within the Pietist circle. At the age of ten he was sent to Francke's Pädagogium at Halle. When the time came for him, in his seventeenth year, to proceed to a university his guardians sent him not to Halle, the stronghold of Pietism, but to Wittenberg, which was sternly orthodox Lutheran. Zinzendorf never lost his inclination to Pietism, but freed himself, at Wittenberg, from Pietist narrowness and introspection. In 1719 Zinzendorf left the university and travelled for two years in Holland and France, moving particularly in Protestant evangelical society. In 1721 he returned to Dresden and entered the Civil Service of the Elector of Saxony.

Zinzendorf's heart was in evangelical religion, not in Government service. From time to time he saw refugees who came out of Bohemia and Moravia, " Hussites " or " Moravian Brethren," fleeing from Austrian persecution into the Protestant land of Saxony. In 1722 he established a home and settlement for such refugees on his estate near the Austrian frontier, in Saxon Lausitz. They called the settlement Herrnhut, the " Lord's Keeping " or the " Lord's Protection." Besides the

Bohemian and Moravian refugees, many hungry and disturbed souls came from other parts of Germany, men and women who felt the want of a more direct and personal appeal to God and Christ than, they thought, was to be found in orthodox Lutheranism or Calvinism. Zinzendorf displayed a high capacity for tactful, orderly government, for maintaining peace, unity, and zeal in his community of diverse evangelical elements.

The settlement grew and prospered, and became a famous religious community. Quarrels and somewhat wild religious views disturbed their peace, but Zinzendorf proved to be a peace-maker, and gradually he was recognized as the spiritual father of the members of the community. In 1737 he was ordained bishop (by Bishop Jablonski, Court preacher of Berlin), and as such he governed the Moravian community at Herrnhut peacefully and happily. He travelled in the interest of his religious community, visited England in 1741, and founded, though he did not visit, a mission station in the United States. He died at Herrnhut in 1760, at the age of sixty. Herrnhut was a place of religious study, prayer, and singing. Men and women, young and old, met to read and study the Bible, to communicate to each other their religious experiences, to give whatever spiritual help they could. There were two daily religious services, and all the community regularly attended. Aiming at a return to the ways of the early Christian Church, the Herrnhuters undertook missionary work in almost every land. John Wesley has told in his *Journal* in 1738 that God gave him to know many of His servants, " particularly those of the church of Herrnhut." In that year, after his return from Georgia, he revisited Oxford with a Moravian Brother, Peter Böhler, who was just arrived from Germany. They went together to Stanton Harcourt, where they stayed with the vicar, John Gambold. " All this time," Wesley noted in his *Journal*, " I conversed much with Peter Böhler." He adds : " But I understood him not." Nevertheless, Wesley was greatly interested by his Moravian connexion. Later he visited Herrnhut, which, for a time, took the place of Geneva as the most vivid centre of the Protestant communion. There, at Herrnhut, on Saxon soil, in the worldly and sceptical and so largely dissolute eighteenth century, was a great and continuing home of simple piety, a centre of ' quietism ' and contemplation, but also of earnest and practical Christian work, which was soon influencing not only the old Continent and British Isles, but the new European societies in America.

In the last half of the century religion and society were enriched by the beautiful life of Johann Kaspar Lavater of Zürich. This man was a minister in the Reformed Church. His earnestness, his high powers of oratory, his intense conviction, brought large congregations to hear him. He became famous throughout the Rhineland and in England. Large numbers of people corresponded with him or came to see him. Lavater frequently travelled in Germany and received an enthusiastic reception. On his visits to Frankfort he came to know the young Goethe, and the two became firm friends. Lavater charmed all who met him by his simplicity and personal goodness. He was indefatigable in his many-sided work—in the ministry, in theology, in philosophical inquiry. He took an enormous interest in the study of character by observation of the human countenance, and published a large treatise on phrenology in 1778. His mystical work, published about the same time in four volumes, called *Aussichten in die Ewigkeit* (*Views into Eternity*), had great influence. During the French Revolutionary War in 1799 the French army under Masséna, after hard fighting with the Russian army in Switzerland, took Zürich. Lavater fearlessly exposed himself in trying to protect the citizens from the maddened, plundering soldiery, and was wounded by a French grenadier to whom he had a few minutes before given food and drink. He lived for over a year in great suffering, borne with the highest courage and fortitude, and died, aged sixty, on January, 2, 1801.

Saintliness can probably be discovered in certain individuals in any age. The eighteenth century, if not particularly rich in other-worldly men, was certainly not without them. A layman of the British North American Colony, New Jersey, John Woolman (1723–72), was the first 'abolitionist,' the first to set himself actively against negro slavery. His *Journal* shows a simple, devout, truthful man, earnest in God's service, wholly disinterested and unworldly. It is a religious and literary classic. France was a Roman Catholic country. The Huguenots or Protestants, *réformés* or *religionnaires* (all these terms meant the same thing), enjoyed no legal tolerance in France. Sometimes their worship was savagely repressed; in the latter part of the eighteenth century they were, for the most part, left in peace, in the general spread of enlightenment and free-thinking. Necker, one of the last and best statesmen of the *ancien régime*, was a Protestant.

The legally recognized French Church, the Roman Catholic, rested, like the whole *ancien régime*, on privilege. The Church was largely exempt from taxation; the clergy paid even less taxes than the nobles. The wealth of the Church in France, comprising land, rents, and tithe, amounted to about 180,000,000 livres a year (£7,200,000). Travellers noted the opulent, substantial aspect of the great ecclesiastical foundations, an abbey with its massive walls and numerous buildings, its extensive and well-kept enclosures, its stately cloisters, its comfortable, if somewhat austere, guest-house, its spacious and sumptuously ornamented church.[1]

The moral and intellectual condition of the clergy was, on the whole, respectable. The *curé*, or priest of the parish, the most numerous and naturally the most influential class of clergy, lived, in the country at any rate, much in the same style as the lesser English country clergy. The house of the *curé* was usually the biggest in the village, close to the church, surrounded by a large garden, perhaps with stables and a barn. The priest was generally a man of decent morals, attentive to his duties, fairly well read. He was the son of a small *bourgeois* or of a small farmer, was trained in a seminary for priests, was appointed to his parish by the bishop or by an abbey or by

[1] P. de la Gorce, *Histoire religieuse de la révolution française* (1921), vol. i, pp. 7–8.

a nobleman who possessed the right of patronage; and in the parish he spent the rest of his life. His usual income might be as little as 500 livres (£20) or as high as 1500 (£60), according as he was entitled to full tithe or not. In addition, of course, he had his house and garden, and perhaps some pasture-land. As a bachelor he was quite as well off as Goldsmith's Vicar of Wakefield, who had a large family, or Goldsmith's brother, the parson in " Sweet Auburn," who was passing rich on forty pounds a year.

The abbeys were mainly wealthy, some of them very wealthy —St Vaast, at Arras, is said to have had a revenue of 500,000 livres (£20,000) a year. Not all the revenue, however, went to the use of the monks or the abbey-church. Most of the abbeys were held *in commendam* (*en commende*)—that is, some powerful archbishop or bishop had one or perhaps two abbeys, visiting his abbey only very occasionally, as a great honour, but receiving about one-third of the revenue. Cardinal de Rohan, Archbishop of Strasbourg, of " Diamond Necklace " celebrity, had the abbeys of St Vaast and Chaise-Dieu; the Cardinal la Rochefoucauld had Cluny; the Cardinal of York, the last of the royal Stuarts, had Anchin and St Amand. The monks, left to themselves under a deputy for the abbot, called a claustral prior (*prieur claustral*), were generally well conducted. There were scandals in a few abbeys. For the rest, there was a decent observance of duty and propriety, but little fervour. The condition of affairs seems remarkably like that of the English monasteries on the eve of the Reformation. In France in 1789 " the normal condition was by no means corruption, but slackness (*relâchement*)." The profession of monk was not popular. There were few recruits, few novitiates. The total number of abbeys was 755 for men, 253 for women. The average number of monks or nuns in an abbey was some seven or eight. The age had passed by them. They were out of date; the last monks languished " in this growing solitude " (*en cette solitude croissante*).

Bishops, according to the Concordat of 1515, were nominated by the Crown, and received institution (which was seldom refused) from the Holy See. On the eve of the Revolution there were 130 archbishoprics or bishoprics in France, all served exclusively by noblemen. About one-third of the total number of bishops are said to have been habitually absent from their diocese, engaged on ecclesiastical or civil business at the Court of Versailles. Being all of high noble family, and enjoying large episcopal incomes or abbatical revenues, they lived the life of the great world, but nearly all of them decently and respectably, and often engaged on public work, such as presiding at the Provincial Estates (the ancient feudal assemblies of the Pays d'États), acting as royal almoners or even as departmental Ministers, and attending to their religious duties with propriety, if not with assiduity.

Such was the practice of the French clergy, as described by an historian who is both thoroughly scientific in his method and also sympathetic, perhaps even ' clerical,' in his outlook.[1] To the regular, officiating clergymen, thus described, must be added a number of *abbés*, ordained priests, of gentle birth and of moderate private wealth, who lived the life of fashionable *philosophes* at Paris, were *habitués* of the *salons*, excellent conversationalists, correspondents, writers of pamphlets, contributors to the *Encyclopædia*, authors of scholarly treatises. Such were the Abbé de Saint-Pierre, the author of the *Projet de paix perpetuelle*, and the Abbé Raynal, a member of the brilliant circles of Diderot and Grimm, a contributor to the *Encyclopædia* and the author of a once-famous *Histoire des Indes*.[2]

The French Revolution deprived the Church of its privileges and property, and reduced it to poverty; but after twelve years, with the conclusion of the Concordat, " the Catholics and priests of France, purified by persecution, strengthened by martyrdom, entered again into their abandoned temples, at the dawn of a new age." [3]

[1] P. de la Gorce, *op. cit.*, vol. i, p. 34.

[2] For Saint-Pierre and Raynal see above, pp. 75–77, 215, 218. Raynal's *Histoire philosophique et politique des établissements et du commerce des Européens dans les deux Indes*, a geographical and ethnographical as well as historical work, was first published in 1780.

[3] P. de la Gorce, *op. cit.*, Preface.

CHAPTER XVIII

BACK TO NATURE

THE admiration of the men of the eighteenth century for
nature had notable effects upon philosophy, literature,
law. It produced a passion, but a restrained passion, for liberty
in a despotic age. Mental and spiritual freedom and equality
before the law were conceptions which these men derived
from their reflections on the state of nature. They also derived the conception that freedom must be social, a condition
not merely of the individual or the family, but of a whole
people. Rousseau placed his ideal of such a free people in
Corsica. " I have a presentiment that this little people will
one day astonish Europe," he wrote in 1765.[1] Corsica astonished Europe by producing Napoleon Bonaparte; its liberty,
however, expressed itself—partly, at any rate—in those days
by 800 assassinations a year.[2]

In any age in which people are inclined to reflection and
criticism there is a tendency for them to consider that virtue is
declining, and that the age is too luxurious. The men of the
eighteenth century had some such notion; and while some, like
Wesley and Zinzendorf, tried to correct this by appealing to the
religious and ascetic instincts, others, like Rousseau and the
Abbé Raynal, called people " back to nature."

The idea of Rousseau and the Abbé Raynal was not new.
In *The Conquest of Granada*, by Dryden, published in 1670,
Almanzor says to Boabdelin, the last King of Granada:

> Obeyed as sovereign by thy subjects be;
> But, know, that I alone am king of me.

---

[1] C. B. Tinker, *Nature's Simple Plan*, p. 34. *Cf.* Rousseau's *Projet pour
la Corse*, in Vaughan, *The Political Writings of J.-J. Rousseau* (1915).
[2] *Ibid.*, p. 38.

I am as free as Nature first made man,
Ere the base laws of servitude began,
When wild in woods the noble savage ran.[1]

Johnson, Boswell, Goldsmith, and General Oglethorpe (at
a dinner of the General's) discussed the reputed decline of
the age in which they were living. Goldsmith attacked the
age; Johnson stoutly defended it. Boswell writes:

On Tuesday, April 13, he and Dr Goldsmith and I dined at
General Oglethorpe's. Goldsmith expatiated on the common
topic, that the race of our people was degenerated, and that this
was owing to luxury. JOHNSON: " Sir, in the first place, I doubt
the fact. I believe that there are as many tall men in England
now as ever there were. But, secondly, supposing the stature of
our people to be diminished, that is not owing to luxury; for,
Sir, consider to how very small a proportion of our people luxury
can reach. Our soldiery, surely, are not luxurious, who live on
sixpence a day; and the same remark will apply to almost all the
other classes. Luxury, so far as it reaches the poor, will do good
to the race of people; it will strengthen and multiply them. Sir,
no nation was ever hurt by luxury; for, as I said before, it can
but reach to a very few. I admit that the great increase of commerce and manufactures hurts the military spirit of a people;
because it produces a competition for something else than martial
honours—a competition for riches. It also hurts the bodies of
the people; for you will observe, there is no man who works
at any particular trade, but you may know him from his appearance to do so. One part or the other of his body being more used
than the rest, he is in some degree deformed: but, Sir, that is
not luxury. A tailor sits cross-legged; but that is not luxury."
GOLDSMITH: " Come, you're just going to the same place by
another road." JOHNSON: " Nay, Sir, I say that it is not *luxury*.
Let us take a walk from Charing Cross to Whitechapel, through,
I suppose, the greatest series of shops in the world, what is there
in any of these shops (if you except gin-shops) that can do any
human being any harm? " GOLDSMITH: " Well, Sir, I'll accept
your challenge. The very next shop to Northumberland House
is a pickle-shop." JOHNSON: " Well, Sir: do we not know that a
maid can in one afternoon make pickles sufficient to serve a

[1] Part I, Act I, Scene 1.

whole family for a year? nay, that five pickle-shops can serve all
the kingdom? Besides, Sir, there is no harm done to any body
by the making of pickles, or the eating of pickles.[1]

Goldsmith believed, or professed to believe, that Piety,
Loyalty, and Faithful Love, the Muse of Poetry and Freedom,
or " self-dependent power," were departing with the emigrants
to North America.[2]

> O luxury! thou cursed by Heaven's decree,
> How ill exchanged are things like these for thee!
> How do thy potions, with insidious joy,
> Diffuse their pleasure only to destroy!
> Kingdoms, by thee to sickly greatness grown,
> Boast of a florid vigour not their own.
> At every draught more large and large they grow,
> A bloated mass of rank unwieldy woe;
> Till sapped their strength, and every part unsound,
> Down, down they sink and spread a ruin round.
>
> Even now the devastation is begun,
> And half the business of destruction done;
> Even now, methinks, as pondering here I stand,
> I see the rural virtues leave the land.
> Down where yon anchoring vessel spreads the sail
> That idly waiting flaps with every gale,
> Downward they move, a melancholy band,
> Pass from the shore, and darken all the strand.
> Contented toil, and hospitable care,
> And kind connubial tenderness, are there;
> And piety, with wishes placed above,
> And steady loyalty, and faithful love.
> And thou, sweet Poetry, thou loveliest maid,
> Still first to fly where sensual joys invade;
> Unfit in these degenerate times of shame
> To catch the heart, or strike for honest fame;
> Dear charming nymph, neglected and decried,
> My shame in crowds, my solitary pride;
> Thou source of all my bliss, and all my woe,
> That found'st me poor at first, and keep'st me so;
> Thou guide by which the nobler arts excel,
> Thou nurse of every virtue, fare thee well!

---

[1] Boswell, *Life of Johnson*, sub anno 1773.
[2] C. B. Tinker, *Nature's Simple Plan* (1922), p. 3.

Farewell, and O! where'er thy voice be tried,
On Torno's cliffs, or Pambamarca's side,
Whether where equinoctial fervours glow,
Or winter wraps the polar world in snow,
Still let thy voice, prevailing over time,
Redress the rigours of the inclement clime;
Aid slighted truth with thy persuasive strain;
Teach erring man to spurn the rage of gain;
Teach him, that states of native strength possessed,
Though very poor, may still be very blessed;
That trade's proud empire hastes to swift decay,
As ocean sweeps the laboured mole away;
While self-dependent power can time defy,
As rocks resist the billows and the sky.[1]

The European interest in primitive nature and in savage life was stimulated by the remarkable achievement of the eighteenth century in geographical discovery and observation. Admiral Anson sailed round the world in 1739–40, and his chaplain wrote an interesting description. Cook's voyages among the islands of the South Seas and to Australia resulted in an immediate and vast increase in Europe's knowledge and interest concerning savage peoples and primitive countries. The gentleness, friendliness, and natural courtesy of the natives of the Tonga Group, called by Cook the Friendly Islands, confirmed the preconceived idea which poets and philosophers entertained concerning the noble savage. Cook later paid with his life the penalty of too much trust in the friendliness and peacefulness of savages, but the men of the *salons* and libraries at home were little affected by such an incident. It is a curious fact that even the highly civilized countries of Europe had interesting survivals or examples of primitive life. While Captain Cook was exploring the South Seas Peter the Wild Boy, who had been caught in the woods near Hanover in 1725, and who could speak no language, was still living in England.[2] George I had taken a kindly interest in him, and had him brought over to England. There Peter the Wild Boy lived until his death in 1785. The French scientist Condamine published an account of a savage girl, caught in the valley of

---

[1] *The Deserted Village, ad fin.*   [2] C. B. Tinker, *op. cit.*, p. 6.

the Marne, living like a wild cat in a tree, and unable to speak any known language.[1] Bruce's *Travels to discover the Sources of the Nile*, 1768–73 (published in 1790), and Buffon's *Natural History* (1749–67) contributed genuine scientific knowledge of savage life to Europe. The journeys and studies of Carl Linnæus produced the *Species Plantarum* in 1753, and established for all time the science of botany.

It was this haunting tendency to hark back to nature and freedom from the artificialities and restrictions of society which led Rousseau, though not a systematic thinker, to write his celebrated treatise on politics, the *Contrat social*.[2] Man, he was convinced, was naturally good and naturally free; he was born unspoiled and unrestricted in body and spirit, but " is everywhere in chains "—chains of law and custom, chains of passion and vice. How has this change occurred? he asks, and at the same time replies, " I do not know." He soon comes to the conclusion, however, that society, as it has been developed, is the cause; the existing state of society has corrupted the noble nature of man. This corruption was itself caused by the very lack of freedom, by the servitude of mind and body in which the citizens were kept by their despotic or oligarchic Governments and society. The way to restore the original virtue of men is to restore their freedom, to release them from the servitude which dishonours and debases them. Nevertheless, by what may be considered to be a curious contradiction in Rousseau's views, he will not leave men, thus freed from corrupting servitude, in anarchy, without control, without government. He concluded that man (although by nature noble) could only really live as a civilized man in a state subject to, controlled by, the general will, of which his own will is a part. This belief in a self-governing political community prevented Rousseau from being a merely destructive thinker, made him constructive, positive. His kind of state, however, would be very different in its form of government from the authoritarian states of enlightened despots.

---

[1] Burnet, Lord Monboddo, *The History of the Wild Girl* (1768).
[2] Rousseau, *Du Contrat social*, Book I, Chapter I.

Montesquieu, *le grand penseur* of the eighteenth century in politics, as Sorel calls him, had surveyed existing laws and states, and had analysed their ways of functioning; his method was historical, based on the careful collection of facts and instances. Rousseau, not exactly ignoring history, but ignoring everything that did not suit his point of view, went " back to nature," owing to his revulsion from a society into which he himself fitted so ill. Yet it is difficult to see that any other kind of society could have treated him better.

Rousseau was himself the natural man, living by whim and instinct; and it was a great privilege for him to be allowed, by that trim, self-satisfied society which he so powerfully casti-gated, to live his own life at large, incurably romantic, erratic, capricious. " I arrived at the age of forty," he wrote in *Les Rêveries du promeneur solitaire*, " floating between indigence and wealth, between wisdom and error, full of vices of habit without any bad tendency in my heart, living at hazard without well-defined principles in my mind, and distracted in my duties without despising them, but often without clearly discerning them." Eighteenth-century Europe was a society where a man must have the correct manner, and must conduct his affairs by the rule of reason; but Rousseau had neither *savoir-faire* nor *raison*. Nor did he make the slightest effort to adapt himself to the ways of this ' artificial ' society, which, nevertheless, went on tolerating him and maintaining him to the end of his strange and wayward life.

This rebel against the age was born at Geneva, the son of a watchmaker, on June 28, 1712. Here was an antique city-state, where man, who had been born free, not, as in other countries, in chains, but obeying the will of all the citizens, *la volonté générale*, obeyed in this way himself. A free city, an enchanting lake, a rushing river, green hills and woodland, majestic mountains in the distance, were food for thought to the imaginative and precocious youth. He read omnivorously, was much alone, sometimes neglected, sometimes petted, never regularly educated, never inured to discipline or to habits of self-control. An inner life of romance, an outer scene of splendid nature—Lake Léman, the Rhône, Mont Blanc, Mont Salève—formed the education of the sensitive and suffering Jean-Jacques. Rousseau was one of the earliest lovers of mountain scenery. The Englishman, William Beckford, who delighted in " those lofty peaks," came to Tyrol a generation later (1782). De Saussure climbed Mont Blanc in 1787.

The boy, who was an orphan, being brought up by an uncle, was put to more than one trade or profession, but failed to make good in any. His delight was to escape into the country-side for long, solitary rambles; but once, in 1728, he rambled too far and too late, and found himself shut out by the closed city gate. The incredible youth simply accepted the fact of exclusion, and turned away from home and friends, to roam in the wide world beyond. Thus began that amazing early course of wandering, for which the only authority is Rousseau's *Confessions*, written in his later years.

Evidently it was on the south side of the city that Rousseau, aged sixteen, found himself shut out from Geneva. It is only a short walk into Savoy, at that time part of the dominions of the King of Sardinia. The boy wandered among the pleasant valleys and farms of that green and fruitful country. A *curé* gave him lodging one night, and introduced him to Madame de Warens, a well-to-do Genevese lady, who, being converted to Catholicism, had naturally left the city of Calvin, and now had a small country-house at Annecy. Madame de Warens was attracted by the handsome, intellectual boy, and sent him to a religious house at Turin, where he made no difficulty in being converted. He was then sent forth with twenty francs in his pocket to make his own living. A good-looking, personable young man, he easily obtained a place, two places in fact, one after the other, as lackey or footman, and seems to have been neither honest nor industrious in one or the other. Soon he was off, vagabonding with another adventurer, the worst sort of companion for a youth who had much imagination and no fixed principles; but after a time he shook off his companion and turned up at Madame de Warens'. She received him kindly, and tried to set him up in life again by sending him to a seminary, to be made a priest; but he soon escaped from this sphere of regularity, and went out into the open—into France, to Lyons, then to Switzerland, Lausanne, Neuchâtel; then to Paris. He lived somehow, partly by giving lessons in music, although he never had much skill in this. Whatever employment he had, he soon lost it, through recklessness or downright misbehaviour—a rolling stone, yet indomitably independent, not afraid of life, not looking for money, never in doubt that he could keep himself. What he liked was " the great roads, the long days of walking, the wide horizons, the uncertain lodging, the chance supper with a stranger, the nights under the stars." [1] All the same, he was glad enough to be welcomed by Madame de Warens again when he turned up at her new home, Les Charmettes, outside Chambéry. She made him a kind of secretary, and he lived comfortably for a time. He was mostly alone, reading, dreaming, walking in the country—two years of delicious solitude (1738-40). The desire to express himself grew; he began to write—just a few essays. After a year or two his solitary habits and self-will proved too much for the temper of Madame de Warens; so he went away, and found a post as tutor in the family of a rich burgher of Lyons. This post lasted him the usual time, and he proved, as usual, undependable and ungrateful. Unabashed by failure, he went to Paris, with the manuscript of a comedy, and his new method of musical notation. He found a little work in copying music, and shortly afterwards had the luck to be taken to Venice as secretary to M. de Montaigu, Ambassador of France. It was at Venice in 1743 that he conceived the idea of writing the *Contrat social*, his treatise upon natural man, upon the artificial, despotic society which has corrupted man, and upon the new political society which will restore him to freedom and virtue. The Government of Venice was arbitrary, interfering, despotic; the people of Venice (Rousseau judged) were corrupt. He reflected upon this, and thought out a better way, suggested to him by reminiscences of the Free City of Geneva.

---

[1] G. Lanson, *Histoire de la Litt. française* (1898), p. 765. *Cf.* Francesco Ruffini, " Voltaire e Rousseau," in *La Cultura* (Genn.–Marz. 1933), p. 84.

Of course, Rousseau soon quarrelled with his employer and
had to leave the embassy. He returned to Paris, to copy music,
give lessons, write articles. Diderot gave him some work to
do for the *Encyclopædia*. He made friends—Diderot, the
bourgeois philosopher, Fontenelle, the exquisite man of the
world and Academician, Marivaux, the writer of comedies,
Condillac, the " philosopher of philosophers." He was admitted
to some *salons*, but he lacked the two indispensable qualities of
eighteenth-century Society—*raison* and *savoir-faire*. He felt a
repugnance to this artificial society of the *salon*: he wanted to
return to nature. Besides, he had married a blousy, untidy,
uneducated wife, Thérèse le Vasseur, with a dreadful mother.
No wonder that he looked back yearningly to man's original,
innocent Golden Age. It is said that he had children by
Thérèse, and that he abandoned them to the foundling hospital.
Thérèse told him that he had the children, but he appears never
to have seen them, for he was a very inattentive and absent
husband.

In 1749 Rousseau seized the opportunity of a prize-essay
competition, offered by the Academy of Dijon, to write on the
prescribed theme, *Si le Progrès des sciences et des arts a contribué
à corrompre ou épurer les mœurs*. Naturally he defended the
paradoxical view, against the accepted view of the result of
progress. He won the prize this year, though he failed in 1753,
when he submitted his other essay, *Un Discours sur l'inégalité*.
From this moment his eccentricity grew. He considered it a
point of honour to live up to his theory, to be the natural man,
l'homme à la nature. He had failed through lack of *savoir-faire*
in the *salon*; now he escaped from the ridicule of men of fashion
by becoming genuinely rude, *farouche*, almost savage. Nevertheless, he could compose a pretty good opera, *Le Devin du
village* (*The Village Soothsayer*), with several spirited tunes,
including the one called " Rousseau's Dream."

In 1756 one of his rich, charitable friends, Madame
d'Épinay, offered him a home of his own, a cottage called the
Hermitage, on her estate in the Forest of Montmorency.
Here, and after the inevitable quarrel with Madame d'Épinay,

at another cottage, Montlouis, not far off, put at his disposal
by the great Maréchal Luxembourg, he had his most fruitful
time. Amid long days of rambling in the forest he completed
his plans for three great works on nature; and he wrote *La
nouvelle Héloïse, Du Contrat social,* and *Émile.* His *Discours
sur l'inégalité* had ascribed all social and political ills to the
withdrawing of man from nature. *Émile* strives to lead man
back to nature by education; *La nouvelle Héloïse* by the
depth and sincerity of passion; *Du Contrat social* endeavours
to construct a society in conformity with reason—that is,
organized according to the principles of natural right, and,
in a sense, according to the imitation of nature.[1] *Émile,* published in the same year as the *Contrat social,* contained strange
views on kings and Governments, as, indeed, both books did.
It also contained (Livre IV) the bold deistic *Profession de foi
du vicaire Savoyard;* Rousseau had to flee from France. Even
Voltaire did not approve of the *Profession.* " To write in form
for or against all religions is the work of a madman," he said to
the Prince de Ligne. Nevertheless, he was willing to give
Rousseau a refuge. So was the Prince de Ligne. " You will
have the key to my library and gardens," the Prince wrote;
" you will have a little house in the country to yourself." [2]
Nevertheless, Rousseau, who might be called the spoiled child
of nature, preferred to go off by himself.

The child of nature found shelter for a time in the Val de
Travers, in the principality of Neuchâtel, which belonged to
the tolerant Frederick II of Prussia. Afterwards he boarded
in the house of the steward—the only house on the island—of
Saint-Pierre, in the Lake of Bienne, continuing the study of
botany, which had for years been one of his great interests.
" Of all the places where I have lived (and I have had charming
abodes)," he wrote in *Les Rêveries du promeneur solitaire,*
" none has made me so truly happy and has left such tender
regrets as the Île de Saint-Pierre. . . . The precious *far
niente* was the first and chief of these joys, and I wished to

[1] G. Beaulavon, *Du Contrat social,* Introduction (1914), p. 64.
[2] Prince de Ligne, *Mémoires,* vol. iv, p. 1.

enjoy all its sweetness." Botanizing in the daytime, strolling
by the lakeside after supper, reflecting upon nature and life—
such was Rousseau's *far niente* on the Lake of Bienne. His
books were bringing in a little money, and he was almost
independent. Friends helped him—de Peyron of Geneva, the
" Earl Marischal " Keith, Governor of Neuchâtel. In 1766,
on the invitation of the large-hearted David Hume, most
friendly of philosophers and men of letters, he went to England,
and lived for eighteen months at Wootton, in Derbyshire.
There he compiled a useful and interesting *Botanical Dictionary*,
and began to write his *Confessions*. He had now the " persecution mania," and was tortured by suspicion that everybody
was conspiring against him—friends, officials, servants, they
were all spies. He fled from England to France, and first the
Marquis de Mirabeau (father of the later famous statesman),
next the Prince de Conti, sheltered him. Later he found a
garret in Paris, and plied his trade of music-copier; but everybody, in his eyes, was still spying upon him, still persecuting.
He had occasional good days, joyous rambles, seeking flowers
in the Bois de Boulogne, and wrote his perfect *Rêveries du
promeneur solitaire*. In 1778 the Marquis de Girardin gave
him a cottage to live in on the estate of Ermenonville, and there
the stormy spirit suddenly expired, July 2, 1778.

Rousseau's lucid prose has the flame of genius in it, and
kindles all who read. " I have read," said Tolstoi, " the whole
of Rousseau, the whole twenty volumes, including the lexicon of
music. What I felt for him was more than enthusiasm; it was
worship." His political ideas at once caught the imagination
of the people of the eighteenth century. In his view of nature
applied to politics Rousseau claimed to be conservative.
" I wish to find out," he wrote, in the preface to the *Contrat
social*, " if there can be in the civil organization some sure and
legitimate rule of administration, taking men as they are, and
laws as they could be." He finds that rule in the principle of
government of his native state.

Born the citizen of a free State, and sharing in the sovereignty,
however feeble, the influence that my voice can have in public

affairs, the right of voting in it, is sufficient to impose on me the
duty of instructing myself about this: happy, every time that I
reflect upon governments, to find ever in my researches new
reasons for loving that of my country.[1]

There follows the opening sentence of Chapter I, Book I:
L'homme est né libre, et partout il est dans les fers. Even the
man who believes himself to be the master of others is more a
slave than they. On what is this universal servitude based? Not
on force, for if it were that fact itself would justify revolution.
But order is a sacred right, the basis of all other rights. The
cause of servitudes is not force, nor is it anybody's natural
right to superiority; it is just convention. Rousseau understood
the old Greek antithesis between nature and convention, and
he had no doubt from which of the two came the ills and
sufferings of mankind.

The most ancient and the only natural society is the family.
As the children grow up they become exempt from the
obedience which they owe to the father, they become free.
This common liberty is a consequence of the nature of man.

The family is the first model of political societies. The chief
is the image of the father; the people are the image of the
children. All being born equal and free, they only alienate
their liberty for their own good.

A people can give themselves over to a ruler; but to do this
they must first be a people. Therefore, before examining the
act by which a people elects a king, it would be well to examine
the act by which they become a people. This act, being
necessarily anterior to the other, is the real foundation of
society. This original political society is the result of a convention, a social contract, by which individuals form an association to defend and protect with all the common force the
person and goods of each associate. By this social contract
each individual, uniting himself with all, nevertheless obeys
only himself, and remains as free as before (*et reste aussi libre
qu'auparavant*). Each one, giving himself to all, gives himself

---

[1] *Du Contrat social*, Book I, Preface.

to no single person. The social pact, reduced to its essentials, is the same everywhere: " Each one of us places in common his person and all his power under the supreme direction of the general will, and we receive into the association every member as an indivisible part of the whole [*et nous recevons en corps chaque membre comme partie indivisible du tout*]." This act produces an association, moral and collective. Every individual, every citizen, has thus a double relation: as member of the sovereign towards the individual citizens; as member of the state towards the sovereign.[1]

The chief magistracy in different states is called by different names—king, president, council, or assembly; but it is not sovereign, for sovereignty belongs to the people. In general, democratic government is suitable for small states, aristocratic for medium states, monarchical for great states.[2]

There is an inherent and inevitable vice which from the moment of the birth of the body politic tends to destroy it; this is individual will (or self-interest), ceaselessly striving against the general will. It is this that changes the constitution and makes the tyranny of governments, the oppressing of the sovereign people by the prince. The degeneracy of a state comes from this breaking down of the original contract, this departure from the primal nature of the state. It is the natural and inevitable decline of all Governments, until their abuses end in dissolution and anarchy. The body politic, like the body of a man, begins to die at its birth, and carries in itself the causes of its destruction.[3]

Liberty and the exercise of the sovereignty of the people are the life of the state. In tracing things back to the first times of nations one would find that the majority of ancient Governments, even monarchic, like those of the Macedonians and Franks, had assemblies of the whole people. And if a thing has already existed it must be considered possible now. The cooling of love of country, the activity of private interest,

---

[1] *Du Contrat social* , Book I, Chapter VI.
[2] *Ibid.*, Book III, Chapter III.
[3] *Ibid.*, Book III, Chapter XI.

the immensity of states, conquests, abuse of government, have made people think of the method of representation by popular deputies in assembly, by what is called in certain states the Tiers État. But sovereignty cannot be represented, because it cannot be alienated. It consists essentially in the general will, and the general will is not representable. The English people deem themselves free. They completely deceive themselves. They are only free during an election of members of Parliament. (*Le peuple anglais pense être libre; il se trompe fort. Il ne l'est que durant l'élection des membres du Parlement.*) The idea of representation is modern. It comes from feudal government, that unjust and absurd system in which the human race was degraded and the name of man dishonoured.[1]

A small state or city admits of the exercise of sovereignty of the people; but will it not be conquered? " No. I will demonstrate later how to combine the exterior force of a great people with the easy police and the good order of a small state." The solution of this difficulty, in Rousseau's view, was " confederation "—" something quite new, the principles of which are still to be established." [2]

Rousseau never wrote the promised demonstration of confederation; but some twenty-seven years later the Federal Constitution of the United States of America was made and came into force. That Rousseau's ideas entered into the making of it is incontestable. Tom Paine's *Common Sense*, published at Philadelphia in 1776, as a pamphlet in favour of the rebellion of the American Colonies, breathes the spirit of Rousseau.

> Society, in every state, is a blessing, but government, even in its best state, is but a necessary evil. . . . I draw my idea of the form of government from a principle in nature, which no art can overturn—viz., that the more simple everything is, the less liable it is to be disordered.[3]

More striking even, in its harking back to nature, and its

---

[1] *Du Contrat social*, Book III, Chapters XII, XV.
[2] *Ibid.*, Book III, Chapter XV.
[3] *Common Sense* (ed. London, 1791), pp. 5, 8.

reproduction of the theme of the *Contrat social*, is the American Declaration of Independence, penned by Jefferson, in 1776:

> When in the course of human events it becomes necessary for one people to dissolve the political bands which have connected them with another, and to assume among the powers of the earth the separate and equal station to which the Laws of Nature and of Nature's God entitle them, a decent respect to the opinions of mankind requires that they should declare the causes which impel them to the separation.
>
> We hold these truths to be self-evident, that all men are created equal, that they are endowed by their Creator with certain inalienable rights, that among these are life, liberty, and the pursuit of happiness. That whenever any form of government becomes destructive of these ends, it is the right of the people to alter or to abolish it, and to institute new government, laying its foundation on such principles and organizing its powers in such form, as to them shall seem most likely to effect their safety and happiness.[1]

The basis of the Declaration is the insistence on freedom and happiness as being part of nature's plan, and on the State as deriving its authority from a social compact designed for these ends. The citizen of Geneva was moving the world.

The storm which ultimately broke upon the world in 1789 came out of France. Yet at one time it had seemed that the revolution would start in Germany. For it was there, for a time, that the greatest spiritual ferment reigned, chiefly in the third quarter of the century, when all the intellectuals were subject to *Sturm und Drang*. The " Storm and Stress " agitation was a revolt against convention in literature, in society. It was an assertion of the individual, of his instinct, passion, genius. It was an appeal to sentiment, to emotion, to nature. *Sturm und Drang* was, in fact, the German expression of the " back to nature " movement, and was much influenced by Rousseau's work; it was actually, however, the prelude not to a political revolution, but to a fuller development of German literature

[1] *Cf.* Carl Becker, *The Declaration of Independence* (1922).

in the Romantic Movement of the end of the eighteenth and the early nineteenth centuries.

The most celebrated work of *Sturm und Drang* is Goethe's novel *Die Leiden des Jungen Werthers*. It outshone Prévost's *Manon Lescaut* over which for forty years the young men of the age had been shedding tears of genuine pity; and though it is like Rousseau's *Nouvelle Héloïse*, which profoundly influenced it, and like Richardson's *Clarissa*, it is a better novel. " No book ever seized all hearts so powerfully as this simple story of unhappy love and suicide ; over no book have so many tears been shed as over *Werther*." [1] The novel, much to Goethe's surprise, chimed with a prevailing sentimental mood of the age, a mood which Goethe thought to be somewhat morbid. Goethe was classical; he believed the ' classical ' to be healthy, and the ' Romantic ' to be diseased.[2] He was disgusted with the ' Wertherizing ' of the young men who read his book; and for all the rest of his life he seems to have been trying to forget his youthful novel and to shake off his fame as the author of it. He was only twenty-five years old when *Werther* was published, in 1774.

It was when Goethe was attending the supreme court of the Empire (*Reichskammergericht*), which was at Wetzlar, that the simple story of *Werther* occurred. There is no doubt that Werther is Goethe himself, for he had conceived a hopeless love, and was passionate and melancholy, although he did not commit suicide, but in the end cast away all morbidness and sentimentality. His beloved was Charlotte Buff, daughter of a bailiff at Wetzlar who managed the estates of the moribund order of chivalry, the Teutonic Knights. Charlotte or Lotte was engaged to be married to Johann Christian Kestner, Secretary of Legation at Wetzlar. They were married in the year after Goethe left Wetzlar, and ultimately had twelve children. He corresponded with the Kestners regularly for the next twenty-five years.

Nevertheless, the " model " from whom Goethe thought that

[1] J. G. Robertson, *A History of German Literature* (1902), p. 315.
[2] B. Croce (trans. Ainslie), *Goethe*, p. 10.

he was drawing his hero was not himself, but Carl Wilhelm Jerusalem, another Secretary of Legation at Wetzlar, a melancholy, sensitive young man who committed suicide in 1772. Goethe, who only knew him slightly, calls him Werther in the novel.

The story opens with a letter of Werther's, opening his heart to a friend who, like him, found pleasure in manifestations of simple nature. Wetzlar, he wrote, lay in a scene of inexpressible natural beauty; and in this scene his soul received the delicious balm of solitude. He wandered about the countryside, making friends with the poor folk and their children, talking to a girl who came to a spring with a pitcher, taking his coffee at a village inn under branching limes.

Werther made the acquaintance of a prince's bailiff, and was invited to the house. He went, was shown in at the front door, and caught sight of the most charming scene he had ever witnessed: an artless grown-up girl, dressed in a simple white frock with pink bows, surrounded by six children for whom she was cutting slices of black bread. The bailiff was a widower, and Lotte, his eldest daughter, took charge of the younger children. Werther made her acquaintance, danced with her in a quadrille, was more and more attracted, and fell desperately in love. Lotte and nature now filled his life. He continued his wanderings about the countryside, amid the fresh fields or under the dripping rain, shelling peas for his simple luncheon, feeling the innocent joy of the man who takes a cabbage from his own garden and brings it to table.

Lotte was already engaged to be married to Albert, an honourable young man, whom she sincerely loved. Albert was calm and happy; with Werther he was frank and friendly. Werther now roamed distractedly in the woods, grinding his teeth, miserable everywhere unless he was near Lotte. " My heart's full," he wrote to his friend, " and ardent sympathy with nature, which flooded me with such bliss and made the world round about into a Paradise, has now become an unbearable torment, a torturing spirit which pursues me everywhere."

Werther resolved to leave Wetzlar. He obtained a post at another embassy, where, however, there was a very unsympathetic ambassador, a meticulous, jealous old fool. One evening he dined at the house of a friend, Count C. There was to be a reception after dinner to which all the resident nobility were coming. Werther thoughtlessly stayed until the noble company arrived, although the social conventions necessitated that he should not show himself among his superiors. Sulky and angry glances were darted at him until Count C., his host, came up to him and said: " You are aware of our odd conventions. The company, I observe, is displeased to see you here. I would not for anything in the world . . ." Werther hastened away. Later, in a coffee-house, a friend maliciously referred to his rebuff: " Everybody is talking about it." Werther resigned his place and departed to his home. Then he went back to Wetzlar.

In and around Wetzlar Werther haunted the places where he had seen and talked with Lotte. She was now married to Albert. Werther saw her occasionally. The poems of Ossian were a great help to him; they crowded Homer out of his heart; he was fain " to hear from the mountains, amid the roaring of the forest river, the fading groans of spirits in their caves and the laments of the maiden pining with grief by the four moss-covered, grass-grown stones that mark the grave of her noble lover! " Yet continually the torture of his love beset him. Lotte was kind, let him visit at her house, played to him on the harpsichord melodies which made his tears flow, until he cried, " For God's sake stop! " She ceased playing, and looked at him fixedly; " Werther, you are very ill. Go, I beg you. Calm yourself! " He tore himself away. He fancied that Lotte's husband was becoming suspicious and jealous ; actually Albert was only overworked and a little irritable. Nevertheless, Werther had to see Lotte once again. He met her alone, read from Ossian to her, broke down, declared his love, and left in fearful agitation. Next day he sent his servant to borrow Albert's pistols for " a journey he was about to undertake." Lotte, on Albert's request, handed the pistols to the servant.

About midnight Werther drank a glass of wine and shot himself through the head. The neighbours found him expiring next morning. He was dressed in the clothes in which he had last seen Lotte—high boots, blue coat, yellow waistcoat. Lessing's tragedy *Emilia Galotti* lay open on his desk.

The effect of *Werther* was immediate and powerful. It was read in every country of Europe, in the original or in translation. Men and women wept over it; young men dressed like Werther, revolted against the conventions of society, indulged a morbid sentimentalism, and committed suicide. The book is a classic in which all ages will find pleasure, and in which all young men, provided they do not take it too seriously, will find profit. " The narrower interest of the book is as a mirror of a generation before the French Revolution, which was filled with an impotent longing to burst the empty forms of an antiquated social structure, and saw in Werther the outburst of individualism for which it had been waiting." [1]

[1] *The Sorrows of Young Werther*, translated by William Rose (1929), Introduction, p. xlv.

CHAPTER XIX

THE TWILIGHT OF THE *ANCIEN RÉGIME*

FRANCE still exists a little [*La France existe encore un peu*] " [1] wrote the Prince de Ligne in November 1789; so far had the great kingdom sunk since the age of Louis XIV.

Mankind is completely at the mercy of its politicians, arbiters of the destiny of poor mortals, as the Prince de Ligne called them. Men have to live in one or another of the types of association called states. The states have to take action and enact policies; and these decisions can only be made by the men in charge, the politicians. As a whole, this work has not been very well done, though better at some times than at others. The politicians' task is very difficult to perform. They are not all first-rate men, and they are dealing with material —the population of their state—that may be obstinate, prejudiced, and unenlightened. Nevertheless, it is by no means always the fault of the people that their politicians make wrong decisions. In the nature of things the politicians have frequently to act on their own initiative, without consulting the people; and it is truly amazing how often and over what long periods the politicians act wrongly. They are necessary people, and deserve gratitude for undertaking their heavy task. Gratitude, however, cannot deter the observer from concluding, after a survey of the many avoidable tragedies in the long history of mankind, that on the whole the politicians have made a mess of things. They have failed to make consistent use of the available knowledge and enlightenment.

The eighteenth century believed itself to be an age of scientific government: the Age of Enlightened Despots. It was indeed an age of reforms and of government by common sense,

[1] Prince de Ligne, *Mémoires*, vol. i, p. 165. The following reference to the Prince de Ligne is from *Mémoires*, vol. i, p. 217.

yet it had a number of perfectly avoidable wars, and it ended in the negation of civilization, a devastating civil war within the society of European states, the Great War of 1792–1814.

The Revolution which brought about the fall of the *ancien régime* began as an effort to correct certain faults in the eighteenth-century Governments. These Governments themselves had been conscious of the need for reform. In some states, Austria, Russia, Tuscany, where there was a particularly strong monarch, the need for reform was faced and dealt with in time; in France it was faced at last, but too late. France was the only country that had a revolution. Nevertheless, it would be wrong to say that the French Government or the French statesmen of the later years of the *ancien régime* were ignorant of the defects of the system or oblivious to the call for reform. Machault, the well-known Minister of Marine of Louis XV, inspired the writing and publication in 1750 of a book to show that " every citizen should contribute to the needs of the State in proportion to his means." [1] It was the exemption of nobles and clergy from most of the taxes that ruined the State's finances. The earlier French monarchy had accomplished a notable work in making France into a unified, administrative state in place of the collection of feudal units that was medieval France. "Unfortunately for the monarchy at the moment when the work was approaching completion, and when nothing was wanting but the constitutional conclusion, the throne was occupied in succession by two kings incapable, one through frivolity, the other through lack of intelligence, of understanding the evolution which was being accomplished in the course of centuries, and whose process they themselves should have completed. Now, every evolution which is misunderstood turns into revolution." [2]

For an orderly minded race the Government of France was curiously unsystematic. The country was wealthy, but not by reason of its political institutions. " In France," wrote Mirabeau, contrasting it with England and Prussia, " nature does

[1] See F. M. Grimm, *Correspondance* (1877), vol. i, p. 431, and Note 1.

[2] W. D'Ormesson, *Enfances diplomatiques* (1932), pp. 151–152. The two successive kings are, of course, Louis XV and Louis XVI.

everything in Governments' despite." [1] The state consisted of twelve provinces and a few other areas acquired after the provinces. As during the course of the Middle Ages one province after another had been incorporated by war, marriage, or other circumstance in the possessions of the French people, it had retained its feudal laws and customs virtually unchanged. The result was that France had types of almost every known variety of local government, some provinces having their own " Provincial Estates " (or legislatures) and their own *parlements* (or independent law-courts). According to Sir Henry Maine, " province differed from province, county from county, municipality from municipality, in the nature of its customs." It was "the special peculiarity of France that an extraordinary diversity of laws continued without sensible alteration while the central authority of the monarchy was constantly strengthening itself." [2] In spite of this strongly marked provincialism, however, France was not a federal state. It was a " unitary " monarchy, perhaps, as de Tocqueville remarks, owing to " the instinct which makes every Government wish to be the sole director of affairs." The king, subject to the local privileges and immunities of the provinces and districts, wielded absolute sovereignty, and exercised this through two agencies in particular: one, the local *intendants*, royal officials, at the head of the thirty *intendances* into which France was divided; and, two, the Controller-General, the chief financial officer of the kingdom, to whom all the *intendants* reported. The *intendants* were skilled civil servants, young, energetic, with their career to make, always strangers to their provinces. They owed their position not to election, nor birth, nor purchase. They were chosen by the Government from the junior members of the Council of State, and were always revocable. [3] They made the cumbrous and somewhat chaotic local-government system function fairly smoothly. " I would never have believed," said John Law to the Marquis d'Argenson, " what I have seen since

---

[1] Mirabeau, *Secret History of the Court of Prussia*, vol. i, p. xxii.
[2] Sir Henry Maine, *Ancient Law* (1897), p. 64.
[3] A. de Tocqueville, *L'Ancien Régime et la Révolution*, Book II, Chapter II.

I became Controller of the Finances. Know that this kingdom of France is governed by thirty *intendants*." They had the same kind of position as the modern prefect. " *Qui lit un préfet, lit un intendant*," writes Alexis de Tocqueville. The *intendants* were appointed, supervised, and instructed from the office of the Controller-General in Paris or from the Council of the king. " I have known," wrote de Tocqueville, " parishes having to ask leave from the Council to spend twenty-five francs."

The Controller-General was the most important Minister in the kingdom. There was no ' Constitution,' no Prime Minister, no Cabinet. Some previous Ministers—Richelieu in the first half of the seventeenth century, Fleury in the first half of the eighteenth—had been given the position (though, like Walpole, Fleury refused to take the title) of *premier ministre* by the king, but none since 1743. The king could consult his Ministers and Secretaries of State separately or in council.

The English visitor Lord Chesterfield had observed in 1753 : " All the symptoms which I have ever met with in history, previous to great changes and revolutions in government, now exist and daily increase in France." " That Government may be said to be weak and tottering," wrote Smollett towards the end of his tour through France in 1765; " there are undoubtedly many marks of relaxation in the reins of the French Government, and in all probability the subjects of France will be the first to take the advantage of it." [1] It is not to be supposed that the shrewd Scotsman was the only man who saw this. There were plenty of keen wits in French society. Unfortunately the absence of a Constitution or a public Press bereft them of means for bringing their views and influence to bear on the Court and bureaucracy, two agencies which never change if left to themselves. The internal weakness of France showed itself in the area where weakness always does most clearly appear, the financial. By the time Louis XVI succeeded to the throne in 1774 the State was practically bankrupt. The revenue was exceeded by the expenditure, and

---

[1] Chesterfield's remark in his *Letters*, December 25, 1753 ; Smollett's, in *Travels through France and Italy*, letter of March 23, 1763.

the deficit was made up by borrowing—a process which, obviously, could not go on for ever. The extravagance of Court expenses, the size of the bureaucracy, the waste of four great wars—Spanish Succession, Polish Succession, Austrian Succession, and Seven Years War (a fifth, the American Revolutionary War with Great Britain, was to follow in 1778) —threw the finances of the State into chaos. In 1769 the retiring Controller-General (M. d'Invau) sent in a memorandum to Louis XV in which he declared: " The finances of your Majesty are in the most terrible state of decay [*Les finances de votre Majesté sont dans le plus affreux délabrement*]." He added: " Every year has accumulated new debt over and above the debt of the preceding year." Then followed figures of the current deficit and of the floating debt. The revenues of a coming year were ' anticipated ' (by discounting them with bankers and tax-farmers) in order to meet current needs.[1] Taxation had reached a point (as has happened so often since with Governments which will not economize and cannot balance their Budget) where increase in the rate failed to bring increase in the return. Peasants were letting land go out of cultivation, because the tax levied on it exceeded the yields of the land.

Louis XVI when he came to the throne was only twenty years old, and was totally without experience in affairs. He felt the need of a firm counsellor. After going through the various possibilities with the rest of the royal family and with high officials he was convinced that the choice lay between two men, the Comte de Machault and the Comte de Maurepas, both honest men, Ministers of proved merit, who had been a long time in retirement. Machault was an uncompromising, austere man, of high ability, without any gifts of popularity. Maurepas was clever, conciliatory, accommodating, rather sceptical about everything. The King decided for Machault, and, retiring to a separate room, wrote and handed to a page a brief letter, inviting Machault to become his chief adviser or *Chef du cabinet du roi*. On returning to the council-chamber

[1] Invau's memorandum is quoted by Ségur, *Au Couchant de la Monarchie* (1909), vol. i, p. 7.

Louis was met by suggestions for 'second thoughts' by advice that he should choose Maurepas after all. The weak monarch hesitated, considered, and decided to change his mind. A courtier was dispatched at once to catch the bearer of the letter to Machault. As it happened, the page with the letter had delayed a few minutes in starting because, as he was mounting his horse, he found that one of his spurs was missing. These few minutes changed the destiny of France. The departure of the page was stopped, the letter was returned to the King, the address endorsed upon it was altered from M. de Machault to M. de Maurepas, and again it was sent on its way.[1] From that moment neither Louis nor his Government ever displayed a power of continuous decision and steady policy.

The ' affair ' of the *parlements* is an instance of this indecision and lack of steadiness. Ever since the days of the Fronde (1649), and, indeed, long before that, there had been more or less open opposition between the Crown and the *parlements*. These law-courts (there were twelve of them, including the *parlement* of Paris) consisted of magistrates, who were, in effect, hereditary, because their office could be purchased and secured for life ; so each judge of a *parlement* as a matter of course purchased the reversion of his office for his son or nephew. The members of the *parlements*, in effect, were a legal aristocracy, powerful, independent, learned, and upright, though rather tenacious of their privileges. Royal edicts were registered with the *parlement* of Paris, which therefore claimed the right of refusing to register. This was one of the sources of quarrel with the Crown. Finally Maupeou, the last Chancellor of Louis XV, had advised the Crown to abolish the *parlement* of Paris, and either to abolish or to restrict the powers of the other *parlements*. " Is France to be subject to twelve aristocracies? " he said to the King. The King agreed with the Chancellor ; and on January 19, 1771, all the judges of the *parlement* of Paris were exiled, by *lettre de cachet*, to the country. Restrictions were placed on the provincial *parlements*. A new *parlement*, with a new constitution, was organized, and fresh magistrates appointed

[1] Ségur, *op. cit.*, vol. i, pp. 40–41 ; *Mémoires de Madame de Campan.*

MIRABEAU

to it. " I will never change," declared Louis XV. In these circumstances Louis XVI ascended the throne. It was now hoped that system would displace caprice in the royal councils; for, as Mirabeau wrote a few years later, " Order and constancy are more necessary for good government than great talent." [1]

It was not to be expected that the tenacious old judges of *parlement* would acquiesce passively in their fate. From the first, pressure was brought to bear on the young King (he was very conscious of his inexperience and awkwardness) to recall the old *parlement*. Maurepas, his chosen counsellor, advised this. Maurepas was disinterested. When called to the King's counsels he refused to accept any salary. He accepted the duty simply out of desire to serve the King and the public good; but he had not the necessary strength of will and courage to break down opposition and face unpopularity. The upshot was that after months of hesitation Louis XVI signed the papers for the recall of the *parlement* of Paris, and was present in person at their restoration in the Palais de Justice, November 12, 1774 —a public reversal of Louis XV's " *Je ne changerai jamais.*"

The recall of the *parlement* entrenched once more in power the most obstinate opposition to the reform of the *ancien régime*. A shrewd spectator said that the King had laid " the first stone of the Revolution." [2] Maurepas did not look upon the recall as an act of indecision. It was before this time that he gave the King a lecture on will-power. " The indecision in which you leave men's minds to float lowers the prestige of your Ministers and leaves business in suspense." " Yes," agreed the harassed monarch, " it is necessary to decide, it is necessary to change the Ministers." [3] Thus galvanized to action, he signed the papers for dismissing Chancellor Maupeou (the opponent of the *parlements*) and the Abbé de Terray, Controller-General, a clever but superficial and dissolute man. In their places he appointed Miromesnil (a good provincial judge) as Chancellor and Turgot, who had been for some time

[1] Mirabeau, *The Secret History of the Court of Prussia*, vol. i, p. 177.
[2] *Souvenirs du Baron de Frénilly, apud* Ségur, *op. cit.*, vol. i, p. 130.
[3] *Journal de l'abbé de Véri, apud* Ségur, *op. cit.*, vol. i, pp. 113–114.

marked out for high office, as Controller-General. The State could still be saved, for Turgot, if unflinchingly supported, was the man to do it; or, as Voltaire said, " If anyone can re-establish the finances, it is he." [1]

Anne Robert Jacques Turgot was forty-four years old when he became Controller-General. He belonged to an old official family, was educated at the famous Lycée Louis le Grand of Paris and at the Sorbonne. His original intention was to enter the priesthood, but when the time came to make the final decision he was not prepared. He had become *philosophe* and sceptical. He was one of the collaborators in the *Encyclopædia*, and wrote a particularly remarkable article in it on " Existence." Entering on an administrative career, he rose to be *intendant* of Limoges in 1761, and for over twelve years was the model and beloved administrator of that formerly unhappy and misman-aged district. After his intendancy Turgot had a few months as Minister of Marine, before becoming Controller-General.

In character Turgot resembled Pascal. In a dissipated and pleasure-loving age he was a severe moralist, a devotee, indeed a martyr, to duty. To achieve the good of humanity was his religion. His manner was modest and innocent. He blushed easily, but would spontaneously break out with laughter at little comic incidents. His countenance was noble and benevolent; his will, when he saw what was the right thing to do, absolutely immovable. People said that he was in too great haste for reform. His answer was that time was flying, and that in his family the men died at the age of fifty. Besides, there can be no doubt that if the State was to be reformed, and collapse prevented, it must be done quickly. History has proved this.

In Bülow's *Memoirs* the former German Chancellor, speaking of his later years, when he helplessly could see the approaching ruin of the Empire, wrote (quoting Herodotus): " Worst of all the sorrows in the world is to see a future misfortune and yet be impotent to avert it. This worst of all sorrows has been mine." Turgot's practical knowledge and experience at Limoges, as well as his studies in history, economics, philo-

[1] Voltaire, *Lettres*, September 7, 1774, *apud* Ségur, *op. cit.*, vol. i, p. 143.

sophy, enabled him to see where the ills of France were and how to cure them; and the offer by the King of the Controller-Generalship gave him the prospect of wielding the necessary power. " I truly believe that I was born to regenerate France," he said to a friend, words which are reminiscent of Chatham's more sweeping statement, " I know that I can save England, and that no one else can." Turgot took the precaution of securing the necessary power by laying down certain conditions, in a letter to the King, before entering upon office. These conditions were: no default, no increase of taxes, no borrowing. The King accepted the conditions and France had the opportunity of being saved. Turgot entered into office, and at once put his principles into practice. Salaries and pensions were reduced without respect of persons. He swept aside the argument fatal to all Government economy, that because a certain expense was good in itself it should therefore be undertaken. When the naturalist Buffon applied for a grant in support of the great and in every sense valuable Jardin des Plantes Turgot, though as sympathetic as anybody to such a work, simply refused; and he did the same thing, time and again, in regard to similar ' indispensable ' needs. Then came the first great edict (September 1774), abolishing the restrictions on the movement of grain from province to province. The fear of famine dominated the minds of the country people of every province, and they dreaded to see grain sold to a neighbouring province; yet it was this very immobility in the corn trade, sustained by provincial law and custom, which made famine over the whole land all too likely. Turgot was an aristocrat, and it is a fact that aristocrats face this kind of problem better than do democratic legislators.[1] The edict for

---

[1] A similar case came up in 1932 in the British Parliament, concerning the projected transfer of the Imperial War Museum from South Kensington to a site already purchased. In the House of Lords the Earl of Munster, for the Government, gave the following reply (*The Times*, December 1, 1932): " It could not be said that the transfer of this museum was a pressing matter. The Government admitted that it would be an excellent thing if the museum could be housed in a dignified building and in a central and convenient district; but they were faced with the pressing need for national economy."

the free movement of grain was followed, four months later, by a batch of six edicts of a similar nature, the chief being an act to suppress the *corvée* (or forced labour for public works) and another to take away from guilds the monopoly of trades and crafts (February 1776). Briefly Turgot's view was that strict economy on the part of the Government, and the removal of all restraints upon trade, would permit France, a naturally rich country with an industrious people, to recover its prosperity; and in this view he was undoubtedly correct.

But alas! Turgot was not to be permitted to save France. His economies aroused, naturally, the keenest opposition. Marie Antoinette could not bear this Puritan Controller. Her *fêtes*, dances, masqued balls, and gaming (she gambled furiously) grew more frequent than ever. Her horses, servants, carriages, and the pensions for her ladies increased; and the King (himself good, kind, simple-living) could not go on with the unpleasant task of refusing to sign his wife's orders on the Treasury. The queen, princes, princesses, corrupt officials, disappointed pensioners, the greedy horde of courtiers and hangers-on, tax-farmers whose commissions were lowered, monopolists who hated the freedom of provincial trade, were all intriguing against the Controller. The restored *parlement* resisted Turgot's edicts and had to be compelled in a royal *lit de justice* to give its unwilling registration. All this made fearfully difficult the position of the industrious, conscientious King, anxious to please everybody, and puzzled with all the pressure brought to bear upon him against his Minister. Only one thing could have saved the situation—if Louis, having decided to have Turgot as Controller, had also decided just blindly to support him, as George II supported Pitt, notwithstanding anything that anyone else had to say. When influential people told George II that Wolfe was mad the stolid monarch only replied, " I wish, then, he would bite some of my other generals." The debonair Louis XVI, however, though far more devoted to duty than George II, had not that monarch's steadiness of purpose. On Sunday, May 12, 1776, the royal letter of dismissal was conveyed by hand from the

Palace of Versailles to Turgot's lodging. The Minister received the announcement " with surprise and mortification." He at once left Versailles and retired to a friend's house in the country. The King sent after him the offer of a pension. Turgot declined in a dignified letter, adding that, as Minister, he had frankly informed the King of the dangers which he believed to exist. " I hope that time will not justify me, and that your reign will be as happy and as tranquil, for yourself and your people, as your principles of justice and benevolence hold out the prospect of it." After this Turgot never again spoke a word of criticism. He died in 1781, at the age of fifty-four, while the collapse, which he had long foreseen, was still from year to year deferred.

When Turgot was dismissed madness seemed to descend upon the French Government. Through family influence Bernard de Clugny, *intendant* of Guienne, a corrupt, extravagant, and debauched official, was made Controller-General. The *corvées* and the guilds were by royal edict restored. Thus, within three months, practically all that Turgot had laboured for and accomplished was undone. Clugny died of fever, brought on by his debauches, on October 18, 1776, having ruined the financial credit of France. Then two honest men were appointed to share the controllership, Taboureau de Réaux, former *intendant* of Valenciennes, and Jacques Necker, a banker, who had on several occasions lent money to the Government and had also given it good advice. Everybody respected Necker. He was one of the richest men in France, and preserved the simple, straightforward manners and habits of the Protestant Geneva citizen that he was, although he lived in a grand Paris *hôtel*, and his wife had one of the most brilliant and fashionable *salons*. For the last four years (1772–1776) he had been retired from active business, and gave all his attention to literature and to politics. He represented the Republic of Geneva at Paris. In order that he could be made " Director-General of the Royal Treasury," the laws against heretics had to be suspended. The situation must have been indeed desperate to make the proud, ancient monarchy and aristocracy of France ask a foreigner and a Protestant to direct the country's affairs. It was like the nomination of Beust, the Protestant Saxon, to be Foreign Minister of Austria-Hungary in 1866, after the disaster of the Seven Weeks War. Necker had opposed, by writings, Turgot's free-trade views, and so was supported by the party (the most respectable of whom was the eminent retired statesman Choiseul) who were united against that uncompromising statesman. Necker was the first Protestant foreigner in his position, for the Scotsman John Law, who had been at the head of the French finances in 1718, appears to have conformed to the Roman Catholic communion. In accepting the call to office Necker refused any salary. He was only forty-four years old. He entered into office in October 1776.

It is never possible to say that anything is absolutely inevitable; and it may be that if left in peace to carry on his administration Necker could have saved France. Given peace and regular administration, a civilized country has marvellous powers of recovery. Necker's four years as Director-General of the Royal Treasury (the title Controller-General being temporarily suppressed) were, so far as his administration was concerned, a complete success. Less rigid than Turgot, he increased the debt at first, but gradually, by patience, tact, and exactitude, he brought the finances into order. All classes believed in him: Marie Antoinette and the courtiers, who found that he did his best to supply their heavy demands, although he cut down a large number of abuses; the mass of established officials, who found that he did not wage war against their vested interests; the *philosophes*, who admired the governance of a *philosophe*, with his heart in literature and the *salon*; the *bourgeoisie*, who liked his banker's regularity and good order, and sympathized with his strict, *bourgeois* morality; and finally the common people when they found that he did not increase the taxes, and that he genuinely wished their good.[1] It may be that ten years of order and regularity in the French finances would have re-established the *ancien régime* firmly, and led to

[1] *Cf.* Ségur, *op. cit.*, vol. ii, pp. 213-214.

the other and essential reform, admission of the people into participation in government through an elected Parliament; for Necker had been in England, and was a warm admirer of the English Constitution. If Necker's administration was a last opportunity for France the opportunity was soon lost, when the Government, contrary to Necker's advice, joined in the American War of Independence, in 1778, against Great Britain. War is the greatest scourge of mankind, though (unlike most other scourges) mankind has the choice of having it or not. France chose war in 1778; a royal councillor who was in office at the time wrote: " The unhappy recognition of the United States has ruined everybody. . . . It produced the famous deficit which led to the Assembly of Notables, to the Assembly of the Estates-General, and, finally, to the ruin of France." [1]

At the end of four years of administration Necker took an unprecedented step. He drafted a complete statement of the condition of the Government's finances (a *compte rendu*), and issued it to the public in the form which in England would be called a Blue Book, February 1781. The people, delighted at being taken into the Government's confidence, read the *Compte Rendu* (*Account Rendered*) with avidity; 100,000 copies were sold at the published price of one écu (about five shillings). It is a long (116 pages) and frank description of Necker's stewardship, with full details of various receipts and expenses, not concealing the vast pension list which was still the chief abuse of the State. The ' ordinary ' Budget for the year 1781 balanced with a surplus of 10,000,000 livres, or about £500,000 (revenue 264,000,000, expenditure 254,000,000 livres). Necker pointed with pride to this result of the administration for which he was responsible. He added a statement of the ' extraordinary ' Budget, necessitated by the war with Great Britain. This unfortunately required the ' anticipation ' of future revenue, and balanced with a deficit of 90,000,000. Necker's object in showing the war Budget separately from the ' ordinary ' Budget was to make his own responsibility clear, and to let

[1] *Mémoires de Saint-Priest, apud* Ségur, *op. cit.*, vol. ii, p. 238.

all parties draw their conclusions about the advisability of peace.

The result of the publication of the *Compte Rendu*, once its figures were properly understood, was to arouse fury in the war party (with Vergennes, Foreign Minister, now at the head of it) and stupor on the part of the public, who saw their illusion of prosperity dissipated. Opposition to the Minister was further increased, this time among the *juges de parlement* and the powerful mass of the *intendants*, by the publication in April 1781 (two months after the issue of the *Compte Rendu*) of a *Mémoire sur les Assemblées Provinciales*. This was a memorandum composed by Necker two years earlier, for the consideration of the King, advocating the re-establishment, not, indeed, of a national assembly, or Estates-General, but of an assembly of Estates in each province. Necker did not mean to publish this project; it was surreptitiously published by the Comte de Provence (brother of the King), who was opposed to Necker. Feeling that his position was being openly attacked, Necker demanded that, as an expression of the King's confidence in him, he should be admitted into the Royal Council, or *Conseil d'État*. Technically the Director-General of the Treasury was not a Minister of State, and therefore was not in the Council. Vergennes advised the King to decline this request, on account of Necker's Protestantism. The King's brother and Maurepas were also against Necker. On the night of May 20, 1781, Necker received at Paris, where the Finance Office was, a royal letter discharging him from his duties as Director-General of the Royal Treasury.

It seems as if at some epochs of history mankind is almost determined to destroy itself. With a benevolent and dutiful monarch France in the last years of the *ancien régime* had the means of prosperity and stability twice placed squarely before her; yet after a serious trial of these means they were rejected. Turgot's policy—economy, internal free trade, and (though he had not time to bring this plan forward) Provincial Assemblies—would probably have saved the *ancien régime*; so would Necker's, though less effectively than Turgot's, for he was no free-trader. In the seven years after Necker's dismissal financial *laisser-aller* and the piling up of debt completed the State's insolvency, and therefore its feebleness. When at last the Provincial Estates of Dauphiné, which had been long considered dead, suddenly restored themselves, spontaneously, by gathering together at Vizille, on June 14, 1788, and demanding that the Estates-General of the whole kingdom should meet, the Government could only assent (too late !), and then practically leave events to take their own fatal course. The fateful Estates-General was summoned for May 5, 1789. Before the elections were held a universally popular demand brought Necker back into office, this time as Minister of State and member of the King's Council (September 1788); but this also was too late.

Mercier's *Tableau de Paris*, which is a contemporary work, gives a picture of Paris before the Revolution. It was probably not much different from any other of the European capitals —large, dirty, crowded, with much that was interesting, much that was disgusting, much that was grand, much that was shabby. Some improvements had taken place during the century. Everybody drank coffee, even the workmen. It was cheap. A cup or two and a piece of bread for breakfast satisfied the workman until nightfall. The Parisians were rather a pampered people. They knew that the Government had to maintain the prestige of Paris, and could not afford to let a famine occur. People wanted an easy life, and would not marry. Young women set up house together, and bought annuities with the money that would have gone towards their dowry. The *octroi* hampered commerce. There were sixty municipal customs barriers, made of wood or iron. If the money which they cost the country could have been put into them they might have been made of gold. There were masses of police and soldiers to keep the dangerous populace in order. Spies were everywhere. Bankruptcies had become so frequent that they were no longer considered disgraceful. Money was easy. " The bankers are the rulers of France." They were always floating loans. " The wealth of the nation is not in question; it is how to get money for the King that is the problem." [1]

The responsibility for the Revolution, the catastrophe of monarchical France, must be laid at the door of various people and classes, but chiefly of the aristocracy, whose extravagance and dissoluteness were notorious, and whose insolence Arthur Young noticed in his *Travels*. A dissolute, extravagant, and insolent aristocracy ruined France in 1789, Venice in 1797, Russia in 1917. It is said that Madame de Pompadour, one of the mistresses of Louis XV, once remarked, " *Après nous le déluge* "; and the deluge came. French aristocracy in the last years of the *ancien régime* were like the people of the time of " Noe," described in the third Gospel: " They did eat, they drank, they married wives, they were given in marriage, until the day that Noe entered into the ark, and the flood came, and destroyed them all." The course of the French Revolution was indeed fairly accurately forecast by the shrewd men of the age that was passing away. It was at this time, November 1789, barely six months after the first meeting of the Estates-General at Versailles, that the Prince de Ligne, though at Belgrade he was far away from the Revolution, wrote: " France still exists *a little*. . . . Louis XVI at the Tuileries is even on the road to the scaffold." [2] The Revolution, however, besides destroying a monarchy and aristocracy, released from the mass of the French people unsuspected energies. Even when the Revolution had pursued its course for some years Europe had not clearly grasped the fact that an old world was being shattered and that the French were breaking forth into something new, though not necessarily better. Casanova, however, writing a preface to his memoirs from his quiet library at Castle Dux, in Bohemia, in 1797, concluded: " The new impetus which a people has acquired may lead it along roads not hitherto discovered [*Le nouveau élan qu'un peuple a pris peut le conduire sur des voies non encore aperçues*]." [3]

[1] See *The Waiting City: Paris 1782-88*, an abridged translation of Mercier's *Tableau de Paris*, by Helen Simpson, p. 259.

[2] Prince de Ligne, *Mémoires*, vol. i, p. 165 (letter to Kaunitz, November 10, 1789).   [3] Casanova, *Mémoires*, vol. i, p. 15.

CHAPTER XX

THE ACHIEVEMENT OF THE
EIGHTEENTH CENTURY

THE magnificent civilization of Europe has been marred by only one thing, enmity between states; nor has the society of states in any age been able to meet successfully this crying evil. It almost seems, however, that the aristocrats of the eighteenth century had solved the enigma, or were in a fair way to solve it, when the catastrophe of the French Revolution and the Revolutionary War came upon them.

For what are the outstanding needs of the civilized states, in order that they may exploit their joint heritage of culture and attain a perfect poise of life? They need, in their relations with each other, social intercourse, commercial intercourse, the continuance of peace. These three things the men of the eighteenth century (the nobility, and the mass of educated people who were aristocrats in so far as they held the aristocratic point of view) had largely achieved.

For one thing, they had certainly established a habit of social intercourse between various peoples, conducted entirely without national prejudice. It is true that this intercourse was largely between members of the aristocracies, because it was chiefly they who had the means and the leisure for travelling; nevertheless, the *bourgeoisie* frequently travelled too. Smollett, Sterne, Boswell, went to Italy, Dr Johnson and the Thrales went to Paris, Rousseau and Moritz came to England. Even artisans frequently (in Germany regularly) travelled, and, where guilds either did not exist or were breaking down, were able to exercise their craft as they went along. The Lancashire artisan William Cockerill worked in Sweden and Russia before he settled down to become a great captain of industry in

Belgium. As a whole, however, social intercourse between nations was pre-eminently aristocratic; and it is to the credit of the aristocracies that this was so. Their example was followed by others, and a sane cosmopolitanism, without the slightest sacrifice of patriotism, was promoted. This fashion was at its height before the French Revolution. In Winckelmann or Montesquieu or the Prince de Ligne or David Hume or Gibbon the eighteenth-century type attained perhaps most nearly to its perfect expression; in Gibbon especially. " It is difficult to imagine, at any other period in history, such a combination of varied qualities, so beautifully balanced—the profound scholar who was also a brilliant man of the world —the votary of cosmopolitan culture, who never for a moment ceased to be a supremely English character." [1] Society in France and England almost dovetailed into one another. " The social intercourse between certain classes of English and French in the period before the French Revolution is one of the best-known phases in the history of France and England in the eighteenth century." [2] It ought to be better known than it is, for in popular imagination the eighteenth century is often, wrongly, represented as a second Hundred Years War between France and England. The knowledge of the French language was widely spread in Europe. Current works of literature and learning were quickly translated into various European languages. The musical, theatrical, military, academic professions were international. The European ' Republic of Letters ' was a reality. The men of the eighteenth century had gone a long way towards realizing the social-cultural solidarity of Europe.

Surely they had gone far, though they had by no means succeeded completely, towards eliminating the scourge of European war. War, indeed, was the great failure in the performance of the eighteenth century. Europe had the War of the Spanish Succession and the useless massacres of the War

---

[1] Lytton Strachey, *Portraits in Miniature*, p. 156.
[2] E. S. Roscoe, " An Eighteenth-century Abbé in England," in *The Contemporary Review*, September 1932, p. 357.

of the Polish Succession, the War of the Austrian Succession, the Seven Years War. The Spanish Succession War, however, was really an inheritance from the previous century, and belongs to the age of Louis XIV. Just as the nineteenth century, as a political and cultural epoch, ends in 1914 when the twentieth century really begins, so the eighteenth century on the Continent begins with the death of Louis XIV in 1715. After that time war on the grand scale was rare in Europe, and but for Frederick the Great's breach of the public peace in his attack on Silesia in 1740 might have been eliminated altogether. After 1763 there was no general European war; the monarchs were bent on avoiding it. At the end of the period the Triple Alliance of England, Prussia, and Holland seemed to be the last necessary assurance of stability on the Lower Rhine and Scheldt, which had been the subject of so many of the old wars. There was not, and seemed unlikely ever to be, an ' Alsace-Lorraine ' question.

Thirdly, the eighteenth century was very slowly, gradually, by natural adaptation (and that is how the thing ought to have been done), meeting the Industrial Revolution. When the century opened there was a satisfactory—it might be said a perfect—balance between man and nature. The economy of Europe was based on agriculture in the country, on crafts and merchandising in the towns. About the middle of the century water-power was being applied to craftsmanship and industry on an increasing scale. Thirty years later the improvements being made by James Watt in the application of steam-power were beginning to make themselves felt. The whole process, however, was very gradual; there was really no Industrial Revolution in the eighteenth century. Revolution means sudden, unexpected, unprepared change—quick, too-quick, development. There was no risk of this in the eighteenth century until the ' Great War ' came in 1792. War, consuming goods with abnormal rapidity, forces upon industry mass production, the expansion of plant, the erecting of new factories, far beyond the needs of peace activity. It was the twenty-two years of European war, from 1792 to 1815, which destroyed the balance between agriculture and industry and produced the Industrial Revolution.

The men of the eighteenth century were not merely, in their quiet way, meeting the industrial problem; they were handling the commercial problem. The eighteenth century was an age in economic life, an age of merchandising, which required an increasing measure of international exchange. The prevailing sentiment was in favour of this. The French and Italian economists and the English economists were, in questions of trade, substantially in agreement with Adam Smith, who showed that the ' wealth of nations ' depends largely on the production and exchange of goods between individuals of the same country and between individuals of different countries, according to the natural play of the law of demand and supply. Disraeli correctly wrote in *Sybil*, referring to Pitt and to Shelburne, whom he calls " one of the suppressed characters of English history ": " Lord Shelburne adopted from the first the Bolingbroke system; . . . a plan of commercial freedom, the germ of which may be found in the long-maligned negotiations of Utrecht, but which, in the instance of Lord Shelburne, was soon in time matured by all the economical science of Europe, in which he was a proficient." [1] Lord Shelburne was prevented by a colleague's ignorance and prejudice from writing conditions for free exchange into the peace settlement made between Great Britain and the United States. His ideas carried weight, however, with the younger Pitt, and along with the influence of Adam Smith helped to produce the Anglo-French commercial treaty of 1786, which, on the French side, was the last important achievement of the *ancien régime*. An era of free international exchange was inaugurated only to go to ruin in the French wars and the economic nationalism of Napoleon's ' Continental System.'

There remained the political problem. The eighteenth-century Governments on the Continent were despotic or aristocratic. It almost seems as if nothing but the hammer-blows of Napoleon could stir these Governments to make a conces-

[1] *Sybil*, Chapter II.

sion to the growing demands and necessities for more representative institutions. In Great Britain there was a Parliamentary system which required reform, and which un-doubtedly would have been reformed, long before 1832, but for the French Revolution and the French wars. The Prussian monarchy, however, required the shattering defeat at Jena, and the Swiss patriciates required a French invasion, while not even the approach of Bonaparte's army was sufficient to arouse the Venetian aristocracy to the necessity for deciding to introduce political reform. The French monarchy and aristocracy did, indeed, make the decision voluntarily in 1789, but too late. A cumbrous, meddling, rigid administrative system, maintained without concession for nearly two hundred years, brought ruin upon itself. In the eighteenth century admiration of English political institutions was universal, but the despotisms and aristocracies preferred the easier method of waiting to the difficult method of grappling with the political problem and sharing power with the growing *bourgeoisie*. European Liberalism was too much an affair of the study; but it came into its own in political practice when the ' Great War ' was over and the nineteenth century was well on its way.

The eighteenth century, too, had the merit of tackling abuses, not hastily indeed, but courageously and almost systematically. Beccaria's remark, in reference to some abuse of the penal system—" This ought not to happen in the Eighteenth Century "—shows the insistence of the age upon the claims of reason in politics and society. His other great statement, that laws must be directed to achieve *the greatest happiness divided by the greatest number*, supplied at any rate a principle to legislation, which the succeeding century found useful. That the men of the eighteenth century were self-confident, self-satisfied, and convinced that they possessed the key to life and to progress is not to their discredit; it is a better outlook upon the world than pessimism or ' defeatism.' Having finished his grand work, *De l'Esprit des lois*, Montesquieu could declare, with something loftier than mere complacency : " If this work meets with success I shall owe it chiefly to the grandeur and majesty of the subject. However, I do not think that I have been totally deficient in genius. When I have seen what so many great men in both France and Germany have written before me I have been lost in admiration; but I have not lost my courage: I have said with Correggio, *And I also am a painter.*"

The Age of Reason, this trim ' Europe '—compact, satisfied with itself, knowing what it knew, worldly, a little cynical, humane, religious but not ' devout,' tolerant, progressive, slow —came to an end in the French Revolution and the European war, a civil war among the trustees of Western civilization. What precipitated the crash?

The people who lived at the time of the great catastrophe could scarcely be expected to discern its ultimate causes. Ten or fifteen years after the struggle was over William Hazlitt, looking back in the fullness of knowledge, ascribed the ultimate cause to the invention of printing:

> The French Revolution might be described as a remote but inevitable result of the invention of the art of printing. The gift of speech, or the communication of thought by words, is that which distinguishes man from other animals. But this faculty is limited and imperfect without the intervention of books, which render the knowledge possessed by every one in the community accessible to all. There is no doubt, then, that the press (as it has existed in modern times) is the great organ of intellectual improvement and civilization. It was impossible in this point of view, that those institutions, which were founded in a state of society and manners long anterior to this second breathing of understanding into the life of man, should remain on the same proud footing after it, with all their disproportions and defects. Many of these, indeed, must be softened by the lapse of time and influence of opinion, and give way of their own accord: but others are too deeply rooted in the passions and interests of men to be wrenched asunder without violence, or by the mutual consent of the parties concerned; and it is this which makes revolutions necessary, with their train of lasting good and present evil.[1]

[1] William Hazlitt, *The Life of Napoleon* (1852), vol. i, p. 58.

Hazlitt was a Radical, and impatient for reform. The men of the eighteenth century, and perhaps the men of the present day, would agree with him about " present evil " as the result of revolution, but might be inclined to doubt the " lasting good." Talleyrand's view was that he who had not lived before the Revolution did not know the sweetness of life. The men of the eighteenth century believed that they lived in a good age; the more earnest acknowledged that it had defects, and laboured for improvement. Turgot, one of the finest characters of the age, was for reform, not revolution; and reform is always possible, revolution is never inevitable. Hazlitt's explanation of the cause of the great collapse will not do; it only explains why change, amendment, reform, was demanded. And reform was coming, was happening all the time. Why could people not wait?

The answer is that people could wait, would have waited, if they had been properly led. The fault lay in the eighteenth-century Governments, which, as Governments are apt to be, were at a lower level of intelligence and will-power than the educated people of the time. The Governments were formed of educated men; but these men were, as they always are, caught up in the routine of administration, and had no longer the time or the energy to study problems deeply and to keep abreast of the best thought. Moreover, the Governments had the usual weakness; they would rather go on over-spending and tolerating abuses than enforce unpleasant decisions. And then, finally, the Governments believed in war as an instrument of policy —the prime defect even of an enlightened age. Out of these three things on the part of Governments—lack of understanding, lack of decision, belief in war—came the great collapse —the Revolution and the European war. Lack of understanding and lack of decision brought on the French Revolution. Belief in war brought on the great civil war in Europe which lasted for twenty-two years.

Every educated person in France knew that reforms were necessary; most of them knew what reforms were necessary. The men who knew best, however, were not the official administrators; or, if they were, they became, like Necker, immersed in the routine of affairs, or, like Turgot, were driven out by the ignorant and the self-interested. There were plenty of men of talent and knowledge in France, but the Government did not use them. If the royal Ministers and officials had only read and assimilated the works of the Physiocrats (and the work of Adam Smith, which was circulating in France) they would have understood all the reforms that were necessary.

Yet even if they had understood the reforms that were needed they would scarcely have had the capacity for decision to carry them out. All Governments hate facing hard decisions. Only under great pressure, and led by a very strong man, will they do so. To enforce equality before the law upon all privileged people; to tax the aristocrats and clergy in proportion to their wealth; and to stop extravagant spending on the Court and the Army—to do such things requires a ruthless power of decision from which all Governments shrink. Yet, in 1789, when it summoned the Estates-General, the French Government had practically taken the decision—too late, apparently. It should have taken the decision when Necker published his great national balance-sheet, the *Compte Rendu* of 1781.

Nevertheless, though the internal forces of revolution broke the dam of authority in France between 1789 and 1792, there was no need for the revolution to spread. Other peoples would have felt the agitation, would have been stirred, might have risen here or there, but would have been kept in order, and would have received some reforms. Ultimately the achievement of civic freedom and equality in France would inevitably have been copied or adopted in other countries. Thus the Revolution, which was accomplished violently, at needless cost, in France, would have been achieved quietly, without bloodshed, elsewhere. What ruined this prospect was the attack of the monarchical states upon Revolutionary France in 1792. This precipitated the twenty-two years of great European war.

Of course the outbreak of the great European war was not caused by the attacking Powers only. Revolutionary France was insolent and provocative. It rode roughshod over Imperial rights in Alsace. It incited foreign peoples to rise against their masters. It engaged in subversive propaganda against other States. All this, however, the old monarchical Governments could have dealt with, by patience, by firmness, by invoking the respect for law, and the power of public opinion and the law of nations. These Governments, however, believed that they could check and change Revolutionary France by war. They had always reserved to themselves the claim to make war as a means of carrying out policy which they could not achieve, or could not achieve quickly enough, by peaceful means. This was the great defect of the eighteenth century. Although peaceful, especially in its later years, it had never eliminated the idea of war, had never really tried to do so. Frederick the Great seemed to have demonstrated that war could pay; that by war you could carry into effect high policy. The Partition of Poland, which was a supreme act of war, seemed with equal cogency to prove this. So when the French Revolutionary State refused to listen to arguments, to protests, to appeals on behalf of law and reason, the old monarchical Governments, Austria, Prussia, and other princes of the Empire —the traditional representatives of international order and stability—set war in motion in order to enforce their policy. They set their armies marching into France. The French resisted, met the invaders at Valmy on September 20, 1792, won the battle (to the surprise of all Europe), and cleared France of the invaders. Peace was still just possible, as it always is when the first bolt of war has been shot, the first battle lost and won. There is inevitably a pause, while the armies are being refitted, and here negotiation can intervene; but if this moment is not seized by diplomacy for a peaceful move, the armies take up the struggle again, and this time for a fight to a finish. The war becomes a war of attrition, and goes on until one side or both are ruined.

Goethe, then thirty-three years old, was present at the battle of Valmy. In his *Campagne in Frankreich* he described how the officers viewed the check which the Allied forces had received. " People avoided each other's glances. We could not even light a fire. After a time some one asked me what I thought, as I had often amused the circle with oracular utterances. On this occasion I remarked, ' Here to-day a new epoch of world-history begins, and you can boast that you were present at its birth.' " He spoke truly. The eighteenth century perished in the smoke of the artillery at Valmy.

There is a remarkable analogy between the end of the eighteenth and of the nineteenth centuries, if the one be considered to end in 1792, the other in 1914. Europe in the period of Frederick II and again in the Victorian Age was on the whole a happy place, cultured, productive, opulent, and, in spite of much searching of heart, really untroubled in mind. Both those opulent ages, so rich in possibilities for mankind, ' crashed ' in a world war, a ' Great Civil War of Europe.' Yet no student of men and things and ideas can deny that there is a European society, the result of 2000 years of common history, of ' pooled experience ' since the time of the Greeks and Romans and the early Christian Church. The best minds in Europe have always kept steadily in view this idea of European society, not a vain ' ideology ' but a real thing, persisting amid all the clashes of ignorant and selfish interest. Voltaire, Goethe, Franklin, Kant, Pitt, had no doubt of the existence and of the need for a citizenry of Europe, the freedom of which was possessed by all people who followed Western civilization. This is the political faith, embracing and transcending all competing schools of opinion, held by men of goodwill.

INDEX

336 THE AGE OF REASON